THE ENGLISH NOVEL
IN THE
TWENTIETH CENTURY

Martin Green

THE ENGLISH NOVEL
IN THE
TWENTIETH CENTURY
[THE DOOM OF EMPIRE]

ROUTLEDGE & KEGAN PAUL
London, Melbourne and Henley

First published in 1984
by Routledge & Kegan Paul plc

14 Leicester Square, London WC2H 7PH, England

464 St Kilda Road, Melbourne,
Victoria 3004, Australia and

Broadway House, Newtown Road,
Henley-on-Thames, Oxon RG9 1EN, England

Set in Bembo
by Inforum Ltd, Portsmouth
and printed in Great Britain
by T.J. Press (Padstow) Ltd, Padstow, Cornwall
© Martin Green 1984

British Library Cataloguing in Publication Data

Green, Martin

The English novel in the twentieth century.
1. English fiction—20th century—History and
criticism
I. Title
823'.912'09   PR881

ISBN 0–7100–9971–1 (cloth)
      0–7102–0276–8 (pbk)

TO GERRY AND MAUREEN GRIFFIN,
To celebrate our shared rebellions

CONTENTS

PREFACE

It is clear enough that two large facts made for differences between nineteenth- and twentieth-century British fiction: one was the career of Kipling, which carried with it a confrontation between literature and imperialism; the other was the break-up of the empire and the intellectual proscription of imperialism, after the Great War. But these two facts, or oppositely tending forces, the pressures they exerted and the contrary reactions they produced in writers, were confused by their near coincidence in time. (In 1914, Kipling still had half his literary career to live.) This confused or elaborate pattern I shall try to trace here.

The main outlines should be clear. For instance, three of my authors, Kipling, Lawrence, and Joyce, came to maturity before 1914, while England was still a great empire, and Kipling a prominent author; the other three, Waugh, Amis, and Lessing, came to maturity when the empire was already clearly in decay, and Kipling a literary joke. (I discovered this ideological symmetry after I had decided that these must be six I would work with.) Then in each chapter I associate another appropriate writer with my main subject, though the appropriateness varies from case to case. Thus Forster goes with Lawrence because they shared ideas about women; but Wells goes with Joyce, even though the two writers' ideas were very different, because both were fond of characters like Leopold Bloom. But the ideas about women and the fondness for Bloom were both ways of combating the glamour of England's imperial destiny.

My six main authors chose themselves; imposed themselves upon me as the most interesting fiction writers of
twentieth-century Britain; but I see, retrospectively, that
they represent the rest of British fiction by the (implicitly
working) double criterion of being artists with both large
talents and large audiences. This might be called a nineteenth-century, or consensus, or even philistine, criterion;
but it is not schizophrenic. The two criteria work together
harmoniously to specify a taste. Large talents who aim to
please a large audience develop in response to that audience's response; they make some alliance between their own
and their audience's concerns; they become public artists.
This makes for a difference between them and those who
write only for little magazines, or those who write only for
women's or men's magazines. (The latter have large audiences, but they are not usually large talents.) It also makes a
difference between these six and those highbrow writers
chosen by French critics to represent modern literature –
Mallarmé, Bataille, Artaud, Flaubert. Such a difference
shows itself not only between Dickens and Mallarmé, but
also between George Eliot and Flaubert.

Public artists represent their society more simply and
powerfully than other kinds of artist; because of their relation with their audience. But their links with that audience
run through literary agents and publishers, who are agents
of the book-buying public. And book-buyers, more defi-
nitely than readers, are a branch of the ruling class. But
writers are called upon, by their vocation, to disentangle
themselves from the ruling class. This complex situation
(which literary scholars have failed to study) creates
tensions for the writer which we shall see in Kipling and his
successors. Such tensions are always there, for all writers,
if usually masked. In this case they are extra-prominent,
because of the political situation (the empire's decay).

Masking is sometimes a matter of ignoring. The nineteenth-century British fiction of the Great Tradition had to some extent turned its back on such problems. Centring itself on women and marriage, on personal relations and alternatives to politics, it had constituted itself a liberal resistance movement within the culture. But even those novels include portraits of aristo-military gentlemen, members of the ruling caste, like Rochester in *Jane Eyre* and Lydgate in *Middlemarch*, which show concentrated concern on the writer's part. And writers outside that tradition, like Meredith and Disraeli, Dickens and Thackeray, give even more striking accounts of that caste; accounts we can call preliminary to Kipling's own work.

At the turn of the century, beside Kipling and his cohorts (Stevenson, Haggard, Buchan), novelists like Henry James, Joseph Conrad, and Ford Madox Ford devoted much of their energy to describing and analysing the British master class, especially its men. Implicitly, they were studying the power relations between literature and that class. Much of their attitude can be suggested by one word they often applied to the gentleman – 'stupid'. This did not always or only connote angry or scornful condemnation; it also meant an appreciative recognition of something other.

It meant that the gentleman did not employ the kind of intelligence the writer and reader did, at the moment of being writer or reader. But the novelists' point was often that intelligence of their kind would preclude the kind of courage and loyalty, faith and chivalry, which the gentleman demonstrated in action. In 'Drums of the Fore and Aft', Kipling describes the British subaltern thus: 'For this reason, a child of eighteen will stand up, doing nothing, with a tin sword in his hand and joy in his heart, until he is dropped.' (*A Kipling Pageant*, New York, 1935, p. 103). And 'stupid' also often connoted a physical vitality and perfection in the gentleman, and a sexual charm, which the writer 'reluctantly' conceded and recommended to his reader.

Much of this had been implicit in Matthew Arnold's

Victorian term for the aristo-military caste – 'the bar-
barians'. By using such terms, the writer ruefully recognized in the gentleman caste qualities he himself could never
possess. And this recognition, somewhat peripheral in
the Victorian middle-class consensus, moved towards the
centre of writers' minds at the turn of the century; and is
associated above all with Kipling.

That association was paradoxical, because Kipling did not
paint full-length portraits of such heroes, but it was not
unjust, because indirectly he did celebrate them. He *was* the
minstrel of the castle to the master class. When I speak of
what Kipling meant to later writers, therefore, I sometimes
mean his presence (a culture-criticism concept) rather than
his influence (a literary criticism term). Kipling was powerfully present to people who never read him – who reacted to
the idea of him. He had made a strident act of identification
with the interests of the empire's master class; and so he was
involved in every attack upon or defence of that class. In the
fifty years or so after 1918, he was widely ignored by other
men of letters as a writer, but he was on their minds all the
time as an ideologist.

Lawrence and Joyce were also present to their writer-
successors – not so much to the general reader. And *they*
were also powerful influences, because they were *read* by
those successors. But it seems possible honestly to argue
that those later writers, including the later three of my six,
were as much affected by Kipling as by Lawrence and Joyce.
And I need not stress how surprising that idea is, when
Kipling had been so banished from the literary scene.

My argument in support of that proposition will of
course take up this whole book; and I must immediately
enter a partial disclaimer. The idea will remain something of
a paradox, even if it is accepted. That is, there are good
reasons for keeping Kipling in a different part of our mind
from Lawrence and Joyce; loyalty to them almost precludes
sympathy with him. But those were rather than are good

reasons. We have had the benefit of them these thirty years at least. We have sucked all the juice from them, and there is more flavour now in the opposite ideas.

But I unparadoxically believe that Kipling is a much more pervasive and powerful presence in English literature after 1918 than has been recognized. Let me take as an example a writer who is probably considered, for a number of reasons, Kipling's polar opposite – Virginia Woolf. She in fact took important novelistic material directly from Kipling. That is, she very often described the aristo-military caste which ruled the empire, and the ambivalent attraction/repulsion which the literary artist felt towards that caste. *Mrs Dalloway* (1925) for instance tells how the gentlemen who stood in the windows of Brooks's Club with their hands behind their back saw the Queen's car drive by, and 'At once they stood even straighter, and removed their hands, and seemed ready to attend their Sovereign, if need be, to the cannon's mouth, as their ancestors had done before them.' (p. 26). They are clearly romantic figures. And we are told how a minor woman character (Lady Bruton) had organized a military expedition to South Africa, and had helped a general compose a telegram which sent troops into battle.

And it is not only minor characters who are defined in these Kipling ways. Peter Walsh, who represents all that is most genuine in the book, is defined in terms of India and the noble vocation of being one of India's rulers. He is set against the backdrop of India. 'All India lay behind him; plains, mountains; epidemics of cholera; a district twice as big as Ireland; decisions he had to come to alone – he, Peter Walsh . . .' (p. 72). He has been a rebel, sent down from Oxford, and has been a Socialist; but he names himself to himself as an adventurer and a romantic buccaneer, and he plays with a knife while he talks (p. 80). He is a Kipling hero, like Kim or Stalky.

Usually in Woolf's work, men's sexual glamour is guaranteed by their adventures, which are typically imperialist in their setting and genre. In *Between the Acts* Giles Oliver is by temperament a 'stupid' Kipling subaltern; and his father dreams of his youthful glory as a young man helmeted: 'and in the sand a hoop of ribs; a bullock maggot-eaten in the sun; and in the shadow of the rock, savages; and in his hand, a gun' (p. 17). These are the two most attractive men in the book.

Woolf's women, on the other hand, have as their heritage English poetry, which they know – as Isa, the central character of *Between the Acts* knows it – as a tangle of unidentified lines and images. This is the way Kipling used poetry, in his stories and essays, and even in his own verse. There are no complete poems, and no concentrated response to poetry; all is allusion and familiarity. Used this way, poetry becomes a national treasury, as in Palgrave's *Golden Treasury*, a jewel box in which lines of Shakespeare, Keats, Sidney, lie entangled like necklaces. They are entangled with each other, and with English history.

Both men and women in Woolf know English history as Kipling presented it in *Puck of Pook's Hill*, that is, as a tapestry of picturesque national legends. For instance, in the pageant of English history in *Between the Acts*, Queen Elizabeth appears as

> Mistress of ships and bearded men,
> Hawkins, Frobisher, Drake,
> Tumbling their oranges, ingots of silver,
> Cargoes of diamonds, ducats of gold,
> Down on the jetty, there in the west land. (p. 84).

Woolf, of course, asks the reader to focus attention, not so much on these images as on the spectators' consciousness of them. But then so did Kipling in his book; and in so far as Woolf's characters establish themselves for us, they are characterized by thoughts and feelings in relation to Kipling's images.

But my main concern must of course be with the six

writers I find so interesting. *Their* debt to Kipling can only be sketched in here, in this Preface; my points about Joyce and Lessing, for instance, are too complex to be summed up usefully. But I can say forthwith that Lawrence's fiction should be read as a reply to Kipling's; and also that Waugh and Amis can be read as first denying, and then repeating, Kipling.

For this to be meaningful, even in a preliminary way, I must give some definition of the Kipling I have in mind. Here, obviously, I can only assert, not demonstrate, these propositions; and the fundamental one, that he was a very gifted and important writer, I will not even assert. The Kipling I am concerned with can be said to have five dimensions. First, he was the bard of the empire's master class; which meant that he wrote about its adventurers and its administrators, but also that he wrote for them – that he attached a new primary audience to literature. Second, he alienated himself from prominent parts of the older audience, notably women and the most morally sensitive parts of the clerisy; and in consequence disabled himself for major themes and genres, notably the novel. Third, he was therefore uneasy with the world of letters and with his own role as a writer; he wrote against the grain, and can best be read dialectically, like such superficially different writers as Brecht and Genet. Fourth, his stories come to us from a circle of men, and men in authority, accustomed to dispose of others' lives; implicitly always, and explicitly sometimes, he affronts the humanist belief that individual fulfilment is the ultimate moral criterion – Kipling says that individual lives exist to be used up in the service of social causes. Last, everything said so far applies best to the early Kipling, for his later work was in some ways all too easy for his audience to take; he made himself the entertainer of the master class, declining the larger challenges of art; in his middle period he wrote elaborately romantic stories about English country houses which flatter his readers' sense of owning property and supervising their tenants' lives; and in his late period he wrote a lot of humorous poems and stories, which made humour take on a role proper to powerful emotion and even religious values. (This middle and late work is what we recognize first as influencing Waugh and Amis. It was the early work Lawrence replied to.)

Thus Kipling tried to win a new audience for literature; an audience that was aristo-military by caste, and rulers of the empire by function, and male. Jane Austen and George Eliot, Charlotte Brontë and Mrs Gaskell, had made the serious novel about marriage largely a genre written by, for, and about, women. Kipling tried to change that. (But Lawrence – and Forster – recaptured the novel form for women, by means of their new art and philosophy of eroticism. It is easy to see the anti-Kipling orientation of their work if one compares *The Rainbow* and *Howards End* with his *The Light That Failed*.) As for caste, the old, middle-class audience had had no imperial loyalties, and the empire appeared only peripherally in their serious novels; impoverished characters disappeared to the empire at the end of the story, or nouveaux-riches appeared from it at the beginning. One could read all the works of the Great Tradition, and never know England had an empire. The ruling-class audience of potential readers had had no full-throated way to express their exultance in the empire, because the guardians of the national voice, the men of letters, had been by and large men of conscience. Kipling's poems and stories gave them that way.

A national voice is necessarily choral, so we may say that there was a change in the composition of the national choir under Kipling. He (and Disraeli, Arnold, Milner, etc., as I shall show) 'called home' the men of empire to represent England henceforth, to be the profile England would present to the rest of the world. These were the men who led the Jubilee processions of 1887 and 1897, not the middle class heroes of domesticity, and it was they who figured in

Kipling's stories and poems.

Introducing an anthology of his work published in 1935, at the end of his life, Kipling gave a very candid account of his audience and his own relation to it. (In typically oblique fashion, he represents himself as a Muslim merchant, addressing the Nakhoda or captain of the buggalow or ship which he is sending out, laden with the wares he has for sale.)

> But the chief part of our business lies with men who are wearied at the end of the day. It is for the sake of these men that I have laded the buggalow . . . you are the servant of these men, oh Nakhoda, and the buggalow is theirs as long as they please. For though I am only a trader with no ware upon which there is not an open price, I do not forget how, when I was wearied at the end of the day, certain great captains sold me that which I could not now find in any market. Pay, then, that debt to these men who are my brothers. (They will not bring their womenfolk aboard, so the talk may be trimmed with a slack sheet.)
>
> (*A Kipling Pageant*, p. xi)

That clearly enough announces his artistic loyalty to the great captains of his own society.

This must not be understood too literally, of course. Kipling did not write about dukes and earls, and he described very few battle scenes; he scarcely portrayed any great English men of war; he painted no full-length pictures of heroes at all. By the same token, he sought no aristocratic or official titles for himself – not even the Poet Laureateship; he played no official part; he merely *was* the bard of empire. Nevertheless, all his work is haunted, as his mind was haunted, by the absent images of the English master-class, its captains and magistrates, its men and women of responsibility. (This absence, indirectness and paradox are typical of his art and thought and temperament; Kipling was both a

man of agonized sensibility and a psyche with staggering
problems.) Indeed, he was not himself, by birth or endow-
ment, an aristocrat or a soldier. Kipling was the minstrel of
the castle, the jongleur of a caste he did not belong to.

The most immediate relevance of this fact for the condition of English literature in 1900 as a whole is his attempt to
realign the major castes. In effect, though not consciously,
Kipling was trying to set up an alliance between the aristo-
military and the clerisy – the Brahmins, the nation's writers,
the book-buying public or those who told the latter what to
buy. This would have been a revolution if it had succeeded,
since the writers had been allied to the commercial caste for
the previous hundred and fifty years. This alliance, which
produced the middle-class consciousness, the Victorian
consensus, had been expressed in the triumph of fiction over
other genres, and the triumph of the domestic novel over
other sub-genres of fiction. (Of course, there were always
gifted writers who did not want to serve the commercial
caste; they were often recognizable by their anger and
eccentricity, like Swift, Byron, and Burton.)

The more general effect of this realignment of caste feeling under imperialism was a certain blighting of literary
hope and ambition all through the twentieth century. The
decline is obvious when we compare modern writers with
nineteenth-century ones. When writers saw themselves as
serving the purposes of the rulers, and saw that class as
aristo-military, they lost faith in themselves as 'creative', as
leaders of a great resistance movement within culture,
which is how Hardy and George Eliot (and Lawrence) saw
or felt themselves. We shall be able to trace this effect in
writer after writer in the sequence studied in this book;
notably in Waugh and Amis. Though they began by mocking Kipling, they ended by assuming his position in both
politics and art. They made themselves 'Kiplingesque
writers'; which was equivalent, in the world of letters, to
placing themselves in the public stocks to be pelted. They

announced themselves as masculinist in front of an audience who all shouted feminist slogans.

Thus to follow Kipling was a kind of doom which he imposed on these later writers. His revolution failed, but he himself triumphed. The world of letters expelled him, and his coup d'état failed, but so did the attempt to suppress it, to exorcise it from writers' minds, and to go back to the old ideals. Once the empire had been brought to mind, it could not be forgotten, and writers could not regain their innocence.

Indeed, at the level of commercial success, of readership, Kipling's revolution did not fail. His sales did not shrink significantly during the twenty years of his critical neglect before his death; and since his death his books have continued to be read in enormous numbers, and world-wide. The same is true for those other writers who were his allies, Stevenson, Haggard, Buchan. One sign of their success is the number of films made from their stories – especially when they are compared with the number of films made from novels of the Great Tradition. Another sign is the shame-faced recurrence of those adventures in the work of later writers, like Waugh, Greene, Amis, Paul Scott. Above all, the sign is the imprint Kipling left on his successors' minds, and on British literary sensibility in general.

[1]

THE EMPIRE AND
THE ADVENTURE STORY

IN 1900 ENGLISHMEN RULED a great empire, and their minds
thrilled with power; now in the 1980s they have lost it, and
their minds sag with the sadness of loss. That is the first
meaning I suggest by my phrase 'the doom of empire', and
it constitutes an obvious but enormous change which has
made itself felt in all they wrote and write. And yet, it seems
to me, the literary significance of that change has not been
recognized. The enormousness has perhaps blotted the
obviousness from view. This book will be an attempt to
recover that horizon, to re-draw the landscape of British
consciousness so that that mountainous bulk emerges as a
coherent shape.

I cannot cover – would not wish to – 'all they wrote and
write'. This is an account just of major fiction, and within
that category I choose six writers of major interest to me,
with side glances at parallel figures in each case. I do not
discuss all they wrote, I offer no new information about
them, and no complete accounts of individual works. What
I do offer – besides the diagnosis through them of the
nation's deeper moods – is a new critical estimate of each
author I take up. When one looks at literature from this
imperial point of view, it assumes different proportions, and
so a different scheme of values is implied.

EMPIRE

But we should begin with generally social effects of that possession and dispossession. We may take as a sign of the times, in England at the beginning of this story, Queen Victoria's Diamond Jubilee of 1897, which James Morris has described vividly in his *Pax Britannica* (the sub-title of which, incidentally, is 'The Climax of an Empire'). And as a complementary reference point, for all those other subjects of the empire, its conscious or unconscious, willing or unwilling, victims, we may evoke the presence of M. K. Gandhi, who had in fact left London a few years before the Jubilee, but who had lived there as a law student for three years.

Gandhi can symbolize the Indian liberation movement, and England's final loss of India, which began a series of other losses after 1947, all of which added up to the end of the empire. He can also symbolize the gathering moral accusation of the English ruling class as imperialist; an accusation which, allied to the actual losses, contributed to a victory for England's men of conscience over her men of power in the course of these eighty years. This victory was overwhelming in the world of letters, and although individual novelists rebelled against the consensus, as we shall see, that consensus was to renounce the very idea of national greatness.

Morris lists the territories ruled by Britain in 1897, continent by continent. In Africa, for instance, there was Ashanti, Basutoland, British East Africa, Cape Province, Gambia, the Gold Coast, Natal, Nigeria, Nyasaland, Rhodesia, Sierra Leone, Somaliland, Uganda, Zanzibar. There were forty-three governments within the empire, eleven of them self-governing. Then came the Crown Colonies, and then the Protectorates; Egypt, for instance, had been administered by England since 1882. And this geographical size was reflected in the stature of the individual Englishman, in the eyes of contemporaries. For instance, Gandhi more than once in his early writing declared himself, and all Hindus, to be small and weak beside Englishmen. Indeed, Morris tells us that Britons *were* bigger and fitter than other Europeans. Five members of the Cabinet in 1897 stood over six feet; and the measurements of the private soldiers of the various European armies confirm the impression of British superiority in physique. That sense of size was lost for ever between 1914 and 1918.

Of course not all Englishmen were or felt themselves to be big, even in 1897. Not all Englishmen were imperialists. It was not so long since none had been. Gladstone despised the empire till the end of his life in 1898, calling its triumphs 'false phantoms of glory'. He had refused to participate in the preceding Jubilee of 1887. And John Stuart Mill had called the empire 'a vast system of outdoor relief for the British upper classes'. The Victorian middle class, who had thought that England was especially their country, had been anti-imperialist. But by 1897 even the new intellectuals were attracted to empire: Bertrand Russell, Bernard Shaw, Sydney Webb, H. G. Wells. *Fabian Essays*, which came out in 1889, while Gandhi was in London, laid out the programme for reformist socialism; but the Fabians thought the British empire was a blessing for world history, and were even on the British side against the Boers.

England was self-consciously changing. The journalist W. G. Monypenny said that 'empire' and 'imperialism' had taken the place which had been held by 'nation' and 'nationalism'. English psychology was now that of a master-race.

> At that moment of her history, Britain was settled in the habit of authority – authority in the family, in the church, in social affairs, even in politics. It was the last heyday of the patricians . . . the English posture abroad was habitually one of command. To the educated

Englishman responsibility came naturally. No other
power had been so strong so long. (Morris, *Pax
Britannica*, p. 46)

All this power was a strong stimulus to the writers and
readers of England – to the world of letters. It stimulated
some, like Kipling, to identify themselves with the empire,
in pride and responsibility. It stimulated others, like E. M.
Forster, to dissociate themselves from the empire, in shame
and repudiation. (Of the two, it was paradoxically the first
which was the more rebellious within the system of literature, for English fiction-writers had purposefully ignored
the empire.) But the difference between the two must not
conceal the fact that both were reactions to this parade of
power. When that power was lost, literature would find
itself in a radically different and diminished situation.

But authority was only one face of empire, and at the time
was easily masked by other images, like modern technology. Morris begins his narrative by describing how the
Queen employed the newly invented telegraph to send a
wire to every corner of her empire before she rode in her
carriage to a memorial service in St Paul's Cathedral. Nearly
all the submarine cables in the world were British, though
some ran across foreign soil. And of course ships were even
more British. A favourite map was one showing British
vessels as red blobs on the ocean. At any moment there were
200,000 seamen and 200,000 passengers at sea on British
ships. Of every 1000 tons of shipping passing through the
Suez Canal, 700 were British. Fifty shipping lines used
Singapore. The empire was one great crystallization of the
modern system, and stood for technological and even ideological progress. Kipling described 'The Deep Sea Cables' as
'Joining hands in the gloom, a league from the last of the
sun/ Hush! Men talk today o'er the waste of the ultimate
slime/ And a new Word runs between: whispering "let us be
one!" ' The new technology promised a release from old

forms of dominance and aggression.

The actual parade of 1897 was unmistakably imperialist, however. Fifty thousand troops marched through London, including cavalrymen from New South Wales, Hussars from Canada, Carabiniers from Natal, Dyaks from Borneo, Maoris from New Zealand, Hausas from Nigeria, and Hong Kong Police. There was an empress, kings, princes, grand dukes, and forty Indian potentates riding three abreast. The *Daily Mail* brought out a special issue printed in gold. And of course this was not mere show. The Royal Navy had 92,000 sailors and 330 ships, including 53 iron-clads, 80 cruisers, 96 destroyers and torpedo boats. The next biggest navy was the French, with only 95 ships. And the army, though less cherished as a British institution, was the largest volunteer army in Europe. The Indian army was professional, and much larger; and a third of the British army was normally in India, as well.

When we think of London now, more than eighty years later, very different images come to mind. No longer the capital of an empire, no longer commanding powerful military forces, many of its buildings announce themselves as owned by Arabs, and its streets are filled with foreigners who have come to shop – just as in the old days *we* went abroad with *our* well-filled purses. The black and brown faces in the streets are not troops sent from the colonies to show their loyalty, but new citizens of England, or English ghettoes, who represent a threat or a reproach. These are images which fill the English mind not with pride and a sense of power, but with unease and a sense of decline.

In 1897 too there was a sense of England changing character, but then it was importantly a matter of its becoming more powerful than before, more military. As John Bowle says, in *The Imperial Achievement*,

> Anyone looking through the periodicals at the time of the Diamond Jubilee of 1897 will be struck by how

military the pattern was: by the quasi-Prussian tropical
helmets of the age of Kitchener and Curzon, the
professional touch of the new khaki suited to the
Northwest Frontier and the Veldt, the bemedalled
chests of military magnates, the roar of applause with
which the new popular press greeted exploits that made
news. If Lord Roberts was the dapper and amiable
embodiment of a peculiarly British tradition, Kitchener
could hold his own with the most monolithic titan of
the German army. And the fleet, spic and span, with an
impeccable tradition and officered by professionals who
were almost a caste, was respected and romanticized
even by the solid citizen majority to whom the army
and the Empire in India appeared more of a class
preserve. (pp.301/2)

Bowle reflects on the curious contrasts within the character of the England Gandhi knew – the contrasts between
what I have called its black magic (its explosives) and its
white magic (its freedoms).

Indeed, the Liberal experiment, so civilian and humane,
carried out within the island between 1906 and 1914,
had been made in contrast with the barbarity of the
power politics and armaments of the time; in contrast
with the rampant militarism of the Prussian officer
caste, the nationalist passions that seethed within the
Austro-Hungarian empire, the colossal social upheaval
brewing in Russia. It was incongruous with the
armaments race, with the great coal-burning battleships
with 15-inch guns, the howitzers, cannon and machine
guns . . . . (p. 296)

And these battleships were British, not Russian or Prussian.
   Gandhi was in London between 1888 and 1891, and it is
worth remembering that 1890 was the year of Kipling's
sudden and dazzling success as a writer. One side of Kipling,

his love of moral heroism of a nineteenth-century kind, was very congenial to Gandhi. But of course Kipling's world view allotted very little space to a Hindu law-student, since it was designed to enhance the Anglo-Saxons' sense of power – and responsibility.

Nevertheless, a paragraph from Kipling's *The Light that Failed* (1890) may evoke Gandhi's London for us as well as anything.

> He leaned into the darkness, watching the greater darkness of London below him. The chambers stood much higher than the other houses, commanding a hundred chimneys – crooked cowls that looked like sitting cats as they swung round, and other uncouth brick and zinc mysteries supported by iron stanchions and clamped by S-pieces. Northwards the lights of Piccadilly Circus and Leicester Square threw a copper-coloured glare above the black roofs, and southward lay all the orderly lights of the Thames. A train rolled out across one of the railway bridges, and its thunder drowned for a minute the dull roar of the streets. The Nilghai looked at his watch and said shortly, 'That's the Paris night-mail. You can book from here to St. Petersburg if you choose.' (p. 107)

The Nilghai speaks shortly because of the swell of emotion he and other men feel at the thought of so much power, so much speed, so much adventure available to them (Englishmen travel even faster now, but they don't feel that speed as their national achievement.) Gandhi presumably did not feel that emotion himself, but he felt that others were feeling it. The sights of London had been so named, by Kipling and others, that they had to mean that; and Gandhi did in fact see the English as adventurers.

This word was not a condemnation, but a description of their role within the empire; which, according to the most liberal imperialism, was to be complemented by other roles played by Hindus, Zulus, Maoris, etc. For imperialism included a vivid appreciation of the non-WASP cultures within the empire, and some of the most convinced imperialists were the most generous and romantic in their feeling for other races.

For instance, Edwin Arnold was a popular poet in the line of Keats and Tennyson (he nearly became Poet Laureate) who went out to India in 1857 (at 25) to be Principal of the Government College at Poona. While there, he learned Sanskrit and Marathi, and genuinely appreciated Indian culture. At the same time, he lived the Anglo-Indian life, and shared the imperialists' alarm about a Russian invasion of India. When he came back to England, he became a leader-writer for the *Daily Telegraph*, a new daily begun when the repeal of the Stamp Act made it possible to sell newspapers more cheaply. This paper had a generally imperialist character and financed explorer expeditions like Stanley's three-year voyage from Zanzibar to the mouth of the Congo, which began in 1874. Arnold was much involved in the sponsoring and planning of the expedition, and Stanley named African mountains and rivers after him.

But he also translated the *Bhagavad Gita* into a very popular English verse version entitled *The Song Celestial*. And when Gandhi was in London, some Theosophists introduced him to this version, and the first time Gandhi read this famous poem, central jewel of the Hindu religious and literary tradition, it was in English and was a part of an English Orientalist movement. He also read the very popular Arnold verse biography of Buddha, entitled *The Light of Asia*.

All through the 1870s, however, Arnold promoted the popularity of the empire in England, for instance by printing in the *Telegraph* on New Year's Day each year letters from far-flung outposts, bringing alive the excitement of the idea of the empire. Although begun as a Liberal paper, because of its imperialism the *Telegraph* gradually diverged from Gladstone, in foreign policy, and the break came in 1878 with England's confrontation with Russia over Turkey. The anti-imperialist Gladstone held Turkey morally impossible as an ally for Britain because of her massacre of Armenian Christians; the *Telegraph* went over to Disraeli, who supported Turkey against Russia, who was our national enemy because of her threat to our empire. The *Telegraph*'s shift of allegiance was in some sense typical of how imperialism developed. Disraeli had Arnold write a part of his Speech from the Throne in 1878, and when Victoria was proclaimed Empress of India Arnold was made Companion of the Star of India.

Later Arnold went on to translate from the Koran and other Arabic sources, and finally focused his enthusiasm on Japan, where in 1892, he married a Japanese girl who was only in her twenties. His generosity and susceptibility to new moral ideas were genuine enough – under Buddhist influence he gave up both hunting and meat-eating – but they were allied to a lax taste, in literature and in other matters.

But the most important general truth that Arnold exemplifies for us is that in those decades people could combine an expansive imperialism with an experimental love of the orient. Because of his Buddhism, he became a vegetarian, and met Gandhi, at the West London Food Reform Society; the two even jointly ran a Vegetarian Club in Bayswater for a time. It was from men like Arnold and Kipling that Gandhi learned to believe in British imperialism as a reaching out to other lands (in both senses of reaching out) on the part of an inordinately energetic people, supremely gifted to organize, control, and administrate, who turned, in the overflow of their happy energy, to ask other cultures to teach them the ultimate meanings of life. That, after all, is the message of *Kim*; the Lama, with all his unworldliness, has the secret of life, and the players of the Great Game, with all their worldly responsibilities, will always turn to him in the end; *Kim*, published in 1901, is one of the most vivid expressions of this kind of Orientalism.

But as far as literary criticism goes, *Kim* was a romance, and so not a novel; it was about exotic places and people, and so not about real ones; it told a series of adventures, and so included no significant moral choices; it was about the empire, and so neither about the countryside (like Hardy) nor the city (like Dickens). There was and is a network of categories like these in the mind of literary Englishmen, a centrifuge sorting out the heavier from the lighter elements, which worked to extrude *Kim*, Kipling, and even the empire, as unworthy of serious consideration. This was partly on the grounds that they were morally reprehensible, and so *ought* not to be taken seriously, but partly that they were intellectually insubstantial, and so *could* not be. This feeling was fully alert and armed with reasons in the realm of literary taste – perhaps it was a stronger force there than anywhere else. There were two main genres in fiction, the novel and the adventure; and of these the former was serious – was what could be taught, could be put forward by men of letters in self-justification, when they measured themselves against men of science, men of politics, men of action – and the latter, though it might be preferred by those other men, was trivial.

ADVENTURE

This scheme of ideas of course represents our own state of mind quite as much as that of 1900, and it announces a feeling of implicit antagonism, which has to be brought to light and sympathetically understood, if the rest of my argument is to be followed. None of my other five subjects – the novelists who came after Kipling – was an adventure-writer (though some of them wrote books with adventure episodes). But the opposition between the adventure and the serious novel determined laws of force which bounded and structured the situation of the writer in England. One had to choose either the one form or the other, and all sorts of consequences unavoidably followed. This opposition was closely tied to other cultural polarities, relating to ideas like 'militarism', 'world-destiny', and 'national greatness'.

Empire meant national greatness, as well as occupied territories. Macaulay in the nineteenth century, and Churchill in the twentieth, both in speeches to Parliament, declared that any dissolution of the union joining Ireland in the one case, or India in the other, to England, would mean disaster to the imperial country. England would cease to be England if it were deprived of its overseas possessions. 'The Repeal of the Union we regard as fatal to the Empire and we will consent to it never – never – never –', said Macaulay; and Churchill said, 'India is our bread and butter, and without it we will go out, down, and under.' Thus a person's relation to (opinion of, feeling for) his country's colonies was often his relation to his country's power and wealth, and thus to that class within the country which embodies its power and wealth. This is likely in the case of a writer to be a relation of antagonism.

Of course, empire did and does also mean opportunity, even for writers. The territories lying out there were felt to be inviting every Englishman's coming, promising to reward his (English-born) courage and energy. Sometimes empire even means other countries, not within the circle of officially colonial territories. For men of letters, the empire has often been, especially in this century, all those peoples who lacked and needed English, and who were willing to pay him to teach it to them. He knew he had always his mother tongue to sell, if all else failed. This was his birth-right, as a son of the empire, not to mention his unique ease of travel, in a world where English is the imperial language, and so all the roads are imperial roads. All this exhilarates his blood, as much as the man of action's, with a sense of power and privilege.

But most importantly, what empire has meant to the man of letters has been his sense of what it meant to his rival. He experienced empire via his resentful imagination of the man of action – the empire was an extended field of action for the latter, an extension of his scope. And that scope was moral as much as geographical; more personal power and more heroism and greatness were available at the frontiers than in the home country, and more brutality, more corruption, more monstrosity. ('Heart of Darkness' gave the sense of the latter, but – within literature – the former was much more diffusely conveyed.)

At the level of national myth, everyone always knew about both dimensions of scope. The British empire was, like the American frontier, a space of legend, and *lived* legend, quite independent of the literary legends about it. It was a space out of prosaic reality, a space of imagination, and felt to be so even by those who lived there. Englishmen could pass into it, as into a luminous haze, and then return from it, themselves luminous – although of course after 1918 a lot of literary energy went into tearing those clouds of glory from ex-colonial administrators – they were made a national joke. But before 1918 they came back legendary even if not wealthy, bronzed by the sun of the imagination. That was the final sense in which the empire was a great possession of the English.

But serious literature was suspicious of that kind of imagination because it was hostile to all adventure. This was what the doom of empire had meant to writers – their diminishment by Force, by Power – so they had denied adventure. At least, that was generally true. The year 1900 was indeed an exceptional moment in the history of English literature, different from before and after, because of Kipling's success with professors of literature, with popular critics, and even with fine sensibilities like Henry James. Literature married itself to adventure and empire. But that moment did not last and the old scheme of ideas reasserted

its hegemony. It had been establishing itself for a century and a half before 1900; in genre terms, the triumph of the serious novel was a Second Front in the war which fiction waged against poetry in the eighteenth and nineteenth centuries and by which it became the dominant literary genre.

Little by little, as Richardson refined upon Defoe, and Jane Austen upon Richardson, it became clear that seriousness (of both the moral and the aesthetic kinds) was the prerogative of the domestic novel, as opposed to the other kinds of fiction. (The Defoe who was the precursor here was the author of *Religious Courtship*, not the adventure writer.) And in the nineteenth century Charlotte Brontë, Mrs Gaskell, George Eliot, Hardy, expanded the scope of that sub-genre to include the themes of industrialism, politics, and cultural change, without sacrificing its organizing centre; while the adventures which began with Defoe the author of *Robinson Crusoe* were written and read in much greater numbers (by English *men*, we might say, unlike the novels), but were felt to be meant for boys. This disregard was to their advantage, in so far as they were the energizing myth of empire; myths have to be absorbed uncritically if they are to act upon large numbers of people, so have to present themselves as mere pastimes, juvenile pleasures, idle dreams.

But this scheme of literary values began to change in the 1880s, which was by no mere coincidence the period when those politicians who followed Disraeli's lead began to preach a gospel of proud imperialism. It was then that R. L. Stevenson began to write adventures with a care and skill which showed that he expected men of letters to take pleasure in them. *Kidnapped* and *Treasure Island* were aimed at literary readers, men of taste and discrimination, as well as at the boys' magazine audience. And hard upon Stevenson followed Rider Haggard and Conan Doyle and Kipling himself, and after them John Buchan and several others. This was a significant literary movement, in revolt against

the contemporary system of literature. As the contemporary critic, Walter Besant, said, the boisterous side of human nature was for the first time being allowed expression in English literature.

Of course the cult of adventure, of boisterousness and implicit imperialism, had long been a very important part of English life, and the centre of a network of cultural habits. To take the most innocuous examples, there was the cult of geography, of maps and pictures of far-off places; of travel and exploration and the love of primitive tribes; of oceans and the British navy, and the British sailor, and all sorts of swimming and sailing; of walking and climbing, and amateur geology and botany as practised on hikes; in so far as these activities were felt to be British and healthy and manly, they were felt also to contribute to the cult of adventure and to the energizing myth of empire.

The influence of *Robinson Crusoe* was everywhere, except in the studies of literary critics; by 1895 there had been 196 editions in English (as well as 115 revisions and adaptations and 277 imitations) and that influence was profound. George Borrow, for instance, tells us how he had refused to learn to read until told part of that story and was then forced to get the rest out of a book. For months, he tells us, 'the wondrous volume was my only and principal source of amusement. For hours together I would sit poring over a page till I had been acquainted with the import of every line' (*Lavengro*, p. 210). And Scott, followed by Cooper, Dumas, Kingsley, and ever so many more 'historical' novelists, had rendered a somewhat masked version of the same myth. (The ways both sorts of adventure entered the lives of later writers may be exemplified from Kipling, who played Crusoe in the basement of his childhood home in Southsea, and then went to public school in Westward Ho! a town built on the scene of Kingsley's novel and named after it.) The desert island, the buried treasure, the coded message, the improvised boat, the desperate defence, the treacherous

savage, the manly leader, all such images were seeded in the deepest recesses of every Englishman's – every European's – imagination.

But they were not taken seriously, at least by men of intellect, because the latter belonged to the opposite party in the cultural dialectic. One did not expect to find a first class mind writing an adventure story; he/she would naturally turn, within fiction, to the 'serious' domestic novel, as George Eliot did. Such was the system of literature, at least as we see it now, looking back. In fact, it is only in the last generation that this order has been established so absolutely. In our time literature has taken over more and more of the functions of our other moral authorities, and looking back as critics we are likely to see as absolute moral distinctions which were in their day more tentative, playful, or polemical. Moreover, when we look at the gifted novelists of post-1930 England, we find their interest to be almost the opposite of the critics'. They seem to have been inspired more by the tradition of adventure than by that of domestic fiction.

[2]

RUDYARD KIPLING:
THE EMPIRE STRIKES BACK

HIS LIFE

RUDYARD KIPLING WAS BORN in 1865, in Bombay, where his father taught pottery and sculpture in a recently established School of Art. John Lockwood Kipling had been unable to marry, for lack of funds, until 1864, when he got this job in India; which was created as part of the spread outwards to the empire of the movement of Art-and-Industry, an attempt to ally high standards of craftsmanship and taste to the new industrial techniques and the new commercial opportunities of the mid-nineteenth century.

His career in art-work for the empire carried John Lockwood Kipling from humble beginnings to the dining table of the Viceroy; he created the banners for the Durbar at which Victoria was declared Empress, he was in charge of the India Exhibit at a Paris Exposition, and he designed a room in the Indian taste for the Queen's House at Osborne. It was thus a career closely linked to the fortunes of the empire, those of the arts, and those of industrial modernization. And Rudyard Kipling, who remained close to his father (the latter illustrated in fact his son's *Collected Works*) may be said to have formed his own career on his father's model, and around the same themes.

But whereas John Lockwood Kipling seems to have been a benign and easily loved man, Rudyard was a difficult temperament and complex mind, only with difficulty maintaining contrary impulses in some sort of working order, and his experience was in many ways painful. This can be seen, or at least guessed at, even in his earliest years. His parents sent him to England when he was 6. This was a general practice among Anglo-Indians, but the Kipling parents seem to have severed the ties with no word of explanation to him. Moreover, though his mother had sisters to whom she was closely allied, the child was sent to live with total strangers – who treated him badly. One is bound to suppose that he was treated so roughly by all concerned because he was 'difficult' – both passionate and rebellious. Thus he passed his boyhood with people he hated and who abused him. But he did not complain, to his parents or to other relatives. He swallowed all the bitterness down, in a way one can call either stoic, or sullen, or proud, but which was in any case significant for his development.

His mother was the more incisive of his parents, and by any standards a sharp-tongued, talented, and striking woman. She was one of five daughters of a Wesleyan minister, four of whom married successful men, three of them in the world of painting and sculpture. One married Edward Poynter, who became President of the Royal Academy; another married Burne-Jones, the Pre-Raphaelite painter, and a friend of William Morris, who was thus a sort of uncle to the young Rudyard. Rudyard was very fond of these relations, and much enjoyed his holidays with them. The contrast between these times, with men and women of striking talents, presence, eloquence, charm, and his every-day misery in Southsea with a bully of narrow views and meagre gifts, a woman he described as 'evangelical' for her Bible-based Puritanism, established an important pattern of preference in the boy's mind. This pattern was in some ways a copy of his parents' transition from the world of religion to that of the arts, of course. Alice Kipling is said to have thrown into the fire a lock of Wesley's hair which had been devoutly preserved in her family, saying, 'The hair of the dog that bit us'. Indeed, there was in those times a general movement of escape from moralism towards aestheticism. One may even see imperialism as a sort of political equivalent to aestheticism – Disraeli's gaudy alternative to Gladstone's puritan moralism. But if Alice Kipling escaped the prison of puritanism, and so helped her son in his rebellion, she left him as a child to languish in a more literal prison.

From there he went to the public school (at Westward Ho! in Devon) which he re-creates in his book *Stalky & Co.* In his autobiography he describes this as a 'caste' school, meaning the military caste: 'some 75% of us had been born outside of England and hoped to follow their fathers in the Army' (*Something of Myself*, p. 26). In an essay, 'An English School', he said, 'and so the men she made went out to Boerland and Zululand and India and Burma and Cyprus and Hong Kong, and lived and died as gentlemen and officers' (*Land and Sea Tales*, p. 562). And indeed, in 1914, of his school-mates, Godby was commanding the New Zealand forces, Maclaglan led a brigade of Australians, Rimington was chief engineer in Mesopotamia, and Dunsterville (the original of Stalky) was to lead an expedition into North Persia (Carrington, *The Life of Rudyard Kipling*).

At first bullied and miserable, Kipling gradually won his way to a position of some prestige in the school, and to the friendship of boys he admired. He did so again by bitter but uncomplaining endurance, and by a rebellion against the school's rules which implied an acceptance of their deeper spirit – a continued testing of those in authority which promised to revere those who passed his tests. But at the same time he combined a sort of aestheticism with this strenuous and sullen power-play. He read French and Russian literature, and decorated his study with Japanese fans. And he was precociously talented as a writer.

At the age of 17 Kipling rejoined his parents and his sister in India, and the four immediately formed a very close and co-operative and mutually loyal unity. They called themselves the Family Square, and they co-operated, to some extent, even in the writing Rudyard published. But what about his feelings of resentment, of having been betrayed? We do not hear of these ever being expressed. What we do see (in so far as such things are to be seen) are symptoms of feelings swallowed down and suppressed. Kipling became the greatest of all propagandists for discipline, cruelly sceptical of all simple happiness and simple faith, and himself a man of black moods, frequent insomnia, and terrible abdominal pains. 'Only the free are bond, and only the bond are free,' says Dick Heldar, his novel-hero; and the fairy boy in 'Cold Iron' becomes human by clamping a slave collar around his neck, saying, 'What else could I have done?'

Living with his parents, he became a cub-reporter on the *Civil and Military Review* and *The Pioneer*, under a short-tempered editor, who 'licked him into shape'. Kipling says, 'For three years or so I loathed him'; he does not need to say how much he later valued that discipline. He plunged into Indian life from the angle of a reporter who was sent by his paper to cover princely ceremonies, cholera outbreaks, bridge-openings, divorce and murder trials. He also came under the decisive influence of the Anglo-Indian administrative class. In a talk given to a naval club, in 1908, he said, 'One is influenced forever by one's first commission, and mine threw me among disciplined men of action – the Indian services – where men were required to live under authority and act under orders.' And in *Something of Myself* he said that at his club in India he met 'none but picked men at their definite work'.

What he met in India obviously reinforced that tendency towards caste-pride instilled in him at school. But what he met was not so much Indian social formations as the social stratification and caste pride which the English in India had developed there. Literarily, moreover, he found Indian

culture a help to expressing that sensibility. Thus in 'The
Eyes of Asia' he has a Rajput write home from London,

> It is not true there is no caste in England. . . . The high
> castes are forbidden to show curiosity, appetite, or fear
> in public places. In this respect they resemble troops on
> parade. Their male children are beaten from their 12th
> year to their 17th year, by men with sticks. Their
> women are counted equal with their men. The nature of
> the young men of high caste is as the nature of us
> Rajputs. They do not use opium, but they delight in
> horses, and sport and women, and are perpetually in
> debt to the moneylender. . . . They belittle their own
> and the achievements of their friend, so long as that
> friend faces them. In his absence they extol his deeds
> (*The War and the Fleet in Being*, p. 150).

The Hindu categories are there only as an indirect means to
celebrating the English aristocracy.

Finally we must note the social success of the Kiplings as a
family. The mother and the sister, both good-looking and
witty, were in demand for private theatricals, dinners and
balls, and literary occasions of all kinds. The Kiplings were
all, in their various ways, entertainers of the ruling class in
India. It is important to grasp this role of the writer's, for it is
a shaping influence on his early work. He was not himself
of the aristo-military caste, by physique, temperament, or
heritage. He was its hereditary bard.

Soon he was allowed to insert poems and stories of his
own into the columns of the paper he worked for. These
were later collected and published; in India, and with very
Anglo-Indian titles, *Departmental Ditties* and *Plain Tales from
the Hills*. Later, but while he was still very young, these
became the first volumes of a new series, the Indian Railway
Library, designed to be read by travellers on that newly built
system, one of England's proudest achievements in India.

His beginnings as a writer were thus closely bound up with the imperial situation in India. He was recognized as being knowledgeable about that situation by, for instance, General Roberts, the Army's Commandeer-in-Chief, who in 1889 asked him his opinion of what the men in the barracks were thinking. And in 1890, while he was still only 25, Kipling was recognized by men of letters in England as a new phenomenon – as having found a new mode of literature, a new idea of the writer, to correspond with England's just discovered imperial vocation.

His early work was satiric and worldly in tone, and his literary models were French and American rather than English. His stories of Simla owed much to French writers, his stories of adventurers to Bret Harte and Mark Twain. He had read a lot of American literature at school, and responded particularly to frontier humour and horror. This chapter could have been called 'The frontier strikes back', for in what Kipling learned from Twain the moral recklessness of the frontier penetrated a literature from which it had up to then been excluded. The empire, no doubt because it was trans-oceanic, had felt much more remote from London than the frontier had from America's literary capitals. The way Englishmen behaved on the North-West Frontier was very different from the way they behaved at home, and their anecdotes about themselves there were very different from the novels of the Great Tradition. Kipling learned from Americans how to put those anecdotes into literary circulation, to the scandal of English critics.

His early work was also to the scandal of the Anglo-Indians themselves, at first, for their official values were quite different from their anecdotes. But gradually, though Kipling never affiliated himself to the Victorians, he managed to build into his stories some equivalent for the value scheme of the Anglo-Indians he admired. However, his equivalences were always tortuous and indirect, ironic and allusive, for no one was less able directly to avow an ideal, to believe in a faith, to express a wish.

In 1890 he returned to England (via America, where he presented himself to his father in art, Mark Twain) and found himself famous. *The Times* published a leading article on his work, his novel *The Light that Failed* appeared in *Lippincott's Magazine*, and W. E. Henley's *Scots Observer* published his Barrack Room Ballads. One of these, 'Danny Deever', caused the professor of literature at Edinburgh University to tell his students, 'Here's literature! Here's literature at last!', waving his copy over his head in excitement. The professors generally were enthusiastic, and also the professorial types among men of letters – men like Edmund Gosse, Andrew Lang, and Charles Whibley.

This enthusiasm was strong in the early 1890s, amongst American as well as English critics. Lafcadio Hearn, writing in 1897, called Kipling 'the greatest of all living English poets, greater than all before him in the line he has taken. As for England, he is her Saga-man – skald, scop, whatever you like.' (*Kipling: the Critical Heritage*, ed. Roger Lancelyn Green, p. 173) W. D. Howells, writing in *McClure's Magazine*, March 1897, claimed him as an American poet: 'the laureate of that larger England whose wreath is not for any prime minister to bestow. . . .' (ibid., p. 193) And finally Charles Eliot Norton, in the *Atlantic Monthly*, 'This splendid continuous fertility of English genius, this unbroken expression of English character and life from Chaucer to Rudyard Kipling, is unparalleled in the moral and intellectual history of any other race.' (ibid., p. 195)

It is worth noting the historic, indeed anthropological, sweep of the perspective in which Norton and Hearn set Kipling. It was a setting Kipling invited; and one could find in anthropology not only then but even now, in Lévi-Strauss's *Tristes Tropiques*, an intellectual context favourable to his art. He spoke for his era, his empire, his nation, as

perhaps no writer had done before. And for a time he spoke
in the name of literature.

But the men of letters' enthusiasm soon faded. Henry
James wrote to a friend on Christmas Day 1897 that he
thought Kipling's talent quite diabolically great, and that as
a ballad-writer his future might still be big; but he deplored
the fact that in prose Kipling could 'make use of so little of
life . . . almost nothing civilized save steam and patriotism
. . .' And of course James did not really think either of those
topics civilized. He found in Kipling, 'Almost nothing of
the complicated soul or of the female form or of any question of *shades*'. James had once thought Kipling might
become an English Balzac, but no longer. After 1900 he lost
touch with Kipling and with his work.

This was part of a general pattern of reaction; in 1899 the
critic Robert Buchanan attacked Kipling as giving a voice to
'hooligan imperialism', which was driving the old humanitarianism into retreat; and as betraying the ideal of General
Gordon, the Christian general, by portraying the British
soldier as a drunken rogue. And the guilt and anger provoked by the Boer War, which meant to England what the
Vietnam War was to mean to America later, set the liberal
intelligentsia completely at odds with Kipling.

The hostility between them and him ran of course both
ways, and Kipling was aggressive from the start. He was so,
for instance, in a story, 'A Conference of the Powers', of
1890, in *Many Inventions*, in which a group of young subalterns meet the great novelist, Eustace Cleever, who may be
a partial portrait of Henry James. When this man of letters
looks at these men of action, Kipling notes that he is utterly
puzzled by their 'steadfast young eyes' and their 'curious,
crisp, curt speech'. 'To me', the Jamesian novelist says
softly, 'the whole idea of warfare seems so foreign and
unnatural, so essentially vulgar, if I may say so, that I can
hardly appreciate your sensations'. (p. 29) When one of
them, called 'The Infant', tells him about Burmese dacoits

who crucify their victims, Cleever 'could not realize that the Cross still existed'. These young subalterns deal with such facts daily: they have all killed enemies, all enjoy fighting, and all like their enemies. The novelist's mind is 'stretched' by them and his soul 'over-awed'. When the Infant says modestly that he has only seen Burma, Cleever adds, 'And dead men, and war, and power, and responsibility.'

Kipling's tone about Englishmen at home tends to be this of *Letters on Leave*. 'Above that they seem to be, most curiously and beyond the right of ordinary people, divorced from the knowledge of the fear of death.' (p. 184) On the next page he complains of a man who 'knows all about the aggressive militarism of you and your friends; he isn't quite sure of the necessity of an Army; he is certain that colonial expansion is nonsense.' (p. 185) Kipling's character declares, 'You mustn't treat any man like a machine in this country, but you can't get any work out of a man until he has learned to work like a machine . . . [p. 197] . . . I honestly believe that the average Englishman would faint if you told him it was lawful to use up human life for any purpose whatever. He believes that it has to be developed and made beautiful for the possessor.' (p. 190)

This vein of thought, Kipling's most interesting but most shocking, is again expressed in 'Drums of the Fore and Aft', 1888, his story about a green regiment that broke under fire, and how two drummer boys rallied it by playing 'The British Grenadiers'. 'Wherefore the soldier, and the soldier of today more particularly, should not be blamed for falling back. He should be shot or hanged afterwards – to encourage the others – but he should not be vilified in newspapers, for that is want of tact and waste of space . . . [*A Kipling Pageant*, p. 101] . . . Speaking roughly, you must employ either blackguards or gentlemen, or, best of all, blackguards commanded by gentlemen, to do butchers' work with efficiency and dispatch.' (p. 103)

It was appropriate, but also notable, that Kipling was a

favourite with the Army and Navy, as well as vice versa. He often paid visits to army and navy clubs, camps, ports, ships; he was taken on a cruise on a warship – an honour never offered to the other authors we are discussing. This of course makes particularly clear his role of bard to the aristo-military caste; and carries with it his character as writer for *men*.

To continue Kipling's life-story, he had married an American, the sister of a friend who died, and they settled first in Vermont, where her family lived. Kipling admired Americans (and Canadians, Australians, etc.) more than Englishmen. He liked the Anglo-Saxon qualities when they were developed by the challenges and adventures of the frontier, not when they were stultified by the securities and pomposities of the long-peaceful homeland. But he got involved in a humiliating dispute with a brother-in-law – humiliating because the other man disposed of more per-sonal force in the dispute, and Kipling was reduced to the unadventurous expedient of invoking the law – and so they returned to England and made their home in an old country house. He had made thus a double retreat – from the empire and then from America – and he probably despised himself for it.

For some years he spent his winters in South Africa, for he had become the friend and 'word-smith' (speech-writer, etc.) of the great political imperialist, Cecil Rhodes. Partly for that reason, he became quasi-official propagandist for the British side in the Boer War, and so lost his liberal and literary audience. He served as war-correspondent, and wrote propaganda; for instance, he composed a ballad about the British soldier, which Sir Arthur Sullivan set to music, and which raised £250,000 for the soldiers. The dissent of liberals could be seen within his own family, where Lady Burne-Jones disapproved of the war, refused to read Kipling's dispatches, and refused to celebrate British victories. Kipling also started a branch of the Navy League near where he lived, and built a drill hall and instituted rifle practice. He was convinced that England needed to prepare for war, as was his friend, Baden-Powell, founder of the Boy Scouts, an organization for which Kipling wrote stories.

During the Great War, Kipling was again a propagandist, and became the major symbol of literature serving militarism. His publishers put out a Services edition of his works, for 'the men in the trenches'. After the war he served on the War Graves Commission, and wrote an official history of the Irish Guards, in which his son had served and died. Thus in 1919 T. S. Eliot reviewed a new volume of his verse by saying that no one even read Kipling any more – no one had even a negative opinion about him.

He had paid the price of his attempt to lead a revolution in English literature, to re-shape the vocation of the writer and re-align the writer's cultural alliances. The price, intellectually speaking, was that he was dubbed a conservative; he was rejected by his natural audience of other writers, and forced into alliance, socially and politically, with all that was dull and dying in English life. And though his work from 1918 to 1936 was elaborate and intricate, and technically interesting, it is in fact thematically duller than what he wrote before 1914.

HIS AESTHETIC

Artistically speaking – that is, in terms of his development as a novelist – the price exacted was disastrous. In effect, Kipling wrote only one novel, in the sense of a long narrative about personal relations, with fully developed characters and a sizeable moral problem at the centre. This was *The Light that Failed*, and it is simply bad. This was the only time he essayed two of the novelist's major tasks – the portrayal of himself as hero, and the portrayal of a woman in a love-relationship with him. These tasks (performed so bril-

liantly for instance by D. H. Lawrence in *Sons and Lovers*),
Kipling miserably failed at.

It is impossible to like or sympathize with his hero Dick
Heldar as much as response to the novel requires; and the
reader is impelled time and again to intervene disbelievingly
in the narration of what Dick and his girlfriend Maisie are
said to say to each other, and are said to feel about each
other. Kipling's account of such matters, far from winning
him authority over the reader's imagination, positively
discredits him. He seems to have no sympathetic understanding of women like Maisie, and no reliable criticism of
men like Dick (himself).

This was a fairly public fact, universally acknowledged
from the beginning. Barrie said in 1891, 'It is in their women
that most of our leading novelists excel . . . Here, unfortunately, Mr. Kipling fails.' (*Kipling: the Critical Heritage*,
p. 82) G. Frankau said, 'Kipling puts women in their place,
whether the kitchen or the drawing room. And because he
does so, the woman who appreciates any but his stories of
children is a rarity.' (ibid., pp. 364–5) Kipling broke literature's alliance with women as he broke its other alliance
with the puritan middle class. These alliances were always
virtual and intermittent but still it was a shock for the
guardians of literature to find a major writer espousing the
cause of the military caste.

The Light that Failed is nevertheless interesting. First of all,
because it is so bad; for there can be no doubt of Kipling's
talent, industry, and ambition, and this was the heyday of
the novel, when that form so dominated fiction that Hardy,
for instance, was forced to practise a form quite uncongenial
to him. Only a powerful psychic resistance within Kipling
to that form – resisting it because it spoke for women, and
love, and liberalism – can explain why he failed at it so
completely.

But the book is also positively interesting as a discussion
of art. Dick and Maisie are both painters; and his friends are

journalists; all are much concerned with the question of
what an artist owes to the general public, to the connoisseurs of art, to public morality, and to himself – to his
conscience as an artist. And for Kipling, of course, these
questions refer particularly to the artist of imperialism –
the artist of adventure, of the exotic, of the brutal, of the
amoral, the artist affiliated to the warrior caste and the
master class.

Aesthetics and imperialism both conflict with domestic
decency, and so with the conventions of the novel. They
also conflict with the conventions of moral discourse, as the
nineteenth century understood those. Such themes therefore found expression in 'journalism' rather than literature,
understanding journalism to cover Dick's paintings and
Kipling's fiction, as well as editorials and polemics, rather
than in 'philosophic' fiction or serious books. They affronted
the connoisseurs of art and the guardians of public morality,
and served the general public. But that public is by definition ignorant and unwittingly tries to make the artist betray
himself. Kipling saw himself as an artist, but one who could
not expect to have his artistry appreciated, and so was all
the more defiantly aesthetic. He says of some short stories.
'I worked the material over in three or four overlaid tints
and textures which might or might not reveal themselves
according to the shifting light of sex, youth, and experience.' (*Something of Myself*, p. 190)

Thus the relation of the journalist to his public is cynical
and even aggressive; Dick looks at London and thinks,
'What a city to loot!', but at the same time he acknowledges
a severe and mortifying principle of duty and service as an
artist. When Dick paints an untruthful picture of a soldier,
because the public wants that sort of sentimentality, his
friend Torpenhow puts his boot through it – he will not
allow Dick to betray his art. More paradoxically, he says
that betraying one's art betrays one's public. Torpenhow
says, 'They are the people you have to work for whether

you like it or not. They are your masters. Don't be deceived.'
(p. 45) And Dick tries to teach Maisie the same lesson. (Just
why such obedience is so important, and how the artist
can submit himself to a philistine master, is left to be
answered by our insight into Kipling's sado-masochistic
self-formation.)

One of the modes of operation of the artist's conscience is
this rough warm comradeship between Dick and Torpenhow. Another is the work itself, hard unrelenting work,
with no promise of reward, which carries the authority of
being hard, of being discipline. Dick tells Maisie, 'All we can
do is learn how to do our work, to be masters of our
materials instead of servants, and never to be afraid of
anything.' (p. 81) *Her* fault, he tells her, is that she paints two
strokes for her own sake, for every one she paints for her
work. 'You must sacrifice yourself, and live under orders,
and never think for yourself, and have real satisfaction in
your work . . .' (p. 87)

But perhaps the most important discipline for the artist is
the encounter with danger, combat, and death. Dick is a true
artist, while Maisie is not, because he is familiar with those
truths; he knows how flimsy are the illusions of liberalism –
of peaceable citizens and home-body artists – the illusion
that peace, morality, order, are natural and reliable conditions of life; illusions which are sustained for the fortunate
flocks at home by the risks and exertions of their wolfish
cousins at the frontiers. He knows that beauty is so poignant, both in nature and art, because it is all we have to
console us for the injustice and horror of fate.

And by the same token, beauty is essentially impermanent,
in art as in nature. Dick paints two great pictures, and both
are irretrievably lost, from the moment they are finished.
One is a mural in the hold of a cargo-ship, and it disappears
beneath the grain that is poured into the hold; the other is a
portrait, which is maliciously destroyed by a jealous model.
Beauty cannot be appropriated, or made permanent; it can

only be pursued, across the seas, in thunderstorms, revo-
lutions, uninhabited islands, dangerous forests.

The confrontation over art and life between Dick and
Maisie is worth considering, even though Kipling fails with
the characters, partly because of parallel confrontations
described by Lawrence – between Ursula and Gudrun
Brangwen and their men – which will be discussed later.
Maisie is, like Gudrun, an independent woman and artist.
She says of her painting, 'It's my work – mine – mine –
mine. I've been alone all my life in myself, and I'm not going
to belong to anybody except myself.' (p. 58) Dick acknowledges her will-power and her workmanship, but declares
that she has nothing to say in her paintings, because she has
not 'seen life'. And when he describes 'life' to her, she is
indeed indifferent to it, as Gudrun would have been.

When he shows her ' "the sort of things I paint" . . .
Maisie looked into the wild whirling rush of a field-battery
going into action under fire.' (p.56) Two artillerymen who
are standing behind her, in the crowd on the pavement
looking at the picture in a shop window, are absorbed in the
action depicted, for the picture is real life to them. And their
comments guarantee its authenticity to Dick, and to Kipling.
But Maisie is not interested. 'Your things smell of tobacco
and blood,' she says. 'Can't you do anything except soldiers?'
(p. 69) In Kipling's drama, this reply is mere petulance. In
Lawrence's, for Ursula Brangwen makes essentially the
same protest to Skrebensky, in *The Rainbow*, it is a religious
truth, because Lawrence was preaching a feminist counter-
attack on Kipling.

The Light That Failed does not expound Kipling's
imperialist aesthetic with any systematic clarity, but it
comes closer to doing so than anything else he wrote.
Kipling was not a clear mind, except in his practice as an
artist. But it requires no great effort for us to see what his
theory implies; and especially interesting is what it means
for the act of reading. To respond to Kipling, the reader will

be forced to make sense out of what does not make sense, to see the beauty of the horrible, to find values in a world which destroys the basis of all values. And since the reader is, *as reader*, the guardian of sense, beauty, and values, this will be a profoundly paradoxical effort he must make – a dialectical reading. Every moral dignity and comfort implicit in the act of reading, of judging, will be constantly undermined by the experiences Kipling offers. In this perspective, seen as a writer who *attacks the reader*, Kipling appears as first cousin to modern figures like Genet, Brecht, Mailer, from whom he is politically remote.

Kipling's own later work did not answer fully to this idea of art, which indeed corresponds to frontier and empire experience. After he married and settled down in England, the note of anger, defiance, and aggression against the English tradition in art was muted; one might say it was replaced as a dominant by playfulness and aesthetic lavishness. But the strain of harsh nihilism never entirely died, and it is one of his sources of strength. His verse, for instance, can often be described as a blues of a master-class. Like the more familiar blues, his sonorous and plangent phrases evoke an experience which characterizes his audience and unites them with him, in stoic suffering and pride. Of course these are experiences of responsibility, of authority, of power, not of powerlessness, as in ordinary blues. But they are public poetry – their refrain, repetition, Biblical and Shakespearean allusions replacing the singer's and pianist's melody. Unlike the poems of contemporaries, like T. S. Eliot, Hardy, Frost, or Pound, this is popular poetry.

Among modern aesthetics, it seems to me that Kipling's was the most politically responsible, along with Tolstoy's, which was essentially contemporary, and Brecht's, in the next generation, which borrowed a lot from Kipling. Of course, the politics were very different in the three cases. If Kipling served the master class of an empire, Tolstoy in old age repudiated the equivalent class in the Russian empire (into which he was born) and served the peasants – the disinherited – who had only a folk art; while Brecht served a revolutionary proletariat, whose destiny it was to seize power. Thus an aesthetics of imperialism contrasts with one of anarchism, in the sense of anti-state conservatism, and with another of revolutionism. These are very different aesthetics; but who else besides these three has had an idea of equal power about art and its social function?

ADVENTURE AND CASTE

We must see Kipling in conjunction with the class he served, and must understand what they got from him. Philip Mason, in his book *Kipling*, says that he himself was an idolatrous Kipling fan by the time he was 14, having identified himself in turn with Mowgli, Kim, and then Beetle. Then, as a young man he came to dislike Kipling strongly. Then he got over that dislike.

Such a development bears all the marks of a profound educational experience, shaping a reader's mind more powerfully than serious literature often can. And Mason sums up,

> No one has had so deep an influence on a whole
> generation of a certain class as he did. Here was
> someone who understood the life they were brought up
> to, their mistrust of politicians and intellectuals, their
> inarticulate devotion to a cause, the training they had
> endured, the tenseness that lay beneath the apparently
> insensitive outer crust, the tenderness they longed to
> lavish on dogs and children, their nervous respect for
> those mysterious creatures, women – so fragile
> compared with themselves, and yet so firmly
> authoritarian as nurses and mothers. (p. 307)

C. E. Carrington says in his *Life of Rudyard Kipling* that his qualification for writing the biography is one he shared with

thousands – that he learned to read with *Just So Stories* and
the *Jungle Books*; went to school with *Stalky and Co.*, read
history with *Puck of Pook's Hill*; and discovered *Plain Tales
From the Hills* as his first adult book. In 1914 he formed his
ideas of army life from *Barrack Room Ballads* and 'The
Brushwood Boy', and the story of a centurion's life in *Puck*
'strengthened the nerve of many a young soldier in the dark
days of 1915 and 1941' (p. 296). In the Preface, he says,

> Looking back, I find no other writer who has seen
> through the eyes of my generation with such a
> sharpness of observation. I owe far more to Kipling
> than to some of the great classic figures of
> literature. . . . There is no other writer, great or small,
> whose work I knew so well, and I have been often
> astonished to find how many others, of all ages, knew
> him as well as I did. . . .

From Carrington we also learn that many of Kipling's
stories were based on newspaper items or current anecdotes.
'It was his pride to record traditional army legends, and he
took the liberty of a Scott or Burns in recording them.' For
instance, 'Gunga Din' is based on the water carrier of the
Guides at the siege of Delhi; 'Drums of the Fore and Aft' on
an incident in Orme's *History*; and John Chinn (in 'The
Tomb of His Ancestors') on James Outram, the friend of
the Lawrences. Thus if Kipling's audience knew his works
very closely, he knew them and their stories just as well.

What he wrote for them was of course adventure. But it
seems that Kipling's intensely literary bent, his genius as a
craftsman, perhaps exacerbated by his fate of serving the
copybook maxims, led him to reject the given in formal
terms. In those terms the adventure romance, and indeed its
value-bearing subject matter, is much more easily to be
found in Conrad. The way Kipling avoided it was above all
by dealing in episodes and fragments. The most obvious
evidence of that is that he wrote primarily short stories, in a

period when extraordinary prestige and reward attached to the full-length novel. But even as short stories, one must be struck by how fragmentary Kipling's anecdotes are, and how often they are told with a stress on their setting, or on their narrative frame, rather than on their subject.

'The Man Who Would Be King' is a good example. The events and the characters are enacted on the stage of an elaborate theatre – the newspaper, the editor, etc. – into which we peer from an odd angle. The effect of this is to stress its character as an anecdote. We don't believe that these events occurred, but we believe that they were told. Kipling's method evokes, very fancifully, a whole series of narratives. What is vaguely but powerfully evoked is the social character of British India, where such anecdotes echoed in the background of everyone's imagination, where everyone was, in a consciously fanciful sense, a man who would be king. Though, since the historical figures whom Carnehan and Dravitt caricature are rather African imperialists like Rhodes and Jameson than anyone Indian, it was in fact everyone in the British empire who had half-acknowledged dreams of that sort.

Or take a story like 'The Head of the District', in *Life's Handicap*, or 'William the Conqueror'. Both of them are very brief anecdotes, which leave the reader wanting to know more (about the persons and events involved) but also caring even more about that genre of life, about the administration of such a district, with its multiple layers of nationalities and religions, and the relief of such a famine. Or take the more purely literary case, the Paolo and Francesca story in 'Through the Fire' or the Antony and Cleopatra story in 'Love o' Women', or the story of Keats in 'Wireless' or 'The Greatest Story in the World'. Here you get the fragment of a well-known poem, play, legend, in some sense concealed in alien material, and made evocative precisely by its fragmentariness and its displacement.

Indeed, it is possible to extrapolate out beyond the use of

famous specific stories, and to say that Kipling makes evocative use of familiar fragments all the time. Take for instance 'Without Benefit of Clergy', which is as complete a treatment of its people and events as you will find anywhere in Kipling. Even there much of the effect derives from the fact that we recognize the figure of Ameera as a sort of Madame Butterfly. We don't need to hear a full realistic account of her. As soon as she appears, we say to ourselves 'there she is again,' and that literary commonplaceness is first cousin to the pathos we feel in Ameera's story – the commonplaceness of her fate in the other sense, i.e. that it happens so often. That second commonplaceness, moreover, evokes a third sense, of sad familiarity, associated with the social atmosphere of British India as a whole; one *hears* such stories over and over. This too is an anecdote, whose power of evocation comes from the familiarity of its type; again we don't so much believe that it happened as that it was told. (The Madame Butterfly figure of course turns up often in adventure fiction; in Kipling, one can mention 'Lispeth' and 'Georgie Porgy'.) Thus if one compares him with Conrad, one sees that the latter was much more old-fashioned in his use of adventure motifs.

CONRAD

Conrad began writing fiction with stories about a man called Almayer or Olmeyer, whom he had met in the East Indies, a failed adventurer. This man was, one might say, the antithesis to Rajah Brooke of Sarawak, Conrad's declared hero among successful adventurers, and it is significant that the antithesis, the anti-hero, was the one who really engaged Conrad's creative imagination.

It took him some years to write *Almayer's Folly*, during which time, he says, he was always haunted by the image of that man, and by his social and geographical setting in the Eastern Archipelago. Then his second novel, *Outcast of the*

Islands, also has Almayer as a character, and a third novel
(not finished until much later), *The Rescue*, has the same
general setting, the same themes, and as hero Tom Lingard,
who is a minor character in the first two. The three books
therefore constitute a sort of trilogy, and a considerable
body of work – perhaps Conrad's most sustained engagement with a subject.

In these early novels, there is a dream of treasure, in gold
and diamonds. There is a sinister hag, Mrs Almayer. There
is a naked corpse, of Dain. There is an explosion, on Dain's
brig, while the Dutch are aboard, so that they are killed
(Conrad often makes use of such explosions). There is a
chest full of the money which Dain paid Mrs Almayer for
Nina, and so on. That is enough to show how lavishly –
much more lavishly than Kipling – Conrad used the motifs
of the adventure romance; and he continued to do so
throughout his writing career.

Conrad had read the literature of France and England and
America as a boy, as well as Polish books. At 11 he declared
that all his favourite books were by J. F. Cooper – the
adventure novels about Natty Bumppo. After that he
turned to reading the lives of explorers, from Columbus to
Livingstone. The kind of childhood reading he makes particular mention of, in his late essays, is of geography books.
He says that Mungo Park and James Bruce were 'the first
friends I made when I began to take notice – I mean geographical notice – of the continents of the world into which I
was born' (*Last Essays*, p. 19). He described himself as a
contemporary of the Great Lakes of Africa, in the sense that
he could have heard of their discovery in his cradle, and in
the later 1860s he did his first bit of map-drawing by transferring the outline of the new country of Tanganyika on to a
blank map. His idea of Africa was mixed up with images of
Mungo Park, Dr Barth, and above all, Dr Livingstone – 'the
most venerated perhaps of all the objects of my early geographical enthusiasm'.

This enthusiasm was to lead to a very significant disillusionment when Conrad finally got to Stanley Falls, because that part of the world by then could evoke no 'shadowy friend or great haunting memory' (Livingstone) but 'the unholy recollection of a prosaic newspaper "stunt" ', and the 'distasteful knowledge of the vilest scramble for loot that ever disfigured the history of human conscience' (the 'scramble for Africa'). The occasion was moreover Conrad's trip up the Congo in 1890, which so disillusioned him with Belgian imperialism, and led him to write *Heart of Darkness*. That is the downward curve of Conrad's engagement with the idea of adventure, from boyhood enthusiasm to mature disillusionment. And though one can explain the dynamic of that curve in terms other than the political history of Empire – Conrad's temperament was predisposed to disillusionment on other grounds – still that political history did correspond to and justify his development. Conrad represented and identified with the European conscience as a whole, in that curve.

Conrad was first a great hero and prize of the lovers of adventure among readers, and then the equally great hero of the opposite party. Both phases of his career were partly the result of non-literary causes. He was the first because he was a foreigner who chose to become an Englishman (chose England, very deliberately) and to become moreover an English sailor; and he was the second because the disastrous failure of the Great War (its incompatibility with any chivalric or adventurous view of war) and the Allies' condemnation of colonialism at its end, together created the need for an anti-imperialist literature. Conrad was the obvious candidate for the job of supplying this; because in both literary and intellectual terms he was ambitious but ambiguous: he made a genuine cult of English and adventurous heroism, but was so romantically disaffected that he hollowed out all his icons from within.

But he was never the anti-imperialist artist he has been

taken to be. Even *Heart of Darkness*, canonical amongst the documents of modern literature, has adventure motifs, and even imperialist themes. For it is still necessary to insist that Conrad, far from attacking English imperialism in the opening pages of this story, is assertively glorifying it. The river Thames, we are told,

> had known and served all the men of whom the nation is proud – from Sir Francis Drake to Sir John Franklin, knights all, titled and untitled – the knights-errant of the sea. It had borne all the ships whose names are like jewels flashing in the night of time, from the *Golden Hind*. . . . Hunters for gold or pursuers of fame, they all had gone out on that stream, bearing the sword, and often the torch, messengers of the might within the land, bearers of a spark from the sacred fire. What greatness had not floated on the ebb of that river into the mystery of an unknown earth!   The dreams of men, the seed of commonwealths, the germs of empire (*Three Short Novels*, p. 2).

There is no more outright glorification of English history and its triumphant curve upward to 1900. So when Marlow says, 'And this also has been one of the dark places on the earth' (which comes immediately after and is the starting point of the story), the meaning is clearly contrastive – even *England* was once uncivilized – and depends on the reader feeling unequivocally how great England has become and still is.

KIPLING'S ARTISTIC SUCCESSES

Kipling pleased his audience, and brought into harmony their confused and conflicting values, by rejuvenating the British adventure tale with the spirit and techniques of the frontier yarn, as told by Mark Twain and Bret Harte. (This was not true of Conrad, and the difference is one way that

Kipling is the better writer.) Literarily speaking, it was the frontiersmen who won the empire its glory.

One can see the relation between Kipling and Twain by placing *Kim* and *Huckleberry Finn* side by side. Clearly Kipling was indebted to the latter in designing his story. Twain and he were the two great entertainers of the Anglo-Saxon community in its period of overt imperialism, and they helped each other quite importantly in their work. The two books' major motif alone – the idea of giving the WASP public an Irish orphan boy as hero to focus their feelings on – is quite an important one. It subtilizes the strategy and renews the feeling of the adventure tale. And Kipling also makes Kim a Roman Catholic. And culturally speaking, an Indian, too.

Perhaps 'The Man Who Would Be King' shows more clearly, or more simply, the frontier influence on Kipling. Dravitt and Carnehan are adventurers of a type that Twain and Harte often dealt with – though in a somewhat different way. The comic dialogue and characterization of them can remind us of the King and the Duke in *Huckleberry Finn*, and the scope of their enterprise can recall characters like Slade in *Roughing It*, and Murel's Gang in *Life on the Mississippi*. But Kipling's particular genius, his historical-mythological sense, is shown in the theme named by the title. The story is about the dream of kingship aroused in every Englishman's heart by the thought of India – of the empire in general.

This expansive myth-making was something quite beyond Twain's scope, and by its means Kipling extended adventure into poetry. Another example of this, *The Jungle Book* (1894) is a collection of stories about Mowgli, an orphan boy who is adopted by a family of wolves and grows up with them as a wolf cub, learning how to deal with the jungle as an animal does, and making friends of the panther and the bear, enemies of the tiger and the monkeys. When he comes to a certain age, he realizes that he is human and must go back to the settlements; a moment of adolescence often occurs in Kipling's fiction, usually a moment of diminishment and always of pathos; but Mowgli is strong because of his animal childhood. Above all, he has learned the Law of the Jungle, which is one of Kipling's picturesque formulations of his own beliefs.

This is a law full of wisdom about courage and cunning and strength; about authority, how to exercise it and how to accept it, and about virility, how to acquire it and how to guard it. This is a wisdom Kipling and his audience cherished, and the Indian setting in which he presented it was more than decorative. It was in India (and the rest of the empire) that England studied such truths, and turned its back on the opposite truths – the liberal-democratic faith – taught at home.

Perhaps the finest of Kipling's treatments of the ethos of the empire's master-class, the aristo-military caste, is *Stalky and Co.* Kipling talks of Stalky, his boyhood friend and fictional hero, in military terms: 'For executive capacity, the organization of raids, reprisals, and retreats, we depended on Stalky, our Commander in Chief, and Commander of his own Staff' (*Something of Myself*, p. 30). And he depicts his other friend, M'Turk, as aristocratic: '. . . in his holidays he was Viceroy of 4000 naked acres, only son of a 300 year old house, lord of a crazy fishing boat, and the idol of his father's shiftless tenantry' (*Stalky and Co.*, pp. 10/11). But both the caste elements are only supplementary to the central theme, which is adventure. And it is adventure taken seriously, taken in relation to its historical function.

This is both a more characteristic and a more significant Kipling success than *Kim*, because of the aggressive moral realism of the meaning, and because of the corresponding intricacy of the artistic means. It is an unpleasant and difficult book; but a powerful study of authority. (Kipling said his original idea was 'tracts or parables on the education of the young', *Something of Myself*, p. 144.)

We are told in 'An Unsavoury Interlude' that, 'Outside

his own immediate interests, the boy is as ignorant as the savage he so admires; but he has also the savage's resource.' And this is a persistent theme; 'tribe' is a word often used. Stalky and Beetle and M'Turk, '. . . spun wildly on their heels, jodelling after the accepted manner of a "gloat", which is not unremotely allied to Primitive Man's song of triumph', (p. 27) and are seen on page 38, 'learning, at the expense of a fellow-countryman, the lesson of their race, which is to put away all emotion and entrap the alien at the proper time'. This they do by deceiving one of the masters, and the point of the story is made by the specificity of the analogy – by the credibility of their behaviour and by Kipling's analysis of it.

They play a West African war-drum, a gift from M'Turk's naval uncle, originally made to signal war across estuaries and deltas: '. . . a deep devastating drone filled the passages as M'Turk and Beetle scientifically rubbed its top. Anon it changed to the blare of trumpets – of savage pursuing trumpets. Then, as M'Turk slapped one side, smooth with the blood of ancient sacrifice, the roar broke into short coughing howls such as the wounded gorilla throws in his native forest.' (p. 60) And as Kipling evokes behind the boys this somewhat fanciful picture of primitive man, he evokes before them the more realistic image of the people they will be ruling and fighting in their adult careers.

The book's central moral paradox, around which its other paradoxes are organized, is that of authority. One of the great lessons the boys learn at school is to obey; and yet the heroes are rebels. This is a serious paradox, for obedience is of the essence of the boys' interrelations – Beetle is obedient to Stalky, for instance; and yet Stalky is a real rebel – Kipling once described Stalky's real-life model as displaying 'an unaffected contempt' for all the masters at their school. The paradox is mediated through the mechanism of the head-master; he represents true authority, which the boys recognize, and he in effect legitimizes their rebellion against the untrue authority of the other masters. He implements the paradox by imposing punishments on them which are categorically 'unjust'. What this does is to give irony a role within a system of piety – to give rebellion a role within a system of authority. Kipling builds a very convincing model of how sincerity – and particularly the sincerity of originality and leadership – can be taught; how a model of aggression and resistance can be built into the teacher-student relationship and not destroy it but energize it.

In the boys' future stands the life of heroism-in-service, most typically in India, on the North-West Frontier. It is represented by the old boys who return to the school, and are just as devoted to the Head as they were as pupils. And by the story in which we hear of Stalky's exploits there, where he has 'become a Sikh', but where he behaves exactly as he did at school, and is again in trouble with the authorities. (And in fact the real-life 'Stalky's' career, as Major-General Dunsterville, did parallel the boy's; long after *Stalky and Co.* was published in the Great War, he led an irregular force from India into Persia, and camouflaged his cars to look like tanks, and so on.) Thus the picture is essentially a triptych; primitive man, the school, and the frontier; no panels from what literature calls mature life or civilization, needless to say.

THE LATER WORK

In Kipling's middle stories, we see the contemporary English countryside from the point of view of the possessing class. In 'The Brushwood Boy', 1895, for instance, the vision of England is pure gold. It is all rose gardens and white peacocks and 'The shadow of the old house lay long across the wonderful English foliage, which is the only living green in the world.'

The hero looks at the round-bosomed woods beyond the home-paddock, where the white pheasant boxes are ranged;

and the golden air is full of a hundred scents and sounds. 'Perfect!' he says, 'By jove, it's perfect!' (*A Kipling Pageant*, p. 364) The same sense of England's beauty, as something rich and perfect, valuable and vulnerable, can be found in 'They', 1904, and 'An Habitation Enforced', 1905. In the first, the house is built of weather-worn stone, with mullioned windows and rose-red tiles, yew topiary, and 'a great still lawn'. There is a great rose-grown gate and a heavy oak door sunk deep in the richness of the wall. (Heavy, deep, and thick – words for carpets and upholstery – are key words in this kind of writing.) In the second, some Americans buy an old house and learn how to live in it, and thereupon they get over their nervous problems, and are able to have a child. (This suggests the connection the culture felt between this kind of expensive beauty and a therapy for exasperated nerves and impaired fertility.) He was creating a myth, and it was a myth of possession and inheriting, not of achievement and building, like his early work. The sardonic-grotesque is replaced by the romantic.

Kipling was justly criticized (for instance, by Chesterton) as being un-English in this kind of writing. He was naming the beauties of the English landscape all too blatantly – as possessions and privileges of the master-class. He was writing like a tourist or an American. It is no accident that the other great describer of English country houses at the same time was Henry James. But by the same token, this is remarkable writing, in the elaborate, sumptuous, Belle Epoque genre – the genre of James, of Proust, of Nabokov. And as in those others, the proud privilege covers impoverishment, the possessions compensate for lost authenticity; the sumptuousness is shot through with guilt and fear. Kipling presents England as an empire to be looted, a rich prey to be ravaged.

For empire meant not only the colonial territories, but the imperial power itself. Kipling's country houses are the embodiment of that wealth and privilege, desirability and vulnerability, in terms of an almost illicit or improper beauty. His language about them renders them sometimes so succulent and sweet and creamy as to be edible, as in 'An Habitation Enforced', sometimes so gleaming, so visibly set and incrusted as to be jewels, as in 'They'. He exaggerates this effect to a point where it is difficult to deal with his more serious meanings, but his self-caricature is truthful. England, in the form of those houses, *was* like a Christmas cake or a set of crown jewels. It was laden with the plunder of the globe.

Kipling's later stories do have some sense of the strengths of rural life, however. He gradually learned, for instance, how to present images of womanhood, and of female kinds of strength, which had been categorically beyond his reach. Indeed, this progress continued after the War. In 'The Gardener' and even more strikingly in 'The Wish House', 1924, perhaps his greatest success in this line, the author's interest, and the plot's momentum, is all in the women; their men are as subservient as the men of Hardy or Lawrence.

Of course this does not mean that Kipling was as great a writer in that line as they. These stories of his are the work of a patient craftsman and a great talent. But Kipling is important not for what he learned from Lawrence and Hardy, but for what he taught to Hemingway and Brecht – by his early work. And of those two, the second is especially interesting, because of the chasms that divide Kipling from Brecht in other ways. The striking similarity of Brecht's *Man Equals Man* (1927) and *Threepenny Opera* to Kipling's early stories and poems indicate the writers' temperamental similarity, in angry protest against polite self-blinding and political sentimentality. If England had lost a major war in 1890 as Germany did in 1918, one might guess, Kipling might have become another Brecht.

Like Kipling, Brecht turned away from artists and intellectuals, preferring the company of boxers and cyclists, in the mid-1920s. He hated concerts, violins, Beethoven, and sang his songs in pubs, drawing on the vaudeville tradition. He used colloquialisms, archaisms, technical jargon, Anglicisms; but his great source was the Bible. He constructed a world of adventure from Kipling and others (Gay, Swift, gangster stories, London underworld myths). 'Everything in the mythical Anglo-Saxon empire, which extends from Alaska to the South Seas, is bigger than life-size, savage, adventurous, and free,' says Martin Esslin, in *Brecht: The Man and His Work* (p. 110). In *Man Equals Man* the Kipling-esque soldiers ransack ancient pagodas for the price of a beer, and storm the mountain fortresses of Tibet.

Like Kipling, Brecht saw himself as a craftsman, and hated the Wagnerian idea of the artist. And in his later development he attached himself to Communism and to the East German regime as eagerly/sardonically as Kipling did to the British empire and its master-class. 'The immoralist, anarchist and nihilist Brecht felt that he *must* find a positive creed,' says Esslin (p. 45). Kipling felt that too, but found his creed in the behaviour of the inexpressive and non-theoretical master-class of the British empire.

It is probably in terms of this affinity with Brecht that we should now think of Kipling. Already at the time of his death Kipling's rejection by England's literature-as-system was obvious. Of the eight pallbearers who bore him to Westminster Abbey, none was an important poet or novelist – which was unprecedented for a writer; his eight included the prime minister, an admiral, a general, and the master of a college. He was honoured by the rulers, and rejected by the writers. But we should remember that beneath the Edwardian plush and the Union Jack lay something very incongruous with them – a spirit as sardonic, as parodic, as bitter, and as twisted, as a Weimar Republic cabaret.

D. H. LAWRENCE:
THE TRIUMPH OF THE SISTERS

OBVIOUSLY LAWRENCE AND KIPLING make very different fundamental statements. One might say that they share a conviction that the conditions of modern life in England – in the great centre of modernizing technology and imperial domination – made simple happiness impossible. But from that conviction Lawrence deduced the need to move outside England and outside those conditions, to create a new life of simple happiness; whereas Kipling stayed inside to build a complex (one might say dishonest) happiness, symbolized in the combination of sumptuous privilege with burdensome responsibility. Kipling tells us to rely on dead forms and social guarantees; Lawrence tells us to find the sources of new life and truth, spontaneous and original.

That is why Kipling and Lawrence are not ordinarily thought to have anything in common or to do with each other – except by those critics who (too eagerly) use the word Fascist as a literary-political category. In their work, Lawrence often figures as a Fascist, while Kipling usually does. That is a challenge which must be dealt with – later – but there is another and more important connection between them – the question of what these two writers have to say to and about each other. One may, I think, take Lawrence's major statements, artistic and ideological, as a dialectical attack upon Kipling. And although they were not primarily intended as such, of course – otherwise the point would scarcely have gone so long undetected – to see them this way is an important clarification.

Lawrence's major work was something we can call *The Sisters*, using his own preliminary title. This was the story (in the grandest sense of story – it is one of the century's greatest philosophic-poetic texts) which he began to write after he eloped with Frieda Weekley in 1912, and the second half of which did not get published until 1920. In the writing it split into two novels, *The Rainbow* and *Women in Love*, the second of which became different enough from the first, in the course of multiple revisions, to be read without reference to it. But if one is to take a large view of Lawrence and what he stands for, one must reunite them. They belong together and they belong in separation from the work he did before 1912 (*Sons and Lovers* is a partial exception) and from what he did after 1920. And one of the dimensions of that separation is quality: *The Sisters* is his greatest work.

Now if we look at this work with Kipling's myth of the imperial caste in our minds, we can see it as an answer, a counter-statement, a denial, and one of a quite deadly character. The sisters, Ursula and Gudrun, triumph over and destroy men who represent Kipling's heroes (and thereby represent the British master-class and the empire it ruled). They elevate in the place of those men Rupert Birkin, the man who represents Lawrence, and who is putatively to represent England as well.

The Sisters is the story of, that is, the analysis of and judgment upon, five attempts at marriage: Tom and Lydia Brangwen, Will and Anna Brangwen, Ursula Brangwen and Anton Skrebenski, Gudrun Brangwen and Gerald Crich, Ursula Brangwen and Rupert Birkin. Of these, the first two are in some sense emblematic cases: they are treated more symbolically and abstractly, in less realistic detail, and in less significant relation to the society around them. In them, moreover, the men are in the crucial conflict with their wives defeated and subdued, but the marriages are in some sense fulfilled and fulfilling.

In the first case, for instance, it is clearly Tom who has to accept limitations imposed by Lydia, not vice versa. When she gives birth to his baby, he has to accept diminution to the status of a child; he and Anna console each other. This is one of the great scenes of the book, and there is no equivalent scene where Lydia is defeated by Tom.

When Lydia thinks over her two marriages, we are told,

> Lydia still resented Lensky. When she thought of him, she was always younger than he, she was always twenty or twenty-five, and under his domination. He incorporated her in his ideas as if she were not a person herself [p. 240] . . . Children had come, he had followed his ideas. She was there for him, just to keep him in condition. She was to him one of the baser or material conditions necessary for his welfare in prosecuting his ideas, of nationalism, of liberty, of science. (p. 241)

Her second marriage was quite opposite in character, in her memory.

> Tom Brangwen had served her. He had come to her, and taken from her. He had gone his way into death. But he had made himself immortal in his knowledge with her . . . [p. 242] . . . she had loved out of fulfillment, because he was good and had given her being, because he had served her honourably, and become her man, one with her. . . . During her first marriage, she had not existed, except through him, he was the substance, and she the shadow running at his feet. She was very glad she had come to her own self. She was grateful to Brangwen. (p. 243)

The passage from which I make these rather long excerpts surely makes clear the dominant theme of *The Sisters*; the triumph of Woman (mother as well as wife) over men, even heroes of nineteenth-century ideas like nationalism, liberty, and science, and the triumph of the man Woman prefers, the man who serves her.

The conflict between Will and Anna is more painful, and the defeat of Will more abject. We are told that he clung to her 'fiercely and abjectly. . . . And she beat him off, she beat him off. . . . For his soul's sake, for his manhood's sake, he must be able to leave her. But for what? She was the ark, and the rest of the world was flood. The only tangible, secure thing was the woman.' (p. 175)

Nevertheless, once Will accepts his secondariness within the household, his position as prince consort, his exile to the workshed and the church, the Brangwen cottage becomes, like the Marsh Farm, a happy family home, full of the abundant vitality of the children and their dependence on their parents. Will has been defeated, as Tom was, but he is not destroyed.

But neither he nor Tom are Kipling men. In the contemporary attempts at marriage, the sisters deal with ruling-class men, and those men are not only defeated but destroyed, and Gerald, the climactic figure, is driven to literal death. (Birkin is, of course, an exception, but one that proves the rule; he is the anti-Kipling man, the servant of Woman.) Anton Skrebensky is one of those subalterns Kipling idolized – like the young men in 'A Conference of the Powers' or those described in 'Drums of the Fore and Aft'. All the main lines of his career refer us to Kipling – specifically, one might say, to *The Light That Failed*: he argues with Ursula about the Mahdi in the Sudan, he goes to fight in the Boer War, he goes to India to become an engineer. So do the main lines of his character: he is modest, inarticulate, physically attractive, eager, ready to die for his country. It is not even entirely trivial that he is often described as 'horsy'. The climactic conversation between them, for the book's themes, occurs before the wedding supper dance.

He has told her how he has learned to shoe horses and

select cattle fit for killing; and she asks him if he likes being a
soldier.

'I am not exactly a soldier,' he replied.
'But you only do things for wars,' she said.
'Yes.'
'Would you like to go to war?'
'I? Well, it would be exciting. If there were a war I
would want to go.'
A strange, distracted feeling came over her, a sense of
potent unrealities.
'Why would you want to go?'
'I should be doing something, it would be genuine. It's a
sort of toy-life as it is.'

This can remind us of the Kipling dialogue quoted before,
from 'A Conference of the Powers'. But Ursula, unlike
Cleever, is unimpressed by this familiarity with fighting
and killing. She declares that it is war that is the game, life
that is serious. Anton replies, 'It's about the most serious
business there is, fighting. . . . [because] You either kill or
get killed – and I suppose it is serious enough, killing.'

'But when you're dead you don't matter any more,' she
said.

He then shifts the ground of his argument, and says, 'It
matters whether we settle the Mahdi or not.' But this she
flatly denies. She does not care about Khartoum.

This is what Maisie might have said to Dick Heldar (who
at the climax of *The Light that Failed* insists on going to
the Sudan campaign). Later Anton evokes the nation, but
Ursula, again like Maisie, refuses to take this seriously.
When he says, 'I would fight for the nation,' she replies,

'For all that, you aren't the nation. What would you do
for yourself?' And finally, 'It seems to me,' she answered,
'As if you weren't anybody – as if there weren't anybody
there, where you are. Are you anybody, really? You seem
like nothing to me.' (pp. 291–3)

And this is in fact the judgment the novel enforces –

Skrebensky is not there. By that reasoning, Dick Heldar, and all Kipling's heroes, are not there. In the next episode, Ursula makes contact with a barge-man, and is

> gladdened by having met the grimy, lean man with the ragged moustache. He gave her a pleasant warm feeling. He made her feel the richness of her own life. Skrebensky, somehow, had created a deadness round her, a sterility, as if the world were ashes. . . . [And even Skrebensky, we are told,] was envying the lean father of three children, for his impudent directness and his worship of the woman in Ursula. . . . (pp. 278–9)

Skrebensky could not desire a woman in that way, we are told. And in the dance scene that follows, Ursula becomes a priestess of the moon-goddess, and destroys him.

She has a strength that Kipling's Maisie, of course, knows nothing of. There are other such scenes, and Skrebensky has finally to acknowledge that he cannot satisfy Ursula, cannot command her imagination, and that in contact with her he has to accept a dependent role, a subsidiary identity, which is cruelly humiliating to him. He withdraws from the relationship, he retreats, he accepts a lesser destiny, in India. That is how every sympathetic reader of the novel sees his fate, and 'India' may legitimately be interpreted as 'Kiplingland'.

Gerald Crich, in *Women in Love*, is not taken so directly from the pages of Kipling, but he even more clearly represents the master-class whose interests Kipling spoke for. He is presented by Lawrence thus: ' "He's a soldier, and an explorer, and a Napoleon of industry," said Birkin, giving Gerald his credentials for Bohemia. . . . "And then he explored the Amazon," said Birkin, "and now he is ruling over coal-mines." ' And he is described as embodying that power. 'His blue, keen eyes were lit up with laughter, his ruddy face, with its sharp fair hair, was full of satisfaction, and glowing with life.' (pp. 56–7)

But we have been shown him before, from a slightly different angle, as someone who must be in charge. And we soon learn to connect that need to command with a strain of hysteria in him, for which the narrative correlative is the fact that as a boy he accidentally killed his brother with a gun. These two themes are brought together in the 'Water Party' chapter, where he allows Gudrun Brangwen to take charge of him for once – allows her to row him, because he has wounded his hand.

> His mind was almost submerged, he was almost transfused, lapsed out for the first time in his life, into the things about him. For he always kept such a keen attentiveness, concentrated and unyielding in himself. Now he had let go, imperceptibly he was melting into oneness with the whole. It was like pure, perfect sleep, his first great sleep of life. He had been so insistent, so guarded, all his life. (p. 170)

And we have just been reminded that, 'He suffered badly. He had killed his brother when a boy, and was set apart, like Cain.' (p. 163) But his sleep is not permitted to continue, because an accident occurs and he must again take charge. 'He was looking fixedly into the darkness, very keen and alert and single in himself, instrumental. . . . It was as if he belonged naturally to dread and catastrophe, as if he were himself again.' (p. 171)

It will be clear in what sense Gerald represents Kipling's world, Kipling's men, by virtue of his capacity for control and command, and by his incapacity for the relaxed and healing relation with a woman. The great example of this is his work in industry. At the end Gudrun reflects on him, on 'what he represented in the world'.

> She thought of the revolution he had worked in the mines, in so short a time. She knew that if he were confonted with any problem, any hard actual difficulty,

he would overcome it. If he laid hold of any idea, he
would carry it through. He had the faculty of making
order out of confusion. [p. 407]

She would marry him, he would go into Parliament
in the Conservative interest, he would clear up the great
muddle of labour and industry. . . . Her heart beat fast,
she flew away on wings of elation, imagining a future.
He would be a Napoleon of peace, or a Bismarck – and
she the woman behind him. She had read Bismarck's
letters, and had been deeply moved by them. And
Gerald would be freer, more dauntless than Bismarck.
(pp. 406–7)

This side of him we can associate quite clearly with the
Kipling who believed in 'using men up'. Gerald too believes
in:

the pure instrumentality of mankind. There had been so
much humanitarianism, so much talk of sufferings and
feelings. It was ridiculous. The sufferings and feelings of
individuals did not matter in the least. They were mere
conditions, like the weather. What mattered was the
pure instrumentality of the individual. Of a man as of a
knife: does it cut well? Nothing else mattered. (p. 215)

This comes from the chapter entitled, 'The Industrial
Magnate'.

And even the strain of hysteria at the bottom of Gerald's
nature is something Kipling often touched on in his treatment of men of power. He portrays them all as fragile,
prone to nervous collapse; even Kim has a sort of nervous
breakdown at the end of his adventures. What Lawrence
added to this diagnosis was the connection with Gerald's
accidental killing of his brother. And we surely need not
limit our reading of that to the most literal plot-meaning,
when we are dealing with so allegorical a fiction as *Women in
Love*. That accident surely represents the fatal fascination

with guns of Kipling's caste (the first scene of *The Light That Failed* presents Dick Heldar and Maisie as children practising with a revolver). It probably also represents the cult of aggression, of hunting, of adventure, of war, of mastery over all the means of death. 'During his childhood and his boyhood he [Gerald] had wanted a sort of savagedom. The days of Homer were his ideal, when a man was chief of an army of heroes, or else spent his years in a wonderful Odyssey.' (p. 213)

But he is a Kipling hero above all because of that naïveté and passivity in his depths that he shares with Skrebensky. Though intelligent enough to see through all the official values of his caste and nation, he has not the faith in himself – or therefore in anyone else – to find out other values. He cannot take charge of his own destiny, and shape it into accordance with his deepest feelings. For that reason, his relations with women are doomed to be either trivial, as they are with Minette, or tragic, as they are with Gudrun. And he is unable to respond to the offer of a creative sexual comradeship which Birkin makes him. Like Skrebensky, Gerald is very attractive to Lawrence (in this context, the vexed question of the homosexual strain in Lawrence need not be raised, since we are dealing with what the novel intends to say rather than what is realized in the text). And Birkin/Lawrence offers himself to Gerald/England, as a friend and potential saviour. He could save Gerald/England from what is now called male chauvinism, from being a male-dominated, death-directed, civilization.

But Gerald turns to Gudrun instead, his female equivalent, a woman who has allowed civilization to limit her freedom and impair her integrity. He finds himself as dependent on her as Skrebensky was on Ursula, or as Will was on Anna. Their conflict is so severe that he tries to kill her, and then goes out into the snow, wanting to die. (The moon again presides over the man's defeat.)

And so he, the Kipling hero drawn on a larger scale than

Kipling himself could essay, is driven to his death by Woman. Gudrun, we may remind ourselves, is another Maisie, a woman artist who drives a hero of empire to his death. But she does so out of strength, not weakness. (She is also, again unlike Maisie, a true artist.)

E. M. FORSTER

In case that should seem too doctrinaire a reading of *The Sisters*, let us look at the other attempt in that decade at major fiction by a 'feminist' writer. That is E. M. Forster's *Howards End* of 1910, also inspired by German ideas of Woman and her power. Lawrence and Forster had many ideas in common. (Edward Carpenter was an important source or station of transition of these ideas for both English writers.) And in *The Longest Journey* (1907) Forster presented his 'natural boy', Stephen Wonham, in explicit conjunction with Lawrence's divinity, the Demeter of Cnidos, just as Lawrence associates Ursula with Cybele and Syria Dea in *Women in Love*.

In *Howards End* we meet again two sisters, this time Margaret and Helen Schlegel, who are in conflict with a family of Kiplingesque men, the Wilcoxes. The Schlegels' father was an anti-imperialist German, 'the countryman of Hegel and Kant'. (p. 28) Of Mr Schlegel Forster tells us that he left his country when it became an empire. 'Germany a commercial Power, Germany a naval Power, Germany with colonies here and a Forward Policy there, and legitimate aspirations in the other place, might appeal to others, and be fitly served by them; for his own part, he abstained from the fruits of victory and naturalized himself in England.' (p. 29) But of course England was an empire too, and only comparatively better. Mr Schlegel implicitly condemned English writers like Kipling. 'When their poets over here try to celebrate bigness they are dead at once, and naturally.'

The Wilcoxes are businessmen, active in the Imperial and West African Rubber Company. But though the Schlegels stand for culture and sensitivity – for vulnerability – by the end of the story the men have been defeated and even destroyed; and the women are in possession of the house for which the novel is named – and which used to be the Wilcoxes' home. Howards End is symbolically England, and so the meaning is in Forster's story what it is in Lawrence's – that England must and shall return to the keeping of women, out of the custody of men. At the end, Helen has a fatherless child, Margaret an invalid husband, and the future is theirs; the Schlegels have triumphed as completely as the Brangwens.

Howards End is an explicitly anti-imperialist novel, for the Wilcoxes are deeply involved with the empire, as part of the larger world of 'telegrams and anger'. Paul Wilcox is on his way to work in Nigeria when we first meet him, and his father describes his going there as a patriotic duty. ' "Someone's got to go", he said simply, "England will never keep her trade overseas unless she is prepared to make sacrifices. Unless we get firm in West Africa, Ger – untold complications may follow." ' (p. 131)

Mr Wilcox's relation to England too is imperialist. 'The world seemed in his grasp as he listened to the River Thames, which still flowed inland from the sea. So wonderful to the girls, it held no mysteries for him. He had helped to shorten its long tidal trough by taking shares in the lock at Teddington . . .' (p. 131)

The overt discourse of the book brings together the Wilcoxes and the Schlegels; culture and civilization must yield something to each other, if they are to meet and England is to be saved. The plot makes it clear that the Schlegels are to triumph, but the discourse insists on honouring the Wilcoxes too. Thus Margaret Schlegel, the book's central intelligence, says,

'A nation who can produce men of this sort may well be proud. No wonder England has become an Empire.' '*Empire!*' says her brother indignantly. 'I can't bother over results', said Margaret, a little sadly. 'They are too difficult for me. I can only look at the men. An Empire bores me, so far, but I can appreciate the heroism that builds it up.' (p. 111)

But her appreciation is sad, is conscientious; it goes against the grain of her *feelings*, and her author's. What the book *shows* us is the defeat of the Wilcoxes, as complete a defeat as that of the Criches in *Women in Love*.

It is interesting that *Passage to India*, Forster's other, and much more brilliant, major novel, is also an anti-Kipling fiction, which may be said to carry the war into Kipling's home-country. Unlike Kipling, Forster was not born in India, spent very little time there, and was a well-established novelist about purely English themes before he wrote anything about the East. He was known as a spokesman for the liberal-democratic faith, and against the Kipling truths. But his Indian work has a privileged position in the Forster canon, because his *Passage to India* (1924) is much the finest thing he ever wrote; it is a very fine novel by any standards, and by most standards better than any single work of Kipling's.

Its subject is the failure of empire to comprehend and subjugate India. At a primary level it presents the British empire, and brilliantly mocks that administrative class which Kipling had so celebrated. As depicted by Forster, these men are completely unable to understand or deal generously with their Indian colleagues or subordinates, and unable to create any life for themselves in India – any life better than a tepid recreation of suburban England. At a secondary level, Forster makes empire include the remnants of the Moslem empire, and Moslem culture in India, which

also failed. This doubling of the material reinforces the
anti-imperial thesis.

The best of the Kipling Englishmen in Chandrapore is the
Collector, Mr Turton. When a 'Bridge Party' is given, to
bring Indians together with English people, he tries to make
it work. 'He made pleasant remarks and a few jokes, which
were applauded lustily, but he knew something to the dis-
credit of nearly every one of his guests, and was conse-
quently perfunctory. When they had not cheated, it was
bhang, women, or worse, and even the desirables wanted to
get something out of him.' (p. 44)

A much inferior kind of Anglo-Indian is represented by
Miss Derek, companion to a Maharani, who has taken leave
from her post without permission.

> Now she wanted to take the Maharajah's motor-car as
> well; it had gone to a Chief's Conference at Delhi, and
> she had a great scheme for burgling it at the junction as
> it came back in the train. She was also very funny about
> the Bridge Party – indeed she regarded the entire
> peninsula as a comic opera. (p. 48)

Mr Turton is more dignified and more generous than that
– until the moment comes when an Indian is accused of
molesting an English girl. Then, 'His face was white, fana-
tical, and rather beautiful – the expression that all English
faces were to wear at Chandrapore for many days.' (p. 163)
But behind his heroism lies blindness and deafness.

> 'I have had twenty five years experience of this country'
> – he paused, and 'twenty five years' seemed to fill the
> waiting-room with their staleness and ungenerosity –
> 'and during those twenty five years I have never known
> anything but disaster result when English people and
> Indians attempt to be intimate socially. Intercourse, yes.
> Courtesy, by all means. Intimacy – never, never.'
> (p. 164)

What Forster is putting his finger on there is precisely the weakness/stiffness which discounted the responsible virtues Kipling had celebrated in Anglo-Indians. Forster spoke for the new anti-Kipling consciousness of the 1920s – a consciousness triggered by the Amritsar Massacre of 1919 if by any one event. *Passage to India* has many other virtues now more important to literary critics, but when it was published it looked more simply like the decade's most brilliant statement of anti-Kiplingism.

LAWRENCE'S LIFE

In terms of class and education, Lawrence's point of origin was not so very different from Kipling's – whose parents, as I have pointed out, were born far below the aristo-military caste they later entered. If we think of the two sets of parents in their adolescence and early youth, we might decide that Lydia Lawrence and Alice Kipling had something in common; both were clever and lively women from genteel-poor families within the Nonconformist culture of the industrial Midlands. Indeed, the two fathers – though they were more different – were both manual workers in Burslem and Eastwood, not far apart, in their early manhoods.

If we think of the two writers' work, it was Lawrence who remained truer to his early upbringing, despite the atmosphere of scandal that pursued him. His indifference to imperial politics, his hostility to armies and wars, his cult of marriage and domesticity, these were caste traits which his mother had fostered in him, and which he made prominent in his writing. It was Kipling, or rather his parents, who betrayed their original caste, to become the minstrels of Simla, entertaining the Viceroy's court with stories, plays, banners, repartee.

However, Lawrence cannot be said to have written for his parents' class, because of his eroticism. That philosophy, and the art that went with it, was a third option, alternative to both the aristo-military imperialism of the adventure story and the moralist humanism of the domestic novel (the literature which his mother may be said to have represented). Eroticism was something new and different; but it can be considered, as I shall show, as the legitimate heir of the latter.

His audience is therefore not so easy to define as Kipling's. We can perhaps suggest it in terms of the conflict between culture and civilization. Fictionally, we can identify these two concepts with the two families of *Howards End*, the Schlegels and the Wilcoxes, and say that Lawrence wrote for the former. (Being a prophet of eroticism, Lawrence presented himself to some degree as the enemy of the Schlegels and of culture; for instance, he spoke against love, and for desire; but that was a dialectical development within culture, and still a resistance to civilization.)

Speaking more analytically, we can associate culture with the fine arts, civilization with technology, industrialism, and the big machines; culture with domestic life and personal relations, civilization with institutional life and impersonal relations; culture with individuals and small groups, civilization with large masses and the means by which they are controlled; culture with women, civilization with men. The contrast between *Sons and Lovers* and *The Light That Failed* as autobiographical novels shows the immense advantage the men of culture have over the men of civilization when they attempt that theme and form. The ineptitude of *The Plumed Serpent* as a political novel shows the disadvantage of the man of culture in that genre.

Lawrence was born in 1885, twenty years after Kipling. His mother had had some education, and loved the world of literacy, but his father was a miner. Miners were something of an untouchable caste in England (and elsewhere); they laboured underground, in cruel discomfort and constant danger, they worked in darkness and came up black at the end of the day, they were badly paid and at the bottom of the social scale, and imaginatively speaking, they were slaves, prisoners, the damned. Lawrence's mother was determined that her sons should not go down the mines, and her consequent stress on education and culture – which excluded her husband from the family life – caused a strain in the writer's childhood. But via his father, Lawrence had access to a layer of English labouring life known to no writer before him – and to few since.

His father proved domestically unreliable, and the mother took on all responsibility, gathering the children around her, and bitterly reproaching him. She fixed strong feelings upon the eldest son, and when he died, she transferred them to 'Bert', who became D. H. Lawrence the writer. He grew up very close to his mother, and in retreat from much of the life surrounding his home, which was rough and sometimes savage.

In adolescence he found himself sexually timid and fastidious, and attracted to men more simply and sensually than to women. Because of a stream of ideas then in circulation in England, as elsewhere, sexual experience was of crucial importance to Lawrence, morally and philosophically as well as personally. We can call this stream of ideas the erotic movement, because it aimed to expand the moral/spiritual importance attributed to sexual experience, to replace Christianity and other ascetic religions, and the purely intellectual disciplines. These ideas were available to anyone who read Nietzsche or Tolstoy's novels, as Lawrence did, and were represented in England itself by Edward Carpenter. One can understand Freud as a part of that movement, and Freudian ideas also reached Lawrence, though a little later – in fact, while he was re-writing *Sons and Lovers*, in 1912. He then understood his sexual problems to derive from his close relation to his mother, and to the failure of her marriage, and he was able to write his remarkable autobiographical novel, which became a manifesto for a whole generation of young people in England.

This was by no means Lawrence's first fiction, but it was

very much better than his first two novels, *The White Peacock* (1911) and *The Trespassers* (1912). It seems likely that it was so in part because Lawrence wrote the final version after his elopement with Frieda Weekley, and with her help. He had shown much of the earlier version to Jessie Chambers, his long-term sweetheart, who figures in the novel as Miriam Leivers. She found the final version a great betrayal, because it told the story of their relations in such a way as to blame her for what went wrong between them, and to give Lawrence and his mother much more flattering roles than he had ever claimed for them before.

It seems likely that she was quite justified in this complaint, but that the novel was much improved by these changes. The image of himself Lawrence had presented in his earlier fiction had been marred by an unprofitable complex of self-reproach and false pride – 'I am great as an artist just because I am guilty as a man' – like that complex which Joyce depicts in Stephen Dedalus. For instance, and crucially, *Sons and Lovers* does not name the homosexual tendencies in the Lawrence character; in *Sons and Lovers*, Paul Morel appears as a sexual naif, naturally ardent but hampered by other people's problems. Lawrence does not falsify his own experience, but he does simplify it. And *Sons and Lovers* works so well because this simplification liberates a powerful dynamic of sympathy. The reader is able to see and to feel what is right and what is wrong – though keeping a strong sense of complexities, impasses, and the suffering of all parties. The reader is able to identify with Paul and to reject Miriam, and to see what was noble as well as what was guilty in his mother's possessiveness.

Exactly what changes Frieda Weekley made or inspired in the manuscript remains unknown, but it seems almost certain that they were important. Frieda had known a circle of German thinkers in the erotic movement, whose ideals of womanhood and erotic freedom and noble innocence she seemed to them (as to Lawrence later) to embody. Her sister

Else had been a brilliant student, and a figure in the women's movement in Germany. And though Frieda sought a different mode of achievement, she knew about the fight for sexual equality, and was equally determined to have a great destiny as a woman. It was through her sister that she had met Otto Gross, the eroticist who meant most to her. He was a disciple of Freud who had, by the time Frieda met Lawrence, gone beyond his master in the direction of erotic liberation and life experiment. Frieda always kept Otto's letters to her, in which he named her the Woman of the Future, but she chose the more reliable Lawrence to be her life-partner, when she ran away from her professor husband.

Both she and Lawrence were very aware of the ideological character of their elopment, of its being a step forward in the erotic movement. She sent her husband Otto's letters, in self-explanation; he spoke of 'making history', and had Frieda read *Anna Karenina*. He saw them as re-enacting but carrying further the story Tolstoy told. Where Tolstoy had lost his faith in erotic values, and began to punish Anna for leaving her husband, Lawrence and Frieda would re-write the story and carry the lovers' fortunes through to a triumphant (morally triumphant) climax.

Having published *Sons and Lovers* with a great *succès d'estime*, Lawrence began work immediately on *The Sisters*, which was in some sense Frieda's life-story, though blended with other materials. It was a triumphal conception, announcing both Frieda's triumph and his own, the woman's and the artist's.

Trapped in England by the outbreak of war in 1914, Lawrence and Frieda suffered badly for the next five years. They were suspected of being disloyal – on occasion suspected of being spies for the Germans, and harassed by the police. *The Rainbow* was prosecuted when it was published, and no one would bring out *Women in Love* for fear of another prosecution. Above all, England's wartime mood was the opposite and enemy of the atmosphere in which the erotic movement could flourish; it was a mood ordained by the master-class, a mood of which Kipling was the official bard. Lawrence had believed that European man had over-come military and male chauvinist habits of feeling, could pass on to a new phase of development; the cruellest experi-ence of the war years for him was the realization that he had been wrong, that men were trapped in a continuing cycle.

Once the war was over, Lawrence and Frieda left England, and never returned to live there in any permanent way. They travelled to Italy, to Sicily, to Australia, to Ceylon, to America, to Mexico. Lawrence wrote prolifically, but not works of the scale and ambition of *The Sisters*. Nor were his themes and attitudes the same. His relations with Frieda were stormy, and they were often on the point of separat-ing. His writing reflected this by concentrating on the relations between men, in *Aaron's Rod, Kangaroo,* and *The Plumed Serpent*. Moreover, Lawrence's health was bad (he had suffered on and off from incipient tuberculosis since 1910) and this added to his restlessness, rebelliousness, and general misery. But in the last years of his life he wrote again out of his relation with Frieda, though this time in a more conservative mood, interpreting eroticism as a modern philosophy of marriage. It is ironic that around this novel, *Lady Chatterley's Lover*, so much scandal should have gathered, since it is really less adventurous – as well as altogether smaller in scale – than *The Sisters*. Lawrence was perceptibly tired; and in 1930, at the age of only 45, he died.

Unlike Kipling, he was not buried in Westminster Abbey, nor did representatives of the armed services or the governmental establishment carry his coffin. In fact, his ashes were involved in a series of minor scandals typical of artistic Bohemia. Frieda had her next husband bring them from the South of France, where they had been interred, to New Mexico, where she was then living, and where he was to build a chapel for them. On the way, however, they got left behind on railway platforms more than once; and in

New Mexico a jealous rival of Frieda's planned to steal them
and scatter them over the soil before Frieda could enshrine
them. All this is ludicrous enough, and cannot be said to
contrast well even with Kipling's case, from most points of
view. But literature – the world of readers and writers – has
found in Lawrence's favour, even in this matter of death and
burial. Kipling was dead for twenty years before 1936.
Lawrence, one may say, is still alive; his books continue to
inspire readers to forms of new life, as well as to critical
appreciation.

HIS ARTISTIC SUCCESSES

If we re-unite *The Rainbow* with *Women in Love*, we have a
novel which moves from the marsh to the mountains. The
Brangwen family have always lived on the Marsh farm, we
are told in the first pages, and marshes to Lawrence meant
low-lying fecundity, a mixture of mud, soil, water, the
home of snakes and lilies and succulent vegetation – the
locus of eroticism. The Brangwens' life there, in the time
before the story begins, is described in Biblical-archaic
language, so as to seem recurrent, cyclical, and in some sense
blind, unconscious. This period in the family history is made
to correspond with the pre-industrial and pre-intellectual
period in cultural history. The story begins when the
Brangwens are awoken, called to consciousness, by the
building of the canal and the railway across their land – by the
industrialization of their landscape. Thenceforth they looked
towards the new town, Beldover, and beyond that to the
world's cities, through the arch of the canal bridge.

This arch is the first of many in the book, which carry
some meaning of time, historical and non-historical, and
some sense of increasing human achievement, but point also
to a size and meaning beyond human scope. For instance,
the cathedral which symbolizes all Will Brangwen's mysticism and aestheticism is described in terms of such an arch.

The greatest of these is the rainbow itself, which recurs as a symbol of spiritual aspiration, and which at the end of *The Rainbow* transfigures as well as transcends the town of Beldover. For Ursula, and for the reader, the rainbow there is a vision of the hope which alone can give men the courage to go on struggling against the brutalization and debasement of life by civilization.

The Rainbow is very much a novel of architectural forms, and of time themes, recurrent and cyclical but also historical time; for its cycles expand man's scope with each generation. *Women in Love*, on the other hand, is timeless; its setting is said to be contemporary, but even so large a fact as the War is not mentioned in it; and it is timeless in the more fundamental formal sense that it is diagrammatic. The crucial mandala is a diamond of which Ursula is the peak, and Gerald the opposite and lowest point, while Birkin and Gudrun (opposite to each other and essentially unrelated to each other) both aspire to and yield precedence to Ursula, and so turn from Gerald and contribute to the triumph of Woman over empire. The light pours down upon the four main characters from directly above, and they cast no shadows, so that the origins and genealogy depicted in *The Rainbow* seem irrelevant. All the readers' attention is directed to the maze the four are in, the paths they must choose between. The ground they stand on is marked out like a philosophic chessboard, into black and white squares, and they move like chessmen according to pre-determined patterns, repeating each other except at the crucial moments of self-determination. And yet, because this is erotic philosophy, and a brilliant novel, the black and white squares are also living marshes, rivers, animals, houses, mountains. And at the end of the story the four find themselves on a summit of the Alps, where they act out their opposite destinies; Gerald goes to his death in the snow, Gudrun chooses decadence, Birkin and Ursula commit themselves to each other, and go down from the white mountains into the fertile darkness of Italy, where life can flourish again.

Those scenes in the mountains belong to the architectural-geographical sequence begun in *The Rainbow*. But mountains are also the phantasms of beauty, pure and abstract beauty, which Gudrun worships, carrying to a further limit her father's inhuman cult of beauty. They are the place of snow and ice and athletic prowess, and so appropriate to Gerald, who has a keen, northern, crystalline beauty. And by the same token, they are the destiny of Western-Northern man, the genius of bright-oiled machinery, and scientific laws, and abstract formulae. They are all that Birkin and Ursula flee for the warm soil and flowers and orange trees of Italy. For *The Sisters* is, together with *A Passage to India*, the supreme achievement of the symbolic fiction of early twentieth-century British literature.

One last continuity to note between the two novels is the 'phenomenological' or thematic treatment of states of consciousness. Lawrence describes his characters' moods to us in terms that are clearly not their own, and yet are equally remote from ordinary discourse. These are states of mind or non-mind for which the best common-sense word is mood, but which are both more portentous than that suggests and more remote from ordinary self-awareness or self-control. These moods accompany or underlie states of physical excitement, like love-making or thunderstorms; but also emotions like mutual antagonism; and even ordinary activities like algebra or 'English' homework, or going to school.

Lawrence's writing of this sort, which is rhythmic, and repetitive, and uses an abstractly melodramatic rhetoric of, for instance, blackness and drowning and waves and shudders of consciousness and so on, is what many people have mostly associated him with. It is what made his contemporaries think him more sex-obsessed than he was; for this rhetoric must not be read as a simply coded message of

sensual excitement – the level of being he is describing may
be said to be as much beyond the senses as it is beyond the
reason.

Women in Love was re-written often during the War, and
the process cost it some ideological self-confidence, though
it conferred formal perfection in compensation. It is a
remarkably crystallized novel; each scene completely
dramatized, with its figures symbolically and brightly
costumed, and each move made by one sister corresponding
to and contrasting with the other's. The sense of place, the
sense of class, above all the erotic meaning of every move is
absolutely clear. The chapters are titled and shaped in such a
way that you can locate a half-remembered passage at will –
something strikingly untrue of *The Rainbow*, where events
are blurred and passages melt into each other. And the prose
is brilliantly pictorial, instead of massively musical.

The death-wish and death-knowledge which Lawrence
had to build into *Women in Love* is to its advantage as a novel,
and the combination of this with the affirmation of life-
values makes for a vivid chiaroscuro. It gives the novel a
tender and rueful honesty, a moving uncertainty, as for
instance in the very last lines. But that is in some ways
ominous for Lawrence himself, for whom much more was
at stake than the achievement of formal perfection in fiction.
Even more ominous are the outbursts of anti-feminine
animus which one finds in later parts of the novel.

> She was on a very high horse again, was woman, the
> Great Mother. Did he not know it in Hermione. . . .
>   And Ursula, Ursula was the same – or the inverse.
> She too was the awful, arrogant queen of life, as if she
> were a queen bee on whom all the rest depended. He
> saw the yellow flare in her eyes, he knew the
> unthinkable over-weening assumption of primacy in
> her. She was unconscious of it herself. She was only too
> ready to knock her head on the ground before a man.

But this was only when she was so certain of her man,
that she could worship him as a woman worships her
own infant, with a worship of perfect possession.

It was intolerable, this possession at the hands of
woman. (p. 192)

And in the chapter, 'Moony', Birkin throws stones at the
reflections of the moon in a pond, trying to destroy this
image of the female goddess. He is protesting against his
dependence on Ursula, and against the dominance of
women in general. The protest is played out on many levels,
from symbol to rational discussion. Thus in the conversation that follows the stone-throwing, Ursula says to Birkin,

'You think, don't you, that I only want physical things?
It isn't true. I want you to serve my spirit.'
'I know you do. I know you don't want physical
things by themselves. But I want you to give me – to
give your spirit to me – that golden light which is in you
– which you don't know – give it me – .' (pp. 241–2)

That is the issue of the book. The spirit is in Ursula, not in
Birkin, but he protests against serving her – he claims what
she has as a free gift. Put in its most positive terms, what
happens between the two is that at the end Birkin has
persuaded Ursula to do that, to understand the relations
between them in those terms, and to live by them. But it is
clear that Lawrence went in considerable fear, and doubt, of
the power he was invoking as a protective deity.

And in the ten years after 1920, Lawrence wrote a good
deal that expressed a rebellion against Frieda and the
doctrine of *The Sisters* His first novel after *Women in Love,
Aaron's Rod,* includes no figure who represents her or her
values – which is a unique case. The central figure, like
Gerald Crich, is offered a saving relationship by a Lawrence-
representative, but refuses it. The suggestion is strong that

he could be saved only by a homo-erotic relationship with another man. The novel has much in common with other literature of the 1920s, notably that of the dandies.

As a political novel, it has much in common with Kipling – its doctrine is what Kipling might have written, if he had been capable of such direct statement. 'We've exhausted our love-urge, for the moment. And we try to force it to continue working. So we get inevitably anarchy and murder. It's no good. We've got to accept the power motive, accept it in deep responsibility, do you understand me? It is a great life-motive.' (p. 345) This is the strain in Lawrence's thought which has earned him the label 'Fascist', which indeed would be acceptable if it could be scrubbed clean of its simply sinister connotations. Clearly Lawrence is here suggesting a political (a cultural) philosophy based on a frank acknowledgment of the relations of power. This diverges from the main thrust of democratic thinking, and aligns Lawrence with Kipling. But this alignment could be called momentary, for neither man was political, and in the body of their work this aspect of their thought counts for very little.

In *Kangaroo* Frieda does appear, and the scenes of domestic comedy between her and Lawrence are funny and charming. But she is allowed no divine or world-saving role. It is the Lawrence-representative who might play that, and he is in some sense kept from it by her. And in *The Plumed Serpent* again the salvation discussed is political rather than erotic, and the eroticism dramatized is between Cipriano and Don Ramon, the magus figure, rather than between Cipriano and Kate, who represents Frieda.

Only in *Lady Chatterley's Lover* and in the related late essays, like 'A Propos of *Lady Chatterley's Lover*', at the end of Lawrence's life, did he restore Frieda and eroticism to a central role in his writing. And speculatively speaking, his writing was quite conservative by that point in his career. He was returning to ideas he had worked out long before, and re-interpreting them in a way that made them more acceptable to the general reader. This was the side of Lawrence, re-creating marriage in modern terms, which has attracted for instance Christian apologists. This work is certainly not contemptible, but the great artist and the bold thinker exhausted himself in writing *The Sisters*.

He began *Lady Chatterley's Lover* by saying, 'Ours is essentially a tragic age. . . . We've got to live, no matter how many skies have fallen.' This is something Kipling might have said, an acknowledgment of duty, a declaration of weary persistence, in the absence of faith. It is well to remind oneself that Kipling was still alive then – he did not die till six years after Lawrence died – and was writing stories that start from a similar point; stories like 'The Gardener' and 'The Wish House'. Both writers were weary by then, and, measured against their own earlier potential, both were conservative. But of course measuring their body of work as a whole, they were absolutely different and pointed readers to opposite directions, in life and in art.

[4]

JAMES JOYCE:
THE EMPIRE OF ART

IT IS WITH LAWRENCE, not with Kipling, that we can fruit-
fully compare and contrast Joyce. But his idea of art and the
artist does nevertheless take Kipling's idea as one of its
starting points, to react against.

In the first chapter of *Ulysses,* the autobiographical
Stephen Dedalus is defined for us as a character, and as the
book's hero, by his difference from his friend, Buck Mulligan. We learn to see Mulligan as 'the usurper', who seems to
be what Stephen really is (the artist as hero), who wins the
Dublin intellectuals' sympathy and admiration which is
Stephen's due. Joyce's aim and triumph – his only triumph,
in handling Stephen – is to win that sympathy and admiration back for his hero, as far as the readers are concerned. We
learn to acknowledge a new idea of the artist.

Mulligan defines himself as a Bohemian boon companion,
genially rebellious against the pieties of both the state
and the home, because he pays his allegiance rather to the
grander, more rigorous truths of art. He offers himself to
Stephen as patron and protector and artistic conscience, as
the one who understands the artist's life-problems. He gazes
upon the ocean with religious emotion, and quotes Swin-
burne. By virtue of these acts of self-definition, he belongs
in the company of Dick Heldar's friends in *The Light That
Failed.* The idea of the artist's life that he embodies is
Kipling's idea. Mulligan offers himself as Stephen's Torpenhow. Joyce rejects that idea.

Mulligan talks grossly and callously of death because of his 'sensitiveness', because, as he says, 'I see them pop off every day in the Mater and Richmond and cut up into tripes in the dissecting room. It's a beastly thing and nothing else.' (p. 8) Stephen is nevertheless offended by such talk, while he, on the other hand, has refused to kneel in simulated prayer when his mother lay dying. This offends Mulligan, who is sentimentally chivalrous and courageous, like Dick Heldar and Torpenhow. Stephen, on the other hand, is intellectually and imaginatively uncompromising.

Moreover, Mulligan is on one side defined or extended by his friendship with Haines, an Englishman who is marked with more simply Kipling traits. Haines is a figure out of *Plain Tales from the Hills*; he is characterized by the fact that – like many Kipling heroes – he has nightmares in which he raves about having to shoot a black panther. He is also presented to us in terms of 'Eyes, pale as the sea the wind had freshened, paler, firm and prudent. The seas' ruler, he gazed southward over the bay. . . .' (p. 18) Again like Heldar and Torpenhow, he represents 'the imperial British state', one of the two masters (the other is the Roman Catholic Church) of which Stephen bitterly declares himself the servant.

Mulligan and Haines are unlike, and in some ways mutually suspect. But they can join each other in a comradeship from which Stephen is excluded: for instance, they swim together, while Stephen fears the water. That is a Bohemian comradeship of young men in which sensibility and prudence, art and social responsibility, can meet on the common ground of genial manliness. Stephen flatly and bluntly disbelieves in the manliness that both profess, rejects even its virtues and attractions, and offers nothing comparable in its place; saying in frank fear, '. . . a man I don't know raving and moaning to himself about shooting a black panther. You [Mulligan] saved men from drowning. I'm not a hero, however. If he stays here, I am off.' (p. 5)

Stephen, and Joyce, reject manliness, the personality structure equivalent to, and necessary to, empire. They reject the
art and the world view which Kipling served, at its very
root. More than anything else, that rejection made them
traitors to all the old standards, and heroes of modernism.

But the more illuminating comparison and contrast is to
be drawn between Joyce and Lawrence. There is as complete a split, a mutual exclusion, a mutual hostility, between
the fictional world of D. H. Lawrence and that of James
Joyce, as we saw between Kipling and Lawrence. One
might say that everything Lawrence omitted from his
characters' 'states of being' in *The Sisters* is to be found in the
'stream of consciousness' of Joyce's characters in *Ulysses*.
(And vice versa; since Joyce's method offers to be inclusive,
it is worth saying that it does not include the moments of
self-determination which Lawrence gives us.) One might
also say that what corresponds within Joyce's world to the
life-inspiring vision of the rainbow at the end of *The
Rainbow* is the quite opposite symbol of the snow at the end
of 'The Dead', the final image of *Dubliners*, an image of easy
and grateful death. Lawrence's reader sees the world 'built
up in a living fabric of truth, fitting to the over-arching
heaven' (p. 494) while Joyce's sees the snow falling 'like the
descent of their last end upon all the living and the dead'
(p. 242).

There was nevertheless a striking likeness between the
two authors' lives, in one important way. Each man
encountered, in his twenties, a woman who came to represent all women to him, and who determined his subsequent
fate, as a man and as a writer. Lawrence was 27 when in 1912
he met Frieda Weekley; Joyce, who was more precocious,
sexually and intellectually, was 22 when in 1904 he met
Nora Barnacle. Both relationships developed very rapidly,
even though there were wide social and intellectual gaps,
educational and experiential gaps, between the two partners
in both cases. Joyce married the peasantry in Nora, as

Lawrence married the aristocracy in Frieda.

Both writers' mothers had just died, in circumstances that left a legacy of grief and guilt in the men's minds, but at the same time set them free to marry. The love-relationship had to be kept secret from the fathers and the rest of the families; and the two couples both went abroad and lived together without marriage. In both cases this stay abroad lengthened into a permanent exile; one might say that the two writers never really came home, after those leavings, in 1904 and 1912 respectively.

Then the two women were both notably 'physical' and 'female' – terms nearly everyone has used about them. Their presence was at all times assertively feminine and distinguished them from the other women Joyce and Lawrence knew. They offered themselves to be known as Woman, and the two writers took them as such. The latter became significantly married men, within what they wrote and outside it, in ways that were not true of, say, T. S. Eliot and Ezra Pound. Lawrence was a good housekeeper, Joyce a bad one, but both were domestic creatures. An important focus of their imaginations and identification of their personalities for us were the home's orderliness in the one case and disorderliness in the other.

In both cases, the marriage helped the man arrive at manhood. Joyce told Nora, 'You made me a man'; and it is obvious that the same was true for Lawrence. Both men had the same difficulty in declaring their feelings for the woman – a difficulty in using the word 'love'. (Both were acutely conscious of living out the end of an age of love.) And both women thought of the men as having more refined and spiritual temperaments than themselves – as being spoiled monks. Joyce, who indulged his fantasies much more shamelessly than Lawrence, wanted to be a child in Nora's womb, and often saw the artist-creator as a female, giving birth. In his different way, as we have seen, Lawrence saw personal and artistic salvation in submitting to woman.

Finally, Lawrence and Joyce both became great writers
by grace of this relationship and what they made of it in
fiction. Nora did not work *with* Joyce as Frieda did with
Lawrence, but Molly Bloom is as great a female figure as
Ursula Brangwen, in her different way. Leopold Bloom
derives his mythic dignity (all that distinguishes him from,
say, Babbitt, Sinclair Lewis's somewhat similar little man)
from his function as cuckolded husband and priest of the
mysteries of the Mother Goddess.

Joyce is therefore, like Lawrence, a figure in the erotic
movement in art, and the erotic movement is one element in
his resistance to empire. The difference between them is that
his cult of Magna Mater is blasphemously comic, while
Lawrence's is religiously serious. Comedy is the mode in
which Joyce is successful, at least; the passage describing
Stephen's erotic vocation in *A Portrait of the Artist as a Young
Man* is so catastrophically and categorically false because it is
written in the wrong mode for Joyce – because it is religiously serious in intention. It aligns itself with, for instance,
the descriptions of Ursula stepping into the barge in *The
Rainbow*, or giving herself to the moon-goddess just after;
and in any such alignment Joyce looks false, in any such
competition he fails. (The wonderful Gertie Macdowell
sequence in *Ulysses* shows how Joyce *should* treat a girl on a
beach and a man adoring her at a distance, where he turns
the scene into satiric comedy, at the heart of which is a
blasphemy against erotic idealism.)

> Stephen, on the sea-shore, sees a girl standing in the
> water, gazing out to sea. She seemed like one whom
> magic had changed into the likeness of a strange and
> beautiful seabird. Her long slender bare legs were
> delicate as a crane's and pure save where an emerald trail
> of seaweed had fashioned itself as a sign upon the flesh.
> Her thighs, fuller and softhued as ivory, were bared
> almost to the hips where the white fringes of her

drawers were like featherings of soft white down. Her slateblue skirts were kilted boldly around her waist and dovetailed behind her. Her bosom was as a bird's soft and slight, slight and soft as the breast of some darkplumaged dove. But her long fair hair was girlish; and girlish, and touched with the wonder of mortal beauty, her face. (p. 433)

This is a classical example of how a writer can have two intentions and how they can cancel each other. On the one hand Joyce wants the girl to be empirically real – 'the white fringes of her drawers' are realistic. On the other he wants her to be a symbol, an epiphany – and so he chants rather than describes – 'Her bosom was as a bird's soft and slight, slight and soft as the breast of some darkplumaged dove.' The result is that the bosom, the girl, is neither real nor epiphanic, but a work of art in the sense of a stage property, a dressmaker's dummy; we see her in terms of textures and contours, upholstered, inert, and static.

Joyce is therefore a somewhat (a comically) Satanic figure within the erotic movement. To use Lawrentian terms, he is the poet of appetite, not of desire. But Molly Bloom, the anti-Penelope, who dominates *Ulysses* by lying on her bed, the presence to which both men turn at the end of the day, the end of the book, is by virtue of that domination a royal or divine figure in our imaginations. Joyce said of her episode, 'Though probably more obscene than any preceding episode it seems to me to be perfectly sane full amoral fertilisable untrustworthy engaging shrewd limited prudent indifferent *Weib.*' (*Letters*, I, p. 170)

Woman becomes then a majestic presence, but within the realm of comedy, according to the rules of art; that marks the difference between Joyce and Lawrence. The passage quoted from *Portrait of the Artist as a Young Man* is part of Stephen's vocation as an artist, and that is what Joyce/ Dedalus went on to become, the architect of a palace of art, as impressive and enormous in its own terms as the palaces of empire. It is typical of the many differences between him and Lawrence that the latter did not portray himself in fiction as an artist. This means that Joyce's effectiveness as an enemy of empire has been within the sphere of art – as artist rather than as priest of Eros; readers of Lawrence rather than readers of Joyce have been inspired to stand up in opposition to the state, to come out of society, to try to create a new life. But Joyce has found an audience in the academy; and this is a more institutionalized and subsidized group than Lawrence's audience; so Joyce's contribution to (passive) social dissidence may be the greater in the long run.

Predictably, Lawrence and Joyce did not care for each other's work; Lawrence described *Ulysses* as an *olla podrida*, of the offal, detritus, and fag-ends of life; he did not give Joyce a fair reading, any more than Joyce gave him one. But in this one phase of their life and work the two writers did come close enough to differ significantly. That is, the differences between them can be taken as comparable and alternative choices, and so can be taken as dialectically related to each other. This is a dialectical opposition within the erotic movement, however, and both Lawrence and Joyce were engaged, were comrades, in the erotic opposition to the empire and Kipling.

JOYCE'S POLITICS

Within his own lifetime (as distinct from his books' lifetime) Joyce's opposition to empire was manifested indirectly – via his opposition to Irish nationalism. That nationalism was opposed to British imperialism, of course, but the two were not generically different, since the empire was the efflorescence of English nationalism; indeed, nationalism was generally acknowledged to be the nobler form of empire, so to reject the former was a priori to reject the latter. By

family inheritance, as the son of John Stanislaus Joyce the
Parnellite, Joyce was an Irish patriot; and by cultural generation, as one of the sons of Yeats, Synge, Moore, etc., he was
an Irish cultural revivalist. Both these heritages (and that of
the Roman Catholic church in Ireland) he repudiated. In
immediate terms, that repudiation enfeebled his protest
against British imperialism; he refused to stand shoulder to
shoulder with those who were making the effective protest.
But historically speaking, his disavowal of even nationalist
politics implies, all the more completely and contemptuously,
a disavowal of empire.

However, we must not underestimate the degree to
which Joyce was politically anti-imperialist just by heritage.
Malcolm Brown says, in *The Politics of Irish Literature*, that
Joyce lived in Irish history 'With an intimacy and depth
denied to Yeats. As everyone knows, his Irish experience
was extra compelling. . . . Joyce was without rival in his
mastery of its taste and flavour, its "felt history".' (p. 17)
And the significance of this is that, as Brown says, from
Norman times to the nineteenth century, the history of
Dublin was mostly the history of the Anglo-Irish wars.
'After Waterloo the wars recessed while Britain became the
workshop of the world; and amid the celebrated advance of
Victorian times, Ireland was the retarded child.' Between
1840 and 1920 England and Wales's population increased by
250 per cent, but Ireland's decreased by 50 per cent.
The English visited Ireland 'as men visit a wreck on a
neighbouring coast' (Brown, p. 3). Cecil Woodham-Smith
has pointed out that looking at English history, especially
imperial history, from the Irish point of view entails revers-
ing the values, turning the great heroes, Queen Elizabeth,
Cromwell, William III, Pitt, into great villains.

Joyce was in fact a kind of Socialist, though a non-
political kind. He was sharply hostile to what he called the
feudal, as well as to the imperial. In the first draft of *Portrait
of the Artist*, the most autobiographical draft, he saluted the

'generous idea' of Socialism. He signed no protests, but like Bloom he admired Arthur Griffiths, who founded the separatist Sinn Fein (Ourselves Alone) in 1902. Joyce also read Kropotkin, Bakunin and Proudhon (whose ideas on property seem to be reflected in *Exiles*, according to Ellmann). His main political authority was Bakunin, who condemned religion and idealism as well as brute materialism (Ellmann, *The Consciousness of Joyce*, p. 83). Clearly, he was an anarchist as much as a Socialist.

In Trieste, also, Joyce was involved with anti-imperialist groups. Trieste was a part of the Austro-Hungarian empire which felt itself to be Italian; three-quarters of the population spoke that language. Joyce there met many Jewish merchants (who were all for Italian rule) and began to identify with the Jews, the one nation exempt from the guilt of aggression. He told Frank Budgen later that their refusal of Christianity had been a heroic sacrifice, and that Jews made better husbands, fathers, and sons. Some of that feeling is clearly expressed in his depiction of Leopold Bloom in *Ulysses*. But of course in Trieste Joyce represented Ireland, and the enemy he was called to attack was the British empire, not the Austrian. And in 1913 he in fact wrote three articles on the evils of empire for a newspaper owned by his friend, Teodoro Mayer, the third of which was bitter against the English. But his politics were cosmopolitan, not nationalist: for he also called the 'Irish rabblement' the most belated race in Europe – Europe's afterthought.

He hated violence as much as feudalism, and so could never be a political revolutionary. In *Stephen Hero* he described his autobiographical hero thus: 'The attitude which was constitutional with him was a silent, self-occupied, contemptuous manner and his intelligence, moreover, persuaded him that the tomahawk, as an effective instrument of warfare, had become obsolete.' (D. Manganiello, *Joyce's Politics*, p. 68). And in *Ulysses*, Stephen taps his brow and declares, 'In here it is I must kill the priest and king.' And

Bloom declares, 'I resent violence or intolerance in any shape or form. It never reaches anything or stops anything.' (*Ulysses*, p. 643)

This pacifism has deep roots in Joyce, since he is willing to repudiate the whole structure of personality which supports the use of violence. He would get rid of the instinct of pugnacity even at the cost of manliness itself, as we shall see. It is here that we can locate his fundamental opposition to Kipling. Joyce defined his representative, Stephen Dedalus, as not manly in contrast with Davin and Cranly in *Portrait of the Artist as a Young Man*; and in contrast with Mulligan and Haines in *Ulysses*, where Bloom is similarly contrasted with the Citizen and with Blazes Boylan. As Ellmann says, Joyce always favours men who retreat from manhood and associate themselves with women. And in so far as Bloom and Stephen both triumph (over Blazes and over Mulligan) by the grace of Molly, we may say that Joyce joins Lawrence in the erotic/dialectical opposition to Kipling.

H. G. WELLS

Joyce invoked the sponsorship of other writers for his rejection of politics/religion/empire, and his declaration of political independence as an artist. He praised James Clarence Mangan as one of those who believe that their inner life is so valuable that they have no need of popular support; [that] . . . the poet is sufficient in himself, the heir and preserver of a secular patrimony . . .' (Manganiello, p. 199). He also invoked Ibsen: he told his brother that his own attitude to socialism and literature resembled Ibsen's.

But the writer I should like to associate with Joyce in this matter of socialism is H. G. Wells. In one phase of his career as a novelist, Wells seems to have invented an objective correlative for a Socialist sensibility which Joyce was able to make use of.

The Wells novels most relevant here are *The Wheels of*

Chance (1896) about Hoopdriver, a Cockney shop assistant on a cycling tour; *Love and Mr Lewisham* (1900) about a teacher of science who hopes to do great things but has to accept the limitations of his marriage and his job; *Kipps* (1905) about another shop assistant who inherits money and escapes his caste, but finds the socially privileged more boring rather than less so; and *Mr Polly* (1910) about a little man who runs away from a wife whose cooking gives him indigestion, and ends up with a motherly type at the Potwell Inn; Mr Polly became the progenitor of many a little man with a big woman, from Leopold Bloom to Charlie Chaplin.

Of these novels the last two were the most important, and were extremely popular. *Kipps* sold 12,000 in the first twelve months after it appeared, and by 1910 had sold 60,000. Wells in general was a world-author, translated into French by 1899, and by 1904 also into Italian, German, Swedish, Dutch, and Polish. In Russia his books were always serialized, and his first *Collected Works* appeared in 1901, and the second, in 13 volumes, in 1908. What he taught was above all the necessity and the imminence of social-political change; and Stalin, Lenin, Churchill, T. R. Roosevelt and F. D. Roosevelt all listened to him.

The significance of his work from our point of view – as an objective correlative for a socialist sensibility – can be gathered from the comments of contemporary readers and reviewers. They spoke of Wells's 'infinite tenderness for the ordinary', and of his 'genius for the commonplace', and said Wells manages to secure a very large amount of sympathy and interest for his 'underbred, lovable hero'. They said, 'Our sympathies are enlisted at once for poor Lewisham, with his small capacities, his meagre opportunities and his vaulting ambitions. . . . The married life of the man (he married on £1 a week and with £50 in the bank) is made intensely interesting to us.' (P. Parrinder, *H. G. Wells: The Critical Heritage*, p. 81) It will be seen how much of this could have been said about Leopold Bloom, had not reviewers been frightened out of their social condescension by Joyce's virtuoso performances of intellectual and stylistic superiority. (This is one of the most important functions of those virtuoso performances.)

But it is *Kipps* which, developing the same idea further and becoming so very popular, almost certainly reached Joyce in one form or another in the years before he began *Ulysses*. Kipps, the contemporary reviewers tell us, 'essays culture'; he labours at the reading of Ruskin's *Sesame and Lilies* and at the tenth edition of *Encyclopaedia Britannica*. This is the same figure we meet as Leopold Bloom in *Ulysses* but also as Leonard Bast in Forster's *Howards End* – a figure which derives in some sense from Kipling's Cockney clerks. But in Wells's hands he is much more fully human. It is symptomatic that the reviewers took him, and the heroes of the other Wells novels in this series, to be autobiographical self-portraits. (Nobody took Forster or Kipling to be portraying themselves in those figures.) And Joyce developed the motif to the status of major art.

There is a remarkable letter by Henry James to Wells which makes the point well. He calls *Kipps* a masterpiece and extraordinarily alive, saying,

> (1) You have written the first closely and intimately, the first intelligently and consistently ironic or satiric novel. . . . (2) You have for the first time treated the English 'lower middle' class, etc., without the picturesque, the grotesque, the fantastic and romantic interference, of which Dickens . . . is so full.
> (Parrinder, p. 126)

If we take this as seriously as it deserves, we will see that it constitutes a high claim for Wells and for the originality of this fictional idea. Finally H. L. Mencken said that *Mr Polly* was about the *average* Englishman. 'It is to this common and intensely human man, to this private soldier in the ranks of Christian civilization, that Mr Wells turns in his new novel,

Mr Polly.' (ibid., p. 179)

Wells of course was not a great novelist, though very gifted; he was not great largely because he did not try hard enough at the craft of fiction. He had always written non-fiction books as much as fiction, and though in that genre too he did not aim high (he wanted and got a broad audience) he took that more seriously. He began calling himself a journalist and not a novelist early in his career.

We may say that Joyce carried through, in serious fiction, the enterprise that Wells sketched out and abandoned. Joyce *was* ready to work hard, and aim high, in artistic terms; and he had no conflicting ambition to reach a broad audience with non-fiction. In the Bloom half of *Ulysses* (of course the Stephen half is another matter) he glorified the Socialist sensibility which was very important to the later English writers. One of those is George Orwell, most notably in *Coming Up for Air*, as we shall see later.

JOYCE'S LIFE

Joyce was born in 1882, the eldest son of a man of striking talents and some inherited property. John Stanislaus Joyce cut a figure in the political-literary-intellectual society of Dublin pubs, but relied for his power to impress himself on others on the ephemeral means of social contact. (His son, in reaction, turned to the marmoreal means of art.) His most lasting employment was politically obtained, as a city rate collector; and his only chance of rising to something better was as a political lieutenant of Charles Stewart Parnell, the leader of the Irish MPs in Gladstone's Parliament. This political affiliation, to the haughty Anglo-Irishman who was betrayed and assailed by a mob of his ex-followers when he got into trouble, was James Joyce's main political heritage and the occasion of his first poem.

This anti-political loyalty to Parnell was common to the leaders of the cultural revival. George Moore adored Parnell;

and Yeats said in his Nobel Prize Speech that the modern literature of Ireland began when Parnell fell from power in 1891. They were all alienated from the national cause, and in some sense from politics, by their devotion to Parnell, but of them all it was Joyce who was most embittered. When he grew up and went to the university, he entered the Irish cultural revival led by Yeats, A.E., Lady Gregory, Synge, etc., which promoted the Gaelic language and Irish history and Irish mythology, as the raw materials for a great literature. But this option of opposition to English culture Joyce also rejected. Instead he chose personally an alienation from Ireland – literal exile – and culturally a form of the European movement of symbolism embodied in Ibsen, D'Annunzio, Hauptmann, etc. And later, as we have seen, he came to a kind of art which broke down hierarchical barriers of class sensibility, and made art focus on the lowest common denominator, politically speaking, the lower middle class man – upon 'average' contemporary culture, and even the below-average sheer detritus of our lives.

John Stanislaus Joyce's fortunes declined steadily after 1890, and the wife and children suffered poverty while the father continued a more improvident and drunken version of his early expansiveness. James Joyce was a favourite son, recognized as brilliant, and to some degree exempted from the deprivations the other siblings suffered, though he was by the same token burdened with extra guilt.

According to *Portrait of the Artist*, he felt some vocation to the priesthood. 'How often had he [Stephen Dedalus] seen himself as a priest wielding calmly and humbly the awful power of which angels and saints stood in reverence . . . accomplishing the vague acts of the priesthood which pleased him by reason of their semblance of reality and of their distance from it.' (*The Portable James Joyce*, p. 418) And we are told later that only in 'vague sacrificial or sacramental acts' did he feel himself drawn to go forth to encounter reality (p. 119). This bears clearly enough on Joyce's attraction to

Symbolism, as an artistic movement with religious aspirations. But it also bears upon his refusal of manhood, for the
passage quoted continues, 'And it was partly the absence of
an appointed rite which had always constrained him to
inaction. . . .'
He cannot act because in some sense he cannot feel.

> He had heard the names of the passions of love and hate
> pronounced solemnly on the stage and in the pulpit, had
> found them set forth solemnly in books, and had
> wondered why his soul was unable to harbour them for
> any time or to force his lips to utter their names with
> conviction. A brief anger had often invested him, but he
> had never been able to make it an abiding passion. . . .
> [He had felt lust but] it too had slipped beyond his grasp
> leaving his mind lucid and indifferent. This, it seemed,
> was the only love and that the only hate his soul would
> harbor. (p. 408)

And for Stephen (James Joyce) to identify himself that way
was to renounce the heritage of his father and of the heroes
of the nationalist movement, who presented themselves as
stage heroes of passion, pride, revolt, and every generous
and manly emotion. This is brilliantly dramatized in the
Christmas dinner scene.

But if drawn to the priesthood, Joyce rebelled against
Christianity and the Church. As the scene of Stephen's
being called to the priesthood makes clear, neither had any
room for something that Joyce offers us implicitly as the
best thing in him – his love of the trivial, the ordinary, the
light-weight. As Stephen stands with the priest who has just
invited him to join his order,

> Towards Findlater's church a quartet of young men
> were striding along with linked arms, swaying their
> heads and stepping to the agile melody of their leader's
> concertina. The music passed in an instant, as the first

bars of sudden music always did, over the fantastic
fabrics of his mind, dissolving them painlessly and
noiselessly as a sudden wave dissolves the sandbuilt
turrets of children. (p. 421)

In that moment, unconsciously, Stephen's decision was
taken: he would never become a priest; he would become an
artist. And the best of Stephen/Joyce's writing was to
endorse that choice. It was the extraordinary energy and
elaboration of his response to trivia, the passion of exact
notation combined with the play of prodigious fancy,
which were Joyce's best gifts – his most spiritual vocation –
as an artist. Other scenes presenting that vocation, like the
one mentioned before, of the wading girl, are far more
pretentious and less authentic, more rhetorical and less
original.

Repudiating Christianity and ordinary social morality,
Joyce grieved his mother's last years. In August 1904, he
wrote to Nora Barnacle,

> My mother was slowly killed, I think, by my father's
> ill-treatment, by years of trouble, and by my cynical
> frankness of conduct. When I looked on her face as she
> lay in the coffin – a face grey and wasted with cancer – I
> understood that I was looking at the face of a victim and
> I cursed the system which had made her a victim.

Before that he had written Nora, 'How could I like the idea
of home? My home was simply a middle class affair ruined
by spendthrift habits which I have inherited . . . I cannot
enter the social order except as a vagabond.' (*Letters*, II,
p. 48)

Leaving Ireland with Nora in 1904, he spent ten years in
Trieste, teaching English at a Berlitz School; then moved
to Zurich, where he began to be funded by rich patrons
of the arts; and then, in 1920, to Paris. The rest of his life
was devoted to his art, in the sense that none of his other

occupations were more than get-rich schemes or domestic tribulations. Like his father, he was quite improvident, and often in debt, and the family was protected and rescued time and again by other people.

HIS WORK

In *Dubliners*, Joyce set out to tell more of the truth about Ireland than Yeats and his friends were telling with their mythological and 'poetic' preoccupations. He described the streets of Dublin in all their meanness, allowing his scene no colour, no warmth, no size. (In *Ulysses* he does give those streets colour, of a different sort.)

Dubliners is then a truth-telling book; with the stress that phrase usually implies, on de-flating and de-afflatusing truths. The book's weakness is that its message is also de-energizing, and not only for readers with Yeatsian expectations about Irish literature. What one might call the principle of life in literature – that is, literature's enhancement of our expectations, our enjoyments, our depth and force of feeling – is cruelly confounded and confused, in writer as well as in reader.

For instance, one of the many categories of disgust and displeasure Joyce invokes is coarseness; the people of Dublin are coarse. This is often rendered physically, in terms of stiff, stolid, materiality. One of the young men characters

> walked with his hands by his sides, holding himself
> erect and swaying his head from side to side. His head
> was large, globular and oily; it sweated in all weathers;
> and his large round hat, set upon it sideways looked like
> a bulb which had grown out of another. He always
> stared straight before him as if he were on parade and,
> when he wished to gaze after someone on the street, it
> was necessary for him to move his body from the hips.
> (*The Portable James Joyce*, p. 61)

In other cases, the coarseness is rendered in terms of a sensual sordidness, as in the central character in the story 'Counterparts'.

> When he stood up [he] was tall and of great bulk. He had a hanging face, dark wine-coloured, with fair eyebrows and moustache: his eyes bulged forward slightly and the whites of them were dirty. (p. 97)

This coarseness extends out to the street life of the city.

> We walked through the flaring streets, jostled by drunken men and bargaining women, amid the curses of labourers, the shrill litanies of shop-boys who stood on guard by the barrels of pigs' cheeks, the nasal chanting of street-singers, who sang a *come-all-you* about O'Donovan Rossa, or a ballad about the troubles in our native land. (p. 41)

Because of this stress, the reader recognizes the writer (and himself) as a figure of refinement and delicacy of taste. The passage last quoted continues:

> These noises converged in a single sensation of life for me: I imagined that I bore my chalice safely through a throng of foes.

But one then finds that Joyce reserves his most vindictive censure for the refined and delicate of taste, like Little Chandler in 'A Little Cloud' and Mr Duffy in 'A Painful Case'. Chandler is presented to us thus:

> His hands were white and small, his frame was fragile, his voice was quiet and his manners were refined. He took the greatest care of his fair silken hair and moustache and used perfume discreetly on his handkerchief. The half moons of his nails were perfect and when he smiled you caught a glimpse of a row of childish white teeth. (p. 80)

After this, it is of course impossible for the reader to identify with the character, who has been defined in terms of a failure in virility. Though we see him in contrast with Gallaher (another coarse and heavy character) and though Chandler is a poet, who sees and suffers what the writer does, we cannot join him in those perceptions. The purpose of self-mortification (the reader's self as well as the writer's – literature's self) undercuts the other purposes of the story.

This is not true of the whole book, and in 'The Dead', Gabriel Conroy, though clearly another Chandler, is allowed to represent Joyce and us without such cruel punishment. By the same token, however, Gabriel is not a deeply interesting figure, and though there is some appreciative warmth in the first part of the story, and some gentle wistfulness in the second (both quite unlike the harsh depreciative truth-telling of the other stories) this is achieved at the cost of abandoning the original enterprise, and even of some degree of inauthenticity. Though a good deal of Dublin is to be met in this story, there is very little of Joyce; that is to say, he writes the first half in the character of Charles Dickens, and the second in the character of a symbolist. The snow equals the mist equals the ocean equals death equals Ibsen.

The real artistic success of *Dubliners* is to be found in the stories 'Ivy Day in the Committee Room' and 'Grace'. In the second, the writer assembles a typical cast of Dublin characters, heavily marked for us as dull, coarse, self-deceiving, sordid. But then, in a second scene, he relents and begins to respect their qualities, though with at first a rather uncertain tone.

> Everyone had respect for poor Martin Cunningham. He was a thoroughly sensible man, influential and intelligent. His blade of human knowledge, natural astuteness particularized by long association with cases in the police courts, had been tempered by brief

immersions in the waters of general philosophy. His friends bowed to his opinions and considered that his face was like Shakespeare's. (p. 171)

Obviously the reader cannot take over these opinions trustingly, and half expects to have Cunningham's claims exposed. But as the action proceeds we gather that he is indeed well-informed and sensible and intelligent.

In 'Ivy Day in the Committee Room', moreover, the technical skills and debunking zeal of the early stories are allied with and redeemed by something very different. It begins with a series of snap-shots of small-time Dublin politicians (as so often, Joyce works by adding figures, one by one, to a scene as static as a stage-set). Each one signifies a kind of physical and moral ignominy.

But then one of them recites a poem he has written on the death of Parnell, because this is the anniversary of his death. Parnell is their symbol of all that politics might be and should be; he is so because he held himself so aloof from the ignominious and malicious games they themselves play. And the poem is both entirely credible as the product of that man, recited to those other men, and entirely credible as the expression of grief and anger in poetic form. The poem is both circumscribed by its fictional context, and yet independently alive within that, which is technically very difficult. But above all it is a brilliant stroke thematically. It reveals a source of their feeling for Parnell, by stressing Parnell's haughty refusal to be a man among men, a man like themselves; but this also makes poignant the way they can acknowledge in him something beyond their own scope. The moral exhaustion of the other stories is here alleviated by this opposite yearning for something greater – for 'Our Uncrowned King'. Without altering the downward thrust of his probe, his scalpel, his pitchfork, Joyce allows a beam of light from above to pass along it.

Portrait of the Artist as a Young Man is even less successful artistically than *Dubliners*. Joyce was scarcely more gifted than Kipling (or at least much less gifted than Lawrence) at the crucial tasks for an autobiographical novelist. He could not portray himself as a character the reader can like enough to trust as his own representative in the world of the novel; nor can he portray the figures with whom that character has his major emotional dealings vividly enough for us to believe in them as independent beings, and yet see them as the character sees them.

Let us take as an example this passage about Stephen's relations with his mother – inserting the preface that these relations are otherwise practically ignored in the book.

> he thought coldly how he had watched the faith which was fading down in his soul aging and strengthening in her eyes. A dim antagonism gathered force within him and darkened his mind as a cloud against his disloyalty: and when it passed, cloudlike, leaving his mind serene and dutiful towards her again, he was made aware dimly and without regret of a first noiseless sundering of their lives. (pp. 426–7)

There is of course self-reproach in the words 'coldly' and 'without regret'; but that is fatally attenuated by the careful narcissism of the prose – perhaps to be located above all in 'dim' and 'dimly' – because so much of the energy seems to go into verbal elegance.

There is, however, one brilliantly written episode in the novel, the Christmas dinner scene, and his success there can help us to understand why Joyce had the difficulties he had with autobiographical fiction. The artistic triumph of this scene is: 1, to render fully but objectively the violence of Irish life (external and internal); 2, to explain Stephen's turning away from both the church and anti-clerical nationalism; 3, to unite naturalistic realism with classical rhetoric and drama. From the slow and casual beginning to the highly theatrical end, there is not a word (with the exception perhaps of a couple of passages of Stephen's musings) which does not contribute both to the empirical reality of the scene, rooting it multiply in its historic-sociological-political contexts, and also to the steadily mounting emotional tension and excitement, as single in its curve as a scene in tragedy by Racine.

Like 'Ivy Day in the Committee Room', this episode achieves an intensity of art-and-truth which is scarcely to be matched anywhere in Lawrence's or Kipling's work. This kind of writing establishes Joyce as one of the great realists. Realism can mean almost anything, but here it means the felt presence of a powerful analytic mind standing outside the scene and selecting the details to name; that mind's action is entirely concealed, since all the action is dramatized and objectified, but it is acutely felt.

But I want especially to point to the diagnostic implications of the scene for Stephen's development. These lie in the contrast between the Dedalus/Casey 'party' to the debate and the Dante Riordan party – which is also a contrast between men and women. The men, who back Parnell and secular nationalism, have all the passion on their side, all the poetry in their speech, all the eloquence, the history, the generosity, the humour, the vitality.

> Stephen looked with affection at Mr Casey's face which stared across the table over his joined hands. He liked to sit near him at the fire, looking up at his dark fierce face. But his dark eyes were never fierce and his slow voice was good to listen to. (p. 278)

The women, and the church, have to offer only Dante's vindictive, repetitive, curtly assertive, rectitude – citing authority in short sharp phrases – or else Mrs Dedalus's plaintiveness, ancillary hostess-ship, insignificance. This contrast of the competing claims upon his loyalty clearly leaves Stephen with no alternative but to love the wrong. The passage quoted before continues, 'But why then was he against the priests? Because Dante must be right then.'

Of course Stephen ceased to see the conflict in such black and white terms as he grew older. But it remained a conflict for him, because he was not able to join his father and Mr Casey as a bold rebel for Ireland's sake. Mr Dedalus/Joyce revealed himself as improvident and exploitative, and as intellectually and morally fraudulent, in every aspect of his life except that of social theatre. James Joyce was chosen by his father, and passively accepted something of an alliance with him against his brothers and sisters, and even against his mother. But he saw clearly that his father was causing his mother's death. His father was indeed 'not right', as Dante had said. But the son had made common cause with him.

Moreover, Joyce was never able to accept the role of manly and fiery rebel, the self-stylization which was the psychological motor of Irish nationalism. We saw this in the crucial sequence in which he was invited to become a priest and chose instead to devote himself to art. We are told there,

> He had never once disobeyed or allowed turbulent
> companions to seduce him from his habit of quiet
> obedience: and, even when he doubted some statement
> of a master, he had never presumed to doubt openly.
> (p. 416)

This is allied, obviously, to his failure to recognize the great passions in himself, and his calling to join the priests as the servants of a great impersonal ritual. The passions are both the outer theatre and the inner structure of manliness, and it is *men* in the great Renaissance-humanist sense who triumph in politics. Stephen/Joyce was not a *man* and so was called to religion instead – to the priesthood; to Dante's side, not his father's; he chose the priesthood of art, an impersonal spiritual labour, which called for no splendour of personality or passion.

The passages which develop his vocation are very interesting, partly because their sequence is in some ways tentative and uncertain. Leaving the priest, Stephen is troubled by the latter's face, a 'mirthless mask reflecting a sunken day', and that image passes into images of 'the troubling odour of the long corridors of Clongowes' his Jesuit school, and 'the warm moist air which hung in the bath at Clongowes above the sluggish turfcoloured water' (p. 421). He rebels against these images, which signal a sordid quality, both sensual and social, to church life. 'What then had become of the deeprooted shyness of his . . . ? [he sees a new image of a priest] The face was eyeless and sourfavoured and devout, shot with pink tinges of suffocated anger.' The psychic cost in self-repression of energizing a priesthood is too great. And he decides, 'His destiny was to be elusive of social or religious orders.' (p. 422)

What is curious is that Stephen thereupon turns towards his home, both literally and metaphorically.

> He smiled to think that it was this disorder, the misrule and confusion of his father's house and the stagnation of vegetable life, which was to win the day in his soul.
> (p. 423)

Obviously this is no less sordid than what he has just turned away from. The difference seems to be that in this case the disorder is disassociated from any lofty purpose, from anything that makes an imperious moral claim on Stephen.

Stephen bears a grudge against order, as that which defeated him, that which he tried to create and failed. 'How foolish his aim had been!' he says, about his one attempt to improve things at home. 'He had tried to build a breakwater of order and elegance against the sordid life without him and to dam up . . . the powerful recurrence of the tides within him. Useless!' (p. 349) He reinforces that feeling, *chooses* disorder as his own.

Moreover, when he finds his brothers and sisters at home, in the scene of vocation, though his description of the house is marked by the same disgust – 'Discarded crusts and lumps of sugared bread, turned brown by the tea which had been poured over them, lay scattered on the table' (p. 424), and so on – he nevertheless joins in with their singing, which is practically the only time Stephen joins in with anyone else in the book. What has become of that deeprooted shyness of his, and his determination to be elusive of all orders? Again it seems that, like disorder, community does not threaten when it carries no implicit moral claim.

Stephen proudly refuses to join any community-in-pride – any community based in self-respect. This is a refusal made in the name of art, but an art conjoined with mess, with a love of the sordid for itself. An ivory tower, rising above a house of misrule, that is what Stephen set out to build for himself, and that is what Joyce achieved magnificently, in *Ulysses*.

Ulysses is of course the story of one day, 16 June, 1904, in one city, Dublin, in so far as that is traversed by two men, Stephen Dedalus and Leopold Bloom. Two other men, Father Conmee and the Viceroy, represent church and state within Dublin, but they play very small parts in the book. The two main characters are very little concerned with political or imperial matters, but their minds bear a recognizable character of anti-imperialism. Stephen mocks both England and Ireland in his Parable of the Plums, and defies the British soldiers in Nighttown. And Bloom tells the rabid nationalist called the Citizen, 'Persecution, says he, all the history of the world is full of it. Perpetuating national hatred among nations . . . [p. 331] . . . But it's no use, says he. Force, hatred, history, all that. That's not life for men and women, insult and hatred.' (p. 333)

Artistically, *Ulysses* is a great achievement, but on a scale so huge that it cannot be treated here. I can say only that here occasionally – and notably in the very first episode – Joyce succeeds with the figure of Stephen as he never did in *Portrait of the Artist*. The contrast and conflict between him and Buck Mulligan, the much more attractive and superficially more gifted rival, works to attract to Stephen the sort of feeling from the reader which Joyce wants. The peculiar difficulties of Stephen's lot – though still created so largely by his own temperament and pride – do seem inextricable from his calling, and that does seem rooted in a serious sense of what he can do and what has to be done.

While as soon as Bloom appears we know we are in the presence of a genial artistic enterprise, in both senses of genial.

> Mr Leopold Bloom ate with relish the inner organs of beasts and fowls. He liked thick giblet soup, nutty gizzards, a stuffed roast heart, liver slices fried with crustcrumbs, fried hencod's roes. Most of all he liked grilled mutton kidneys which gave to his palate a fine tang of faintly scented urine.
>
> Kidneys were in his mind as he moved about the kitchen softly, righting her breakfast things on the humpy tray. Gelid light and air were in the kitchen but out of doors gentle summer morning everywhere. Made him feel a bit peckish. (p. 55)

Everything there, from the vividly sensual prose to the self-pleased attention of the writer to the self-pleasing figure before us, announces a new mode of literature, and with a great scope of possibility – though in fact what Joyce goes on to do far exceeds the scope promised here.

Ulysses was written and re-written over several years, and published in Paris in 1922. It was very much a book of that place and time, with the Great War just over, and all the great states and their politics discredited. Men of letters, like men of culture generally, felt that the best way to prevent another such war was to turn their back on all the forces and habits that produced them. *Ulysses* was a prime example of what to turn to, just because it lay in a diametrically opposite corner of the human map.

It was taken to be a sign of the times, both by those who

loved it and by those who hated it. The latter crassly
denounced it as incarnate decadence, and as marking the
decay of English literature – as intending the decay of
English nationality and Englishness. These feelings were
exacerbated by the issue of censorship, which seemed to
represent the interference of governments – war-making
governments – in the life of free spirits. Censors in fact
prevented the publication of *Ulysses* in various countries for
several years. Soon, of course, the book was rescued from
these political and crudely moralist contexts, and taken into
the protective custody of literary critics and scholars. They
did not treat it as a threat to the British empire but as a
myth-anti-myth, as a gigantic parody of life and art, as a
fantastic encyclopaedia of all sorts of knowledge and image.

All of which, of course, it certainly is. My own point of
view, however, is closer to that of the philistines of 1922.
Ulysses was in fact an anti-imperialist manifesto; not so
much by virtue of Joyce's implicit political statements and
cultural challenges within it as by its character as a work of
art. First of all, *Ulysses* is a palace of art – not merely an ivory
tower such as Stephen Dedalus promised to build, at the end
of *Portrait of the Artist*, but a concatenation of such towers in
an enormous structure that is a maze at the same time. One
has to insist on the size and the elaborateness because,
especially in 1922, before people had learned how to read it,
the effort it demanded from readers was an important issue.
Joyce is supposed to have said that he expected his readers to
devote their lives to reading him; and certainly political
leaders like Gandhi refused to allow their followers to
become involved in modern art, just because the time and
effort it demanded would remove them from political and
social effectiveness. The reader of *Ulysses*, at least in 1922,
needed a longish course of education, some of it quite
esoteric, he needed to overcome many conventions of
decent discourse and polite imagination, and he needed to
make extraordinary efforts of apprehension and sympathy,

before he could understand and appreciate it.

This is a cultural challenge which literary critics, scholars, and teachers usually do not take the measure of, because they *have* devoted their lives to reading Joyce and other such writers. (Moreover, of course, as a result of their labours, *Ulysses* no longer *does* require a life-time's effort to enjoy it.) The way the character of art changes with the change in the size and complexity of individual works is a very significant aspect of the history of art. It is something Tolstoy was very conscious of, and it plays a large part in his denunciation of both modern and Renaissance art, in *What is Art?* *Ulysses* seriously affronted empire by demanding so much from its readers – by seducing them away from the investing of moral energy in political and social matters.

H. G. Wells can be invoked again on this point. Joyce had written to Wells, asking for his help in recommending his *Work in Progress* (which became *Finnegans Wake*) to the attention of the public. Wells wrote back refusing, on 23 November, 1928, on the grounds of a fundamental difference between them, which amounted to an accusation of social irresponsibility in Joyce.

> Your training has been Catholic, Irish, insurrectionary;
> mine, such as it was, was scientific, constructive, and, I
> suppose, English. The frame of my mind is a world
> wherein . . . a *progress* [is] not inevitable but interesting
> and possible. That game attracts and holds me. For it, I
> want language and statement as simple and clear as
> possible. . . . Your mental existence is obsessed by a
> monstrous system of contradictions [the Roman
> Catholic theology, etc.] . . . it seems a fine thing for you
> to defy and break up. To me not in the least. . . . You
> have turned your back on common men, on their
> elementary needs and their restricted time and
> intelligence, and you have elaborated. What is the
> result? Vast riddles. Your last two works have been

more amusing and exciting to write than they will ever
be to read. (p. 620)

In this case we see a Socialist reproaching Joyce, but there is
no full contradiction between this and our previous use of
'Socialist' to describe Joyce's sensibility. The division
between the two writers arises over the issue of statism.
Joyce was an anarchist, in the loose sense – he was in fact so
apolitical that all such terms as Anarchist and Socialist must
be taken as being often metaphorical in their application to
him. Wells, on the other hand, was a statist in his political
thinking – a world-statist, in fact. In the novels mentioned
before, Wells was not thinking politically at all, and his
images of the little man could be assimilated to Joyce's.
But when Wells was being seriously political, and Joyce
seriously artistic, they found themselves far apart and an
alliance between them was impossible, as Wells's letter
points out. Joyce was then attacking empire from an angle
which threatened the Socialist world-state equally. He was
re-building the palace of art on a new and enormous scale,
investing the private life, the aesthetic, the cultural, with
pretentions and resources which made it a counterpart, a
counterforce, to the life of civilization and politics.

All activities on the side of culture and against civilization
are likely to swell to a size corresponding to and challenging
the greatness of the institutions and actions, the wars and
empires, of their times. The great systems of thought in
Germany at the end of the eighteenth century seem to
correspond to and respond to the achievement of the French
Revolution and Napoleon. It is thus that we should understand the writing of *Ulysses* at the moment of England's
greatness as an empire; just as we understand the writing of
Hegel's *Phenomenology of the Spirit* at the moment of
Napoleon's greatness.

This does not mean that the great work of culture will
appear in closest social conjunction with the great work of

civilization; rather the contrary. The development of critical philosophy in Germany, rather than in England or France, was probably made possible by Germany's *distance* from the centres of modern civilization, by the smallness and unimpressiveness of the ducal states, in which a professor could be (especially given the social freedom of the German university system) a great power comparable with a duke. The same is true for Joyce as Irish, as compared with Kipling as English and bard of the master-class. (It is also significant that it was written in small neutral Switzerland during the War.) While in nineteenth-century England, it seems to have been possible for novelists to distance themselves from political and economic power – for instance, by implicitly denying that England was an empire – and thus to find for themselves a protective shade within which to work.

In its character as a palace of art, then (as well as in its character as Socialist realism), *Ulysses* made its signal against empire. The two signals work in oddly disconnected connection, like co-ordinated pistons pushing the wheels of a locomotive. And in this as in other ways *Finnegans Wake* may be seen as a further extension of *Ulysses*, more elaborate and difficult as art, more demotic and disrespectful in culture – disrespectful of all the achievements of culture-in-alliance-with-civilization. Perhaps most notably, it breaks down the structure of personality, making all kinds of minds and experiences inter-permeable, and symbolically breaking down all the other erections of human pride. But *Finnegans Wake* is still, and perhaps for ever, a preserve of the academy, and has not entered into the mainstream of literature, as *Ulysses* has.

Joyce's primary audience can be said to be academic, in a sense which distinguishes it from Kipling's and Lawrence's audience. But *Ulysses* and the other books are by now familiar presences to everyone who cares about British fiction in the twentieth century. They are an important part of literature's resistance to empire.

[5]

EVELYN WAUGH

WAUGH GREW UP AT a time when Kipling was taboo – when he was a symbol of jingoism and imperialism, of everything passé in art and ideas, everything repressive in social and political action – a symbol of the fathers whom Waugh and his friends rebelled against. His brother, Alec Waugh, tells how Evelyn as a boy opened conversation with his prep school teacher by saying, 'My father's a terrible man – likes Kipling, you know.'

In Waugh's written work, Kipling heroics are most directly mocked in *Scoop* (1937) in the person of General Cruttwell, F.R.G.S., an explorer-adventurer who now serves as a glorified shopwalker in the store which outfits William Boot for his career as a foreign correspondent. He is the pre-1914 Kipling hero confronting the post-1918 unheroic youngster.

An imposing man: Cruttwell Glacier in Spitsbergen, Cruttwell Falls in Venezuela, Mount Cruttwell in the Pamirs, Cruttwell's Leap in Cumberland, marked his travels; Cruttwell's Folly, a waterless and indefensible camp near Salonika, was notorious to all who had served with him in the war. The shop paid him six hundred a year and commission, out of which, by contract, he had to find his annual subscription to the R.G.S., and the electric treatment which maintained the leathery tan of his complexion. (p. 46)

The phony adventurer hero was an old joke in 1937. Kipling figures of this kind had long been easy game for humourists; they are to be found throughout P. G. Wodehouse's work, for instance. Waugh's contribution was only to give the joke a classical perfection. But the anti-Kipling sense of humour expressed in it was something much more pervasive, and much more his. He had extended and explored that sense of humour more boldly and brilliantly than any other writer.

In the 1920s he read D. H. Lawrence and Joyce, among the other voices of rebellion who had authority for his generation. He followed them, and turned away from the writers loved by his father and his friends' fathers. And *Decline and Fall*, one of the most brilliant of Waugh's books even though so early (published 1928), is straightforwardly satirical against all fathers.

When Paul Pennyfeather is sent down from Oxford for indecent behaviour, his guardian says sanctimoniously,

> 'Well, thank God your poor father has been spared this disgrace, that's all I can say.' [And we soon discover the sordid motive behind his moralism.] 'I do not think that I should be fulfilling the trust which your poor father placed in me, if, in the present circumstances, I continued any allowance.' (p. 15)

Of course, Waugh's satire is directed against cultural as much as familial fathers; for instance the dons at Oxford.

> Mr Sniggs, the Junior Dean, and Mr Postlethwaite, the Domestic Bursar, sat alone in Mr Sniggs' room overlooking the garden quad at Scone College. . . .
> 'The fines!' said Mr Sniggs, gently rubbing his pipe alongside of his nose. 'Oh my! The fines there'll be after this evening.' (pp. 11–12)

All the men in authority, and all the institutions, like Parliament, the press, prisons, are imaginatively dull and morally shady. Waugh presents them to us as so many all-too-recognizable puppets, dangling limp and lifeless until *he* animates them with his mockerys; *his* expert mimicry of voice and gesture brings them alive for a second, but it is *his* life, not theirs. Only the young people, the rebels, escape the reproach of dullness.

Perhaps the most striking attack on social and parental authority is Captain Grimes's speech against home and marriage, that most sanctified of values, maternal as well as paternal.

> They should have told me that at the end of that gay journey and flower-strewn path were the hideous lights of home and the voices of children. I should have been warned of the great lavender-scented bed that was laid out for me, of the wistaria at the windows, of all the intimacy and confidence of family life. But I daresay I shouldn't have listened. Our life is lived between two homes. We emerge for a little into the light, and then the front door closes. The chintz curtains shut out the sun, and the hearth glows with the fire of home, while upstairs, above our heads, are enacted again the awful accidents of adolescence. There's a home and family waiting for every one of us. (p. 102)

In this first book, Waugh is satirical of the fathers (and mothers) and sympathetic with the sons; satirical of the middle class and sympathetic with the aristocracy. But any such position was, in twentieth-century England, self-evidently paradoxical. And in his next novel, *Vile Bodies*, those basic sympathies were reversed. Lady Circumference, who had been satirized in the previous book as philistine, in this one is sympathetically shown looking at

> a great concourse of pious and honourable people (many of whom made the Anchorage House reception the one outing of the year), their women-folk well gowned in

rich and durable stuffs, their men-folk ablaze with
orders; people who had represented their country in
foreign places and sent their sons to die for her in battle,
people of decent and temperate life, uncultured,
unaffected, unembarrassed, unassuming, unambitious
people, of independent judgment and marked
eccentricities, kind people who cared for animals and
the deserving poor, brave and rather unreasonable
people, that fine phalanx of the passing order,
approaching, as one day at the Last Trump they hoped
to meet their Maker, with decorous and frank cordiality
to shake Lady Anchorage by the hand at the top of her
staircase. Lady Circumference saw all this and sniffed
the exhalation of her own herd. (p. 127)

This passage evokes exactly the feeling Kipling set out to
evoke about exactly the same subject. (Because of his
double irony, Waugh was able for a paragraph at a time to
seem much more direct than Kipling; for he *did*, as much as
Kipling, admire Lady Circumference.)

Indeed in middle life Waugh turned into just as much of a
reactionary as Kipling, in political and social matters; he
blasphemed against every liberal piety; and his literary taste
was shaped by Kipling-like paradoxes and self-contradictions
of temperament. There was now no trace of Joyce or Lawrence in his work, which eschewed the large forms and
themes, and aimed at small-scale and traditional ingenuities.
'Experiment? God forbid,' he said, in his *Paris Review* interview of 1962, 'Look at the results of experiment in the work
of a writer like Joyce. He started off writing very well, then
you can watch him going mad with vanity. He ends up a
lunatic.' In *The Ordeal of Gilbert Pinfold* he said that Dickens
and Balzac had been daemonic masters, but that the twentieth-century's novelists will be valued for 'elegance and
variety of contrivance'. Thus P. G. Wodehouse's 'sheer hard
work' had made him one of the finest literary artists of

the century. Wodehouse was one of Kipling's heirs -- the Kipling of the humorous short stories – so we can fairly connect this declaration with a return to the older author.

Moreover, when Waugh wrote an autobiography, towards the end of his life, he made it seem that his complaint against his father was not that he liked Kipling but that he had not liked him enough – had not been sufficiently Kiplingesque.

> Many little boys look on their fathers as heroically strong and skillful; mighty hunters, the masters of machines; not so I. Nor did I ever fear him. He was restless rather than active. His sedentary and cerebral occupations appeared ignominious to me in my early childhood. I should have better respected a soldier or a sailor like my uncles . . . a man, even, who shaved with a cut-throat razor. . . . I never saw him as anything but old, indeed as decrepit. (*A Little Learning*, p. 63)

As usual, Waugh is making an effect, and the reader may be uncertain how trustingly to believe this account. But we cannot doubt that he, looking back, attributes a Kipling sensibility to the little boy he had been; 'a normal, strong, brave, and clever little boy'; and it seems likely that he was indeed always a Kipling beneath the dandy mannerisms of the 1920s. Of course, he was also a complicated and irritable aesthete and satirist; but then so was Kipling himself. We may, I am suggesting, regard even the early Waugh as – unbeknownst to himself – a Kipling redivivus of the next generation.

Moreover, Waugh was typical of his generation in this progress from asserted anti-Kiplingism, which meant anti-imperialism, anti-militarism, etc., to a gradually discovered self that was something like pro-Kipling. A whole group of his friends grew up reading Kipling, Haggard, Henty, Stevenson, but in early manhood repudiated all they stood for, in some sense repressed the memory, and chose attitudes and tastes as diametrically opposed to those as possible. Graham Greene, for instance, describes that process in his own case, in *A Sort of Life*. He hated gym, games, and the OTC at school, and would hide away to read at the time when such things were scheduled.

What he read was – in adolescence – highbrow stuff; but in his autobiography he recalls rather his earlier, childish reading of Haggard and Henty; and traces its reappearance, transformed, in his own writing. His versions of adventure, for instance espionage and war stories, are of course ambivalent in their celebration of the adventurer's virtues; but in the long run Greene's heroes (for instance, Scobie in *The Heart of the Matter*) are genuine Kipling heroes. The same could be said of Waugh's *Black Mischief, Scoop,* and his novels about the Second World War. In them he returned – though with superficial irony – to the old Kipling model, both in narrative plot and in character sympathy. The ironical tone is flaunted to announce a big difference from Kipling, but the *effect* of these stories is very much that of *Plain Tales From The Hills*.

In the 1930s Greene and Waugh seemed very different talents and temperaments, yoked together by their Catholicism very ill-assortedly. Greene seemed both more serious and more at home in the modern world – the world of gangsters and secret agents – than the romantic and dandified Waugh. But it gradually became apparent that they were always very alike; Greene's autobiography might have been written by Waugh – in some ways it is more like the early Waugh than Waugh's own autobiography. We now see them as alternates and complements of the one temperament; Greene wrote mainly out of the depressive phase, Waugh out of the manic, but it was a see-saw.

Amongst the group I am calling Waugh's generation, probably no one else was so like Kipling as he, at least in talent, and perhaps in temperament. But there was a comparable development and change over the years in someone

as different as Noel Coward; from his shrill mockery of
everything Establishment in the early 1920s to the patriotic
sentimentality of *Cavalcade* later, and his war-time songs
and movies. Although Kipling was not formally reinstated,
or overtly imitated, the conventions by which this patriotic
conservatism was made palatable were retrieved from him
and all he stood for. Like *Where the Rainbow Ends*, *Cavalcade*
closed with a rendering of *God Save the King* by the whole
company. But a more striking case than Coward is Greene.

GRAHAM GREENE

Graham Greene, whom we will take as the comparable and
related author in Waugh's case, begins his 1971 introduction
to *The Heart of the Matter* 'Evelyn Waugh once wrote to me
that the only excuse he could offer for *Brideshead Revisited*
was "Spam, black-outs and Nissen huts". I feel much the
same towards *The Heart of the Matter*, though my excuse
might be different – "swamps, rain and a mad cook" – for
our two wars were very different.' He tells us that he began
this novel in 1946, six years after he finished the preceding
The Power and the Glory. It was published in 1948, and
therefore can be compared with *1984* as well as *Brideshead
Revisited*; three of the great literary successes of immediately
post-war England.

The likeness Greene suggests lies in a certain guilt he and
Waugh share – their need to excuse their books – presumably for a certain extravagance in both technique and
feeling. (And the same might have been said by Orwell
about *1984*.) As Greene's kind of extravagance, we might
cite 'His hilarity was like a scream from a crevasse.' (*The
Heart of the Matter*, p. 208) This extravagance was in both
writers in the mode of the Catholic novel – both writers
were Catholic novelists in this phase of their careers; that
means a mode of sensibility characterized by melancholy,
disgust with modern society, and a vindictive delight in the

failures and poverties of human nature.

This offered itself as a religious conviction, but it can be read equally well as a reaction to England's loss of power, of empire. Both writers were preoccupied with death and diminishment. For instance, the central characters in both novels were possessed by the death-wish, as were the authors. Greene says,

> I had always thought that war would bring death as a solution, in one form or another, in the blitz, in a submarined ship, in Africa with a dose of blackwater, but here I was alive, the carrier of unhappiness to people I loved, taking up the old profession of brothel child. (p. xii)

Waugh, in his subsequent work, the trilogy about the War, entitles a version of *Brideshead Revisited* as *The Death Wish*; and portrays another autobiographical and death-directed hero, Guy Crouchback. And if we compare those novels with *The Heart of the Matter*, we see that both heroes are embodiments of responsibility and pity, burdened with undeserving wives, and generally disliked (found 'not *simpatico*') because of their virtues ('why must you always tell the truth?').

This career of being a Catholic novelist was very important to both writers, and is significant for our argument even when we take it on its own terms. The Catholic novel was essentially an inverted dandy form – a kind of black Romanticism. Its macroscopic significance for our argument is its flouting of the WASP tradition in fiction, in both its adventure and its domestic forms. It was a reaction against the ideology that had carried England to greatness.

The microscopic significance of this genre is its emphasis on fictional cliché (as one way of enforcing its scorn for unregenerate human nature and so for all expansive or generous ambition). Scobie, the hero of Greene's novel, always foreknows exactly what will happen if someone tries out a new plan. When his girlfriend Helen says no doubt she'll be conscripted when she gets back to England, he foresees:

> After the Atlantic, the ATS, or the WAAF, the
> blustering sergeant with the big bust, the cook house
> and the potato peelings, the lesbian officer with the thin
> lips and the tidy gold hair, and the men waiting on the
> Common outside the camp, among the gorse-bushes
> . . . compared to that surely even the Atlantic was more
> a home. (p. 157)

But this technique is particularly striking when it is applied to disfavoured characters. In the first sentence of the novel we meet Wilson, who is characterized by his 'bald pink knees'. Later we hear that he has a very young moustache, his shorts are always flapping, he is plump, innocent, romantic; and for these reasons he is the fool and villain of the piece. These are all the traits of a failure in virility, which is at the same time a failure in crucial caste virtues. Plump, pink, hairless, Wilson is the opposite of Scobie, who is lean, lined, dried out by the heat of experience, reduced to an emblematic virile manliness. And Greene convinces us of Wilson's failure not so much by displaying his behaviour as by evoking this cliché of manhood.

It is not accidental that this cliché is a legacy of Kipling. Scobie is one of Kipling's *men*, Wilson one of his *boys*, as those two were so often contrasted in the Indian stories. This is no accident, because so much else in Greene's novel comes from Kipling or from his collaborators in adventure, Conrad and Maugham; for instance, the post-imperialist setting, with the law courts 'a great stone building like the grandiloquent boast of weak men' (p. 7). One notes too the importance of hints and clues in Greene as in Kipling, a technique Lawrence and Joyce never stoop to. Greene makes as much use as Agatha Christie herself of the distrust evoked by our recognizing all the characters as types.

Above all, the art of cliché is Kipling's – since he perfected it for his fragmentary fiction.

Greene does not openly allude to Kipling, but he does to Buchan and to Stevenson. In this novel, one of the most vivid passages presents Scobie inventing a new version of *Treasure Island* to amuse a boy in hospital. And he attributes to Wilson a shameful habit of reading Palgrave's *Golden Treasury* 'in small doses', like drinking in secret; 'a finger of Longfellow, Macaulay, Mangan' (p. 4). We can take Palgrave as the poetic equivalent of Stevenson, within that imperial literature, the enjoyment of which is a secret vice for Greene's characters.

It is a related point that prep school experience and pre-1918 school memories (Kipling's territory, fictionally speaking) are made so important in both Greene's and Waugh's novels. In *The Heart of the Matter*, Helen is portrayed as a schoolgirl, in terms of her stamp collection and her netball; while Wilson and Harris are concerned with their Old Boys' Association and their memories of school. They have none of them escaped their school identities. Waugh makes the same comic-pathetic evocation of Apthorpe's school loyalties, and of Guy's training camp being a school. In all these cases the pre-1918, prep-school experience, repressed or repudiated in the 1920s, returns with powerful nostalgia in the 1940s, as true-as-well-as-false.

And what most strikingly unites the two Catholic novelists is their common evocation of imperial caste criteria. Wilson and Harris in Greene, Trimmer and Hooper in Waugh, are mercilessly harried and mocked by their authors because of their lack of fire and force, their failure in master-class style. This is so striking because it has so little to do with the 'Catholic' sensibility officially proclaimed, and so much to do with Kipling and his ethos. Though the Catholic movement in fiction was in some sense designed to reverse Kiplingism, these writers in fact perpetuated that

ethos implicitly, covertly developed those values in the
same direction. And this was true of other members of his
generation, Communists as well as Catholics, and those in
between.

WAUGH'S GENERATION

The idea of a generation – of a group of coevals marked off
from other social groups by the sharing of important
experiences – is an important tool in understanding Waugh.
He wrote brilliantly – though in the mode of fantasy rather
than of realism – about that generation, and he wrote for
them. In his case, the audience is best suggested by that
word, rather than by the academy, as in Joyce's, or the
master-class, as in Kipling's. Of course, in all these cases, we
are not implying that no one else enjoyed these writers, but
that we can picture the group named as in some sense
occupying the front rows and primarily present to the
writer; this helps us to understand both the target of the
writer's gestures, and the discipline of self-adaptation
imposed upon the rest of the audience as they learn to
appreciate these gestures. This was the cultural hegemony.
Waugh's audience became very large in England, and
gradually even became international, but readers who
belong to a different generation (or a different social class
even among coevals) would participate only by virtue of
assimilating themselves to that primary group; who had in
the 1920s constituted themselves as a private world, a world
of laughter which refused the seriousness of their fathers – of
the public world. (His later audience was of course somewhat different; it included more men of power.)

This private world of young people, dedicated to
laughter, in fact included many people of taste and talent,
who exerted an important influence on the England of their
day. Because of that revolt against seriousness of theirs,
which Waugh celebrated for them, critics have not done

him justice as a writer – have not taken *him* seriously. I have described this generation in *Children of the Sun*, shown how pervasive it was in English cultural life in the 1920s and 1930s, and how many positions of power it occupied after 1945.

HIS LIFE

Born in 1903, Waugh went to a modest and religiously oriented public school, Lancing, and then to a minor college at Oxford, Hertford. While at Oxford, however, he joined a circle of dandies, aesthetes, and aristophiles who were characteristically Etonian. Joining them meant declaring himself for the Pleasure Principle and for fantasy, rejecting the Reality Principle and realism. It also meant changing caste, for his father was essentially middle class, a minor man of letters who worked for a publishing firm. Waugh's Oxford experience, his choice of new caste identity, he wrote about at length in *Brideshead Revisited*. It was the determining one of his life, indeed of many lives, for a similar choice was made by many of those I have called his generation, as we shall see.

In *Decline and Fall*, Waugh discussed the question of caste in terms of his middle-class hero's being offered money by Sir Alastair Digby-Vane-Trumpington.

'But', said Paul Pennyfeather, 'there is my honour. For generations the British bourgeoisie have spoken of themselves as gentlemen, and by that they have meant, among other things, a self-respecting scorn of irregular perquisites. It is the quality that distinguishes the gentleman from both the artist and the aristocrat. Now I am a gentleman. I can't help it: it's born in me. I just can't take that money.'

Of course he does take it, and the moral exhilaration of the book is all derived from the way he (and Waugh) is joining the aristocracy and deserting the British bourgeoisie. What

makes the exhilaration interesting is the keenness with
which Waugh defines such terms. Paul Pennyfeather
undoes the knot with which Defoe had tied together the
gentleman and the aristocrat, in *The Complete English
Gentleman*, two hundred years before. Defoe had married
the two, and given the bourgeois the moral primacy, at the
beginning of the period of bourgeois domination, and Jane
Austen, Dickens, Thackeray, etc., had celebrated the union.
Waugh divorced them for the benefit of his generation, and
joined the aristocracy.

Having scraped through his examinations at Oxford
(none of this group did any academic work or learned
anything there, according to them), Waugh went to London
to look for, not a career, but a way to earn money. Having
been forced to teach in a prep school, he turned the experience to comic fantastic account in *Decline and Fall*, which
had a considerable success, and was chosen by Winston
Churchill to be his Christmas present that year. Waugh
became a friend of Churchill's son, Randolph; and Churchill
himself was, one may say, *his* politician. (Churchill was then
the most Kiplingesque figure in British politics; and of
course became the national saviour.)

On the strength of this success, Waugh made what turned
out to be a typical 1920s marriage. His wife was also called
Evelyn, and she dressed and behaved boyishly, so that the
exaggerated sexual differentiation of their parents' generation (the Edwardian) was flouted. She was known as the
second Evelyn, and they began their married life in a state of
childlike simplicity which implicitly defied 'adult' styles in
sexual relations and everything else. For various reasons, the
marriage lasted a very short time, and Waugh in bitterness
reacted against his generation's self-liberation and sought
for social guarantees of his values. In his next novel, he
spoke of his new 'hunger for permanence'; and he took
instruction in and was admitted to the Roman Catholic
church.

In the 1930s he wrote travel books and other novels, or rather fictions. Indeed, in so far as he essayed the major themes or tones of the novel proper – as in *A Handful of Dust* – his work suffered in quality; his best books have been called entertainments rather than novels. (Greene's fiction has been divided up in the same way.) He married again, within the church, and had a large family, which he ran on old-fashioned lines. When war broke out, in 1939, Waugh was delighted, both because it would redeem England's honour to fight Germany-and-Russia (an alliance he saw as 'the modern age in arms') and because he had a romantic admiration for soldiers and the army. He was in love (he uses that term) with both the military and the aristocratic components of the aristo-military caste. His romance with the army, however, was ruined by experience, and before the end of the war he wrote *Brideshead Revisited*, his romantic recapturing of his Oxford past and a fantasized Catholic aristocracy.

In the post-war years, he was a very successful writer, but hated the England he lived in. He found no good subjects to write about, though he devoted a great deal of effort to a trilogy about the war. This was his nearest approach to success in realism, but the books are invaded by his long-established, but this time inappropriate, habits of comic fantasy, and even in its other episodes the story lacks vitality. The trouble is at least represented by, if not rooted in, Waugh's central character and representative, Guy Crouchback; who is in some sense a modern Kipling hero – a Kipling subaltern grown up, but doomed to a sequence of disappointments and defeats in a post-Kipling world.

Waugh's most interesting literary project came to him in Jerusalem in 1935, he tells us. Thinking of General Allenby's 'superbly modest entry into Jerusalem seventeen years before' and reflecting that Allenby 'had created the purest and most benevolent government the land had known since

Constantine', Waugh had felt proud of being English, and planned a literary career to express and serve that pride.

> I was of an age then – 32 – when, after I had struck lucky
> with 3 or 4 light novels, it did not seem entirely absurd,
> at any rate to myself, to look about for a suitable 'life's
> work'; (one learns later that life itself is work enough.)
> So elated was I by the beauties about me that I then and
> there began vaguely planning a series of books – semi-
> historical, semi-poetic fiction, I did not know quite
> what – about the long, intricate, intimate association
> between England and the Holy Places. The list of great
> and strange Britons who from time to time embodied
> the association – Helena, Richard Lionheart, Stratford
> Canning, Gordon – would without doubt grow with
> research. . . . The first, flushed, calf love of my theme
> has never completely cooled, though I now know that I
> shall not pursue it further. One element is certainly dead
> for ever – pride of country. ('Work Abandoned',
> Stinchcombe, 1952, in *The Holy Places*)

Helena is the only part he completed, but just before he died he signed a contract for a novel about the Crusaders. Such a series would have been like Tennyson's *Idylls of the King*, an attempt to revive English history and myth in a form morally and politically inspiring. Perhaps the last (at least brilliant) example of this genre was Kipling's *Puck of Pook's Hill*.

Waugh had always been interested in the Arthurian legend and above all in its Tennysonian revival. The most brilliant thing in *A Handful of Dust* is his evocation of Hetton, a country house built in the architectural equivalent of Tennysonian Gothic. It is with a superb paradox of feeling, or a self-stabilizing and self-renewing anarchy, that Waugh celebrates:

> the blasts of hot air that rose suddenly at one's feet,

through grills of cast-iron trefoils from the antiquated
heating apparatus below; the cavernous chill of the more
remote corridors where, economizing in coke, he had
had the pipes shut off; the dining hall with its hammer-
beam roof and pitch-pine minstrels' gallery; the
bedrooms with their brass bedsteads, each with a frieze
of Gothic text, each named from Malory, Yseult,
Elaine, Mordred and Merlin, Gawaine and Bedivere,
Lancelot, Perceval, Tristram, Galahad, his own dressing
room, Morgan le Fay, and Brenda's Guinevere, where
the bed stood on a dais, the walls hung with tapestry,
the fireplace like a tomb of the thirteenth century. . . .
(p. 9)

These are Waugh's most serious values that he is celebrating here. Comic-satirical though this description is, Hetton
remains throughout the book the symbol of all that modern
life disastrously lacks, and Brenda is finally denounced to us
as a modern Guinevere, who has betrayed a whole way of
life by her (typically modern) sexual infidelity.

While in *Brideshead Revisited*, the representative of
modern life is described as indifferent – fatally indifferent –
specifically to chivalry.

Hooper was no romantic. He had not as a child ridden
with Rupert's horse or sat among the camp fires at
Xanthus-side; at the age when my eyes were dry to all
save poetry – that stoic, red-skin interlude which our
schools introduce between the fast flowing tears of the
child and the man – Hooper had wept often, but never
for Henry's speech on St Crispin's Day, nor for the
epitaph at Thermopylae. The history they taught him
had had few battles in it but, instead, a profusion of
detail about humane legislation and recent industrial
change. Gallipoli, Balaclava, Quebec, Lepanto,
Bannockburn, Roncevales, and Marathon – these, and
the Battle in the West where Arthur fell, and a hundred

such names whose trumpet notes, even now in my sere
and lawless state, call to me irresistibly across the
intervening years with all the clarity and strength of
boyhood, sounded in vain to Hooper.

HIS BEST WORK

We have seen that the art, and the enjoyment it offers, is the
same in both *Decline and Fall* and *Vile Bodies*, although the
values the author implies are quite different. Therefore the
artist's ideology is a minor issue, and the major issue is
something else – is in fact the shift from one 'ideological' or
'satirical' principle to another. It is important to recognize
the paradoxical romanticism of passages like these in *Decline
and Fall*:

> As the last of the guests departed Mrs Beste-Chetwynde
> reappeared from her little bout of veronal, fresh and
> exquisite as a 17th century lyric. The meadow of green
> glass seemed to burst into flower under her feet as she
> passed from the lift to the cocktail table. (p. 133)

This satiric-romantic writing Waugh invented, on the
model of the Commedia dell' Arte. This is the genre to
which Waugh affiliated himself – or rather, which he
adapted to literary purposes – and it is important to recognize the implicit anti-imperialism (and anti-nationalism, for
that matter) carried quite silently by this aesthetic. When the
Commedia became intellectually fashionable in modern
times, it was in mid-nineteenth-century France, and
amongst spiritual rebels like Baudelaire. The latter were
fascinated by both the stage performances of the Commedia
troupes and their reflections in paintings by Watteau and
others. The figures of Pierrot, Columbine, and Harlequin
became the emblems of a sensibility, and that sensibility
became dominant in poetry with Laforgue, in painting with
Picasso and Braque, and in the other arts, at the end of the
century. From France it spread to England, and in the 1920s

the Commedia figures were to be found everywhere, from Diaghilev's Ballets Russes to china dolls and telephone covers. And everywhere – with varying degrees of eloquence – they spoke against the orthodox virtues of empire and Kiplingism.

Those figures were in effect a sort of pantheon (though being purely aesthetic, they only *suggested* moral values) which was alternative both to the Hellenic pantheon of the classical aesthetic, and to the Hebraic virtues of fire and strength, action and heroism. The Commedia stood for lyric emotions, romance, exquisite elegance, though also for moments of brutality, madness, terror; it stood for laughter and tears, fragile emotions and fragmentary meanings. Two lines by T. S. Eliot suggest the gamut of the sensibility, 'Midnight shakes the memory/As a madman shakes a dead geranium.' When it came to dominate the imagination it diminished or silenced the major chords of war and adventure, love and marriage. So it is important to see how much of Waugh's best work is done in this genre.

This best work is to be found in his entertainments, and is of course farcical, in the simple sense that it borrows from and imitates stage farce in many obvious ways. The comic situations are stage-farce situations, in tableau and action, in costume, grouping, pose, gesture, plot connection, and so forth.

We may be surprised, once we begin to count it up, by how much farce material we find in the books. They do not, in one sense, *feel* so farcical, because the farce, especially the more physical elements of it, does not involve the reader. We are conscious of wit more than of farce. The amorous chases of pantomime, the grapplings in the dark, the custard pie in the face, these are not elements of Waugh's comedy. There is more of that in the black humourists – there is more in Wodehouse or in Anthony Powell. Waugh's comedy does not, as farce often does, primarily reduce minds to bodies. Waugh is not interested in bodies.

As Waugh transforms the terms of stage farce into literary terms, he makes them the terms of a refined and 'classical' literature. He does this by rather general means, like the elegance of his prose, the moderation of his effects, the severity of his taste, but also by two sets of specific techniques. First, most often he reports the scenes of farce to us, or rather, more complexly, he has them reported by one character to another. For instance, we learn of Paul's debagging in *Decline and Fall* by means of the conversation between the two dons, so that the farcical action itself takes place in the background.

Again, in *Black Mischief*, the Birth Control Pageant is presented to us through the interstices of the exchanges between Dame Mildred Porch and Sarah Tin, which are full of the satiric comedy of their relationship. The skill in complexity of these techniques and the severity of the moral judgments counteract the grossness of the action, and in a sense intellectualize the farce.

The second technique, or set of techniques, which has the same tendency, is the serialization of farcical action. The most famous example of this is the wounding, the sickening, and the dying of little Lord Tangent in *Decline and Fall*. Because the sequence of events is brought in (and immediately dropped out) time and time again, it never happens for us, it is merely used, and so becomes a device of Waugh's wit and not an event in black humour.

Of course Waugh's farce is also intellectualized in the less formal sense that his comedies make such full reference to contemporary events and personalities, and their background in history, politics, and aesthetic taste. They are a kind of history of their times. For instance, the motor races in *Vile Bodies* are described in such a way as to make us see what such events are like, as well as being an occasion for farcical action. The books reduce the history of their times to the dimensions and intensities of farce, but they also give a knowledgeable account of that history. This is a counter-pressure within them, which complicates the form. At moments the ingredient of farce is minimal, because Waugh's eye is on some contemporary phenomenon he wants to record accurately.

But besides farce, the term 'Commedia dell' arte' suggests traditions and techniques which are specifically and deeply related to Waugh's scenarios. 'Commedia' suggests above all that central trio of characters, Pierrot, Harlequin, and Colombine, and their inter-relationships – Pierrot's naïve and hopeless yearning for beauty in general and Colombine in particular, Colombine's tenderness for him but weak and treacherous yielding to the brutal importunities of Harlequin, and Harlequin's heartless and unscrupulous aggressions against the other two which leave him still bound to them for ever, and which never win him any substantial advantage. This complex surely provides the centre for the objective correlative to Waugh's sensibility in these novels. Paul Pennyfeather is a Pierrot hero in a rather negative way, William Boot (in *Scoop*) much more positively – because he is culturally specified by his country origins, his literary prose, his good manners, and his eccentric relatives. Then in *Black Mischief* Waugh creates a Harlequin hero, Basil Seal, who exploits his mother and his mistress quite unscrupulously, and who, having stolen Prudence from her former lover, ends by eating her in a cannibal banquet. And finally in *Put Out More Flags* he created a true Pierrot, Ambrose, who stands in the perfect complementary relation to Basil. The two have maintained 'a shadowy and mutually derisive relation' since Oxford, and they are bound to each other as allies and comrades against the ordinary world, and yet Basil betrays Ambrose to the police on a charge he himself invents, and then has Susie (a Colombine figure) unpick the letter 'A' from Ambrose's crepe-de-chine underwear to replace it with his own initial 'B'.

Ambrose is Pierrot by virtue of his 'absurd light step and heavy heart', because of his self-caricaturing mannerisms of nodding his head and fluttering his eyelashes as he speaks, because of his hopeless yearning for love, because he is a true artist and a Jew and a homosexual. He is the perfect objective correlative for feelings that, for instance, Balcairn in *Vile Bodies* is supposed to objectify but fails to. Basil is a much better Harlequin than Adam, not only because his brutality – and his boringness – is so frankly brought out but also because his sexual psychology (his narcissism and sadistic phallicism) is so boldly and yet delicately drawn. And *Put Out More Flags* is the best of the novels because it exploits these Commedia characters. It has in fact three Harlequins, Basil, Mr Todhunter, and Colonel Plum; and two Pierrots, Ambrose and Cedric; and four Colombines, Sonia, Angela, Susie, and the bride of Grantley Green. Waugh's sensibility here finds its objective correlative, in the world of the Commedia.

Around the three main characters, the Commedia deploys Pantaloons, Pedants, Scaramouche-braggarts, Brighella-intriguers, and so forth. Figures like Lady Circumference, Lord Copper, Dr Fagan, Captain Grimes, and so forth, do not correspond in detail to the former, but they are designed in the same way for the same function. They have as much fictional life, and the same kind; they are plausible and implausible in the same ways and to the same degree. And through some of these contemporary cartoons, these pompous Press lords and shrill interior decorators, the traditional masks of the Commedia may be seen to shine, and this is an effect traditionally employed in the Commedia genres. Ballets and pantomimes often began with young lovers who, in a dream or spell, were transformed into Pierrot and Colombine, and so could express their themes with greater aesthetic exuberance.

Waugh's other claim on our attention is his cultural history interest, which is primarily literary and artistic. It is Waugh's autobiography as a writer that he obliquely discusses with us. In *Unconditional Surrender* he implicitly condemns *Brideshead Revisited* as 'trash', and in a sense it is, but it is also a remarkable fantasy-autobiography, and a culture history of his generation. It is obvious that the central character of the novel, Charles Ryder, represents Waugh. And the life-choice he makes – against Protestant moralism and for Catholicism and the aristocracy and aesthetic fantasy – is parallel with Waugh's choice of Catholicism and the Commedia.

The novel begins in Oxford, and the first thing we see Charles do is fall in love with Lord Sebastian Flyte, a Catholic aristocrat. Sebastian takes Charles on a picnic in somebody else's car, with strawberries and white wine, after which they lie on the grass. 'Sebastian's eyes on the leaves above him, mine on his profile'. The magic door into the walled garden of romance has opened for Charles, we are told. After an austere school life, and alienated family, he finds love and wit and beauty and style all in one. And this love is anarchy, 'The hot spring of anarchy rose from deep furnaces where was no solid earth, and burst into the sunlight – a rainbow in its cooling vapors – with a power the rocks could not repress.'

A contrast is drawn between all that Sebastian represents to Charles and all that his cousin Jasper represents, which is the prudent, middle-class, career-oriented attitude to Oxford. Even more interesting is the effect on Charles's taste which is ascribed to Sebastian. Charles arrived at Oxford with Bloomsbury taste.

> On my first afternoon I proudly hung a reproduction of Van Gogh's 'Sunflowers' over the fire and set up a screen, painted by Roger Fry with a Provençal landscape, which I had bought inexpensively when the Omega workshops were sold up.

Collins, one of Charles's intellectual friends, had exposed to Charles the fallacy of Bloomsbury aesthetics. But it was not until Sebastian, idly turning the page of Clive Bell's book, *Art*, read out loud, 'Does anyone feel the same kind of emotion for a butterfly or a flower that he feels for a cathedral or a picture?' and replied defiantly, 'Yes, I do,' that Charles's eyes were opened.

Ryder comes to know Sebastian's Oxford and then Brideshead, the house to which Sebastian drives him on that first expedition, the great baroque mansion with the fountain imported from Italy; and beyond Brideshead stands Venice, which is the imaginative domain of Lord Marchmain, Sebastian's father, a Byronic voluptuary and magnifico. These are the perspectives of beauty, art, sensuality, magnificence, the Renaissance, paganism. But the pagan Lord Marchmain has been defeated by his Catholic wife, who is a reality principle within the novel, and Sebastian can represent those perspectives only in child-like, playful, nursery form. His addiction to his teddy bear is serious as well as playful, a real refusal to grow up. Sebastian stands for the pleasure principle, that which *must* be superseded by the reality principle. The latter is represented by both Lady Marchmain and her eldest son, Bridey, devout Catholics, who accept the church and all its juggernaut truth. We are told that Bridey's face looks like an Aztec sculptor's version of Sebastian's, and that Lady Marchmain's brothers, also Catholics and war-heroes, have the same primitiveness in their faces. They belong to Kipling's world, repellent but real. Thus paganism inevitably leads to Catholicism, as immaturity leads to maturity. They and Kiplingism constitute together a single option, in opposition to both the alternatives, dull ordinariness and corrupt modernism.

Thus Bridey and his mother (and Sebastian's younger sister, Cordelia, who is simple and good) stand in polar opposition to the brilliantly overdeveloped and decadent mind of Sebastian's homosexual friend, Anthony Blanche, who stands for modern aestheticism. Between those poles Charles is fatally divided. Anthony also flouts middle-class

seriousness and conscientiousness; he also lives for beauty
and wit; he also inhabits exotic terrains of the imagination.
But his challenge to his enemies is much more vigorous
and risk-taking. While Sebastian inhabits Brideshead and
Marchmain House, the English past, Anthony inhabits contemporary Paris and Berlin.

Anthony recognizes Charles's artistic gifts and tries to
claim him for modernism. He invites Charles to dinner,
offers him friendship, tries to turn him against Sebastian,
warns him against the fatal effect on his art of his love for
Sebastian. He says that Charles will be, as an artist,
'strangled with charm'. Charles refuses Anthony's friendship and sees only malice in his warnings. This is the crucial
moment in the story, though its full significance is not made
clear until later. Charles is afraid of Anthony. He is afraid of
his flaunted homosexuality, of the size and scope of his
rebellion against the normal, the traditional, the decent, and
afraid of the modernist art towards which Anthony tries to
direct him. He chooses Sebastian.

He chooses the quaint and the charming, and turns away
from the dangerous and the bizarre. Sebastian is not interested in Charles as an artist or in modern art. His rebellion in
aesthetics as in other things is purely playful. Anthony is
associated with Cocteau, Diaghilev, Picasso, with modern
art at its boldest. Charles prefers the art of painting British
country houses. He prefers charm. But when his first exhibition is held, Anthony attends it, and he alone understands
what Charles is doing and what has gone wrong with his
artistic development. He tells Charles that he has suc-
cumbed to English charm in just the way he had warned
him against in their conversation about Sebastian. And
Charles admits that Anthony is right. Anthony is established as He Who Knows. He has been right all along and
about the author himself. Charles is bored by his wife, by his
art, by his friends, by everything. (In *Gilbert Pinfold*
Waugh portrays a terrifying boredom in a character who is

obviously autobiographical.) Charles has chosen aestheticism, and then, within the world that option opened up, he has failed to recognize the crucial crossroads, has failed to take the strenuous path upwards that might have led to Art. Waugh (and his generation) had turned their backs on Kipling and moral responsibility, but lacked the courage needed for the great destructive alternative, modernism.

WAUGH AS KIPLING

In *Scoop* and *Black Mischief* on the other hand, Waugh comes very close to Kipling (and to the Lévi-Strauss of *Tristes Tropiques*) in his richly romantic treatment of European imperialism. The latter book begins with a proclamation, 'We, Seth of Azania . . .' and we see a native ruler trapped into imitating the style of European empire. Imperial history is as palpable a presence as it is in 'The Man Who Would Be King'.

> They were in the upper storey of the old fort at Matodi. Here, three hundred years before, a Portuguese garrison had withstood eight months' siege from the Omani Arabs; at this window they had watched for the sails of the relieving fleet, which came ten days too late. (p. 8)

Waugh describes how modern progress in Azania had bloomed in the form of a railway; showing a zest for historical absurdity very like Kipling's.

> The train was decked with bunting, feathers and flowers; it whistled continuously from coast to capital; levies of irregular troops lined the way; a Jewish nihilist from Berlin threw a bomb which failed to explode; sparks from the engine started several serious bush fires; at Debra Dowa Amurath received the congratulations of the civilized world and created the French contractor a Marquess in the Azanian peerage. (p. 10)

Waugh's own allegiance goes, like Kipling's and Lévi-Strauss's, to the pre-modern, the non-European, to the exotic landscapes and cultures the imperialists seized upon.

It [a church] could be descried from miles around, perched on a site of supreme beauty, a shelf of the great escarpment that overlooked the Wanda lowlands, and through it the Brook Kedron, narrowed at this season to a single thread of silver, broke into innumerable iridescent cascades as it fell to join the sluggish Izol 5000 feet below [p. 173]. . . . Sixty miles southwards in the Ukaka pass bloody bands of Sakuyu warriors played hide-and-seek among the rocks, chivvying the last fugitives of the army of Seyid, while behind them down the gorge, from cave villages of incalculable antiquity, the women crept out to rob the dead. (p. 57)

This is the reality which underlies and will supervene upon all the gimcrack pretences of European civilization and progress. This is exactly Kipling's emphasis in dealing with such subjects, and there is a strong harmony between *Black Mischief* and 'The Man Who Would Be King'.

And in the first of Waugh's three novels about the War, Guy Crouchback, like a belated Kipling hero, joins the army with a romantic enthusiasm which is clearly also a reaction against an irresponsible hedonism in the world around him.

Like Kipling, Guy needed a war, to force reality upon his contemporaries. He was glad to hear of the Russo-German alliance.

News that shook the politicians and young poets of a dozen capital cities brought deep peace to one English heart. Eight years of shame and loneliness were ended. . . . The enemy at last was plain in view, huge and hateful, all disguise cast off. It was the Modern Age in Arms. (*Men at Arms*, p. 12)

Guy goes to pray at a Crusader's tomb 'for our endangered kingdom'.

But if his inspiration is chivalric, and in some sense medieval, what Guy encounters in the Corps of Halberdiers – and finds exhilarating – is late Victorian or Kiplingesque. 'Nowhere in England could there be found a survival of a Late-Victorian Sunday so complete and so unself-conscious, as at the Halberdier barracks.' (p. 63) There he apprentices himself first to Apthorpe, a Kipling-style hearty, the sort of Englishman the dandies of the 1920s all mocked, and then to Brigadier Ritchie-Hook.

> He [Ritchie-Hook] was the great Halberdier *enfant terrible* of the first World War . . . twice court-martialled for disobedience to orders in the field; twice acquitted in recognition of the brilliant success of his independent actions; a legendary wielder of the entrenching tool; where lesser men collected helmets, Ritchie-Hook once came back from a raid across no-man's-land with the dripping head of a German sentry in either hand [p. 67]. . . . For this remarkable warrior the image of war was not hunting or shooting; it was the wet sponge on the door, the hedgehog in the bed; or, rather, he saw war itself as a prodigious booby trap. (p. 74)

Ritchie-Hook does indeed force reality upon Guy's contemporaries; in this case his fellow-officers, who refuse to take the military vocation seriously. When the training of the Halberdier officers goes slack, the Brigadier punishes them, and 'That evening Guy felt full of meat, gorged like a lion on Ritchie-Hook's kill.' (p. 121)

And surrounding Apthorpe and Ritchie-Hook, embracing Guy, is the regiment.

> Guy loved Major Tichborne and Captain Bosanquet. He loved Apthorpe. He loved the oil-painting over the

fireplace of the unbroken square of the Halberdiers in
the desert. He loved the whole Corps deeply and
tenderly [p. 54]. It seemed to Guy that in the last weeks
he had been experiencing something he had missed in
boyhood, a happy adolescence. (p. 48)

That adolescence could be said to be inspired by, or model
itself upon, Kipling's *Stalky and Co.* – a world of practical
jokes and escapades, but also of authority and responsibility.

The army stands for hierarchy, rarefaction, and caste, a
model of social formation, the opposite of everything
modern and decadent.

the whole hierarchic structure of army life was affronted
by this congregation of so many men of perfectly equal
rank [p. 95]. . . . In all his military service Guy never
ceased to marvel at the effortless transitions of
intercourse between equality and superiority. . . .
Regular soldiers were survivals of a happy civilization
where differences of rank were exactly defined and
frankly accepted. (*Officers and Gentlemen*, p. 319)

However, Guy himself has been (like Waugh) a dandy,
which means that he is fatally alienated from his roots in the
Kipling caste. When he first has a drink with Major Tich-
borne, he cannot respond to the ritual 'Here's how!' with the
same phrase, because that ritual belongs to the Kipling style
he has so long mocked. Once he joins the regiment he
manages that phrase, but he is felt to be always a little
outside the caste. Though he loves Apthorpe, that is in part
because he can – he must – laugh at him; and he must do so
because he is still something of a 1920s dandy, and Apthorpe
is a pre-1914 Englishman. (He is full, for instance, of tales of
his adventures in the African bush.) Indeed, Guy *needs*
Apthorpe to laugh at. Returning from leave to the regiment,
bruised by disappointments in civilian London, Guy con-
soles himself with the thought that:

> The spell of Apthorpe would bind him, and gently bear
> him away to the far gardens of fantasy [p. 138]. . . .
> [Hearing about Apthorpe's wearing of a tin helmet in
> his portable lavatory] 'And when do you put it on,
> before or after lowering the costume? I must know . . .
> I must visualize the scene, Apthorpe. When we are old
> men, memories of things like this will be our main
> comfort' [p. 157] . . . As Guy foresaw, those mad
> March days and nights of hide and seek drained into a
> deep well of refreshment in his mind. . . . He never
> again smelled wet laurel, or trod among pine needles
> without re-living those encumbered night prowls with
> Apthorpe. . . . (p. 158)

Laughter, and we shall see the same in other cases, here does
duty for sentiment.

Guy's feelings are paradoxical. He loves the same things
as he makes fun of; and the things he loves are specifically
the things of the old, pre-1914, Kipling England. For
instance he is intensely excited by the building in which he
receives his training, because it is a former prep school, and
one replete with memories of the First World War. It is
called Kut al Imara house, after a famous battle, and the
sleeping quarters had been the boys' dormitory. Each room
was named after a battle in the First War. His was 'Pasch-
endael'. He passed the doors of 'Loos', 'Wipers' (so spelt)
and 'Anzac' (p. 92).

It is not that Guy's memories of school or that war are
happy; such happy memories as he had are at least blended
with unhappiness, alienation, boredom; but the *blend*
is significant, is truth – though his response to the truth
expresses itself mostly in laughter. When he thinks of his
early (prep school) images of war, he thinks in terms of the
story hero, Captain Truslove, another Kipling figure.
Captain Truslove had been, like Kipling's Stalky, expert in
handling Pathans on India's North-West Frontier. Guy

realizes – but quite unresentfully – that he was taught to think of war in terms of such pseudo-historical romance, not in terms of the actual fighting of 1914–18.

And this mocking delight in the absurd comes together with Guy's admiration for Ritchie-Hook – Guy's sense that only the latter's barbarity can make sense of war and armies (which are reality). They come together in the practical joke, especially the military joke. Ritchie-Hook takes Guy on an illicit raid ashore near Dakar; Guy 'was filled with the most exhilarating sensation of his life; his first foothold on enemy soil.' (p. 229) Ritchie-Hook returns badly wounded, but before collapsing says, '. . . "take care of the coconut" . . . he had laid in Guy's lap the wet, curly head of a Negro.' (p. 231) This is reality, in part because it is horrifying, but in part because it is absurd; in both aspects it is what Guy has been starved of during the fat and flaccid years of peace.

In the second volume, *Officers and Gentlemen*, Waugh makes remarkable use of a configuration from P. G. Wodehouse (and other post-Kipling humourists), the dandy and his valet, Ivor Claire and Corporal-Major Ludovic. The latter 'looks like a dishonest valet'. Both these men, at first favoured by the novelist, turn out to be traitors, and the latter a murderer. This twist of plot expresses Waugh's repudiation of wartime frivolity and dandyism. And yet Waugh reserves for Ludovic the role of becoming a writer, and of writing a novel which, judging by its description, is very like *Brideshead Revisited*. In other words, Waugh suggests that we should see Ludovic as a caricature, or diagnosis, of himself. This calls for a dialectical reading, of the kind described before; but the rest of the book has no use for that.

This second volume is much more simply a comic fantasy than *Men at Arms*, much closer to Waugh's entertainments. And though the third volume, *Unconditional Surrender*, includes Waugh's only serious treatment of a serious war theme – the fate of Jewish and other refugees in Yugoslavia

– fictionally, the book falls apart; it is clear that Waugh has
ceased to believe in the larger enterprise he began.

Like Kipling, he found too much that was recalcitrant in
the form of the novel; or rather, he felt himself too much out
of sympathy with the whole enterprise of literature, with
the whole world of readers and writers, to be able to carry
through a big enterprise. The shadow of Kipling had fallen
across him, fatally.

[6]

KINGSLEY AMIS: THE
PROTEST AGAINST PROTEST

KINGSLEY AMIS WAS BORN in London in 1922, went to Oxford
briefly during the War, and returned after serving in the
army. He began to earn his living as a teacher, and married,
at roughly the same ages as Waugh had done twenty years
before. Seen in this way, the two authors' careers followed a
similar outline, in the first years of their lives. They stood in
roughly the same relation to the two World Wars, in terms
of the generations they belonged to, and both their first
books were satiric comedies which outraged some of the
older men in the literary establishment.

If we look back to the members of Waugh's generation,
discussed in *Children of the Sun*, we shall be struck to see how
many of them went on to variously successful and important careers. Most of them England rewarded richly. John
Strachey became a minister of the crown, 1946–51; Robert
Boothby was made a baron in 1958, Kenneth Clark in 1969.
Clark was director of the National Gallery, 1934–45; Alan
Pryce-Jones was editor of the *Times Literary Supplement*,
1948–59. Cecil Day-Lewis was Poet Laureate from 1968
until his death, when John Betjeman succeeded him, in
1972. William Walton was made a knight in 1951, Betjeman
in 1969, Cecil Beaton in 1972, Harold Acton in 1974. The
award of CBE (Commander of the British Empire) was
given to Cecil Day-Lewis in 1950, Osbert Lancaster in 1953,
Anthony Powell in 1956, Louis MacNeice and Oliver
Messel in 1958, Stephen Spender in 1962, John Lehmann in

1964, Harold Acton in 1965, Nancy Mitford and Cyril Connolly in 1972. After the Second World War, one may say, they staffed the Establishment. In literature, for instance, besides the novels, poems, essays, biographies, and travel books they produced, they filled between them the key reviewing and editorial jobs on the *Times Literary Supplement*, the *New Statesman, Encounter, New Writing, Horizon*, the *Observer*, the *Sunday Times*. They had become the central ganglion in the nervous system of 'England', and some of them felt insulted by Amis's comic satire.

Some of them had also become famous or infamous because of their involvement in scandals relating to political treachery, spying for Russia, and homosexuality. These included Burgess and Maclean and (though not involved in the homosexual part of the scandals) Philby and Blunt. These scandals were a part of the life of that generation – they are a reason why Waugh the satirist is its best chronicler – and they are also a reason why the next generation, of Amis's friends, reacted against them. Though most of the revelations were made long after Amis began to write, the moral, sexual, and political ambiguity of Waugh's group had of course long been obvious. But by 1950 that sleaziness was married to an old-fashioned and self-defensive gentle-manliness, a muted and furtive claim to a master-class style.

Thus Somerset Maugham wrote a letter to the *Sunday Times*, which was published on Christmas Day, 1954, about the social significance of Amis's currently published *Lucky Jim*. This significance was sinister, he said, because the novel described a new class on the British scene, the white-collared proletariat, trained technicians of the mind but not educated gentlemen – not members of an imperial caste.

They do not go to the university to acquire culture, but to get a job, and when they have got one, scamp it.
They have no manners, and are woefully unable to deal with any social predicament. Their idea of a celebration

is to go to a public house and drink six beers. They are
mean, malicious, and envious. . . . They are scum.

Maugham foresaw the futures of the Lucky Jims of real life
as schoolmasters, journalists, and, in a few cases, even the
cabinet ministers of England; and counted himself fortunate
that he would not live to see what they would make of his
country. A considerable controversy followed; Amis was
supported by anti-dandies like C. P. Snow (whose fiction
was roughly in the school I have called Socialist realism) but
above all by writers of his own emergent generation like
John Wain and Philip Larkin. And it is worth remembering
that Maugham, himself a homosexual, whose life-style was
the subject of scandal, had been one of those liberators of
Waugh's generation, one of those older aesthete figures
from whom they had received encouragement in their
rebellion against nineteenth-century moralism. But he now
spoke out for 'civilized' values, and he spoke on behalf of
many of them. Indirectly, this was a claim that the empire
had not entirely passed away. This outrage was just like that
which Waugh had evoked by his *Decline and Fall*, among the
older writers of 1928. But by 1954 those older writers
included Waugh himself, and his generation, who were by
then in the seats of power rather than aspiring to them. For
instance, his friend Nancy Mitford brought out a book
called *Noblesse Oblige* in 1956, which was based on some
articles which had appeared in *Encounter*, on the difference
between upper-class and lower-class word usage. The book
included illustrations by Osbert Lancaster, a poem by John
Betjeman, and above all an open letter to her by Evelyn
Waugh. He reproached her with 'bamboozling some needy
young persons' – the new, working-class-born, university
students of literature; in other words, the Lucky Jims.

Waugh named these new students and teachers of English
l'école de Butler, after the Butler Education Act of 1944,
which had given them the chance to go to the university, by

making available a lot of new scholarships. Such young
people could of course make nothing of the novels of his
friends, Anthony Powell or L. P. Hartley, or (he implies) his
own; because such novels imply an understanding of the
British class or precedence system. These sour and blunt-
minded young people – 'The primal man of the classless
society' – who come off the university assembly lines in
their hundreds every year, are now trying to become poets
and novelists as well as critics, but they really need to be
re-educated before they have a chance of succeeding at
literature.

This was the voice of the master-class at its clearest and
fullest – no doubt much of Waugh's pleasure in using it
derived from his sense of how out-dated it would seem –
and it was directed implicitly against *Lucky Jim* and its
author. Amis was then the spokesman in fiction for post-
war, Socialist England. At Oxford he had been editor of the
University Labour Club Bulletin ('in the days of Help for
Russia Week', says his friend, Larkin) and he wrote a
pamphlet for the Fabian Society.

During this period, the first years after the war, England
seems to have been more than usually describable in terms
of a split personality. On the one hand it had a Labour
government with a large majority, and with large schemes
for nationalizing the country's industries, which were being
put into effect energetically. Moreover, great hope was
placed in social renewal by means of education, discussion
groups, and every kind of planning. And rationing controls
were retained, even in some instances intensified, at a time
when other countries were relaxing them. These were signs
of a seriousness of mood, one of democratic responsibility,
which found a climactic symbol in the Festival of Britain in
1951. The Festival aimed to recapture the seriousness of the
Victorian Great Exhibition of 1851, but without the ornate,
imperialistic, and self-aggrandizing aspects of the Victorian
style – employing a more democratic and 'Scandinavian'

taste. In the world of the imagination, in literature, two of the big successes were George Orwell's *Animal Farm* (1945) and *1984* (1949); while in the world of literary and cultural theory F. R. Leavis began to be recognized as the important British critic.

On the other hand there was a cult of the frivolous, the elaborate, and the playful; represented by revivals of Oscar Wilde plays with sets and costumes designed by Cecil Beaton; in prose by *Brideshead Revisited*, and Osbert Sitwell's many-volumed autobiography; and in verse by Dylan Thomas and 'neo-romanticism'.

Amis and his friends clearly spoke for the first of these two conflicting forces, and against the other. The last issue of *Penguin New Writing* in 1950 contained an essay by John Wain, attacking neo-romanticism in the name of moral realism. The editor, John Lehmann (one of the dandy group) also gave Wain a spot on his radio programme about new writers; but when, in 1951, he lost control of that programme, it was to Wain that the BBC handed it over. And he thereupon introduced readings from *Lucky Jim*, which was able to find a publisher as a result of that publicity.

Wain was a great admirer of Orwell, and in his own fiction, particularly in *Hurry On Down*, he translated some of Orwell's ideas into his own terms – such as the vision of the working-class family in its kitchen, united in physical and emotional warmth, an integral human unit. The heroes of his and Amis's early novels are notably fond of and close to their fathers (unlike the heroes of Waugh's and his friends' fiction), and hostile to aesthete 'uncles'. (So, even more obviously, were the central characters of Raymond Williams's novels and Richard Hoggart's writings.) And in poetry Philip Larkin seemed a clear antithesis to Dylan Thomas and John Betjeman. Thus Amis began his career as and enemy of the imperial caste, and of those 'gentlemen' who tried to hold on to something of that style.

LUCKY JIM

Of course there were likenesses between *Lucky Jim* and
Waugh novels like *Decline and Fall*, just because both were
comedies – indeed partial farces – and satires, with a rich
cultural specificity. Both Waugh and Amis were brilliant
mimics, and namers of the habit, tastes, preferences of social
types. But their basic sympathies were so different that their
techniques also were widely separate. For instance, Waugh
has no real representative among the characters of his entertainments, while Amis *is* Lucky Jim, and everything in the
book is mediated to us via that personality. How we feel
about Jim/Amis determines how we judge the book. And in
so far as we can detect Waugh's own personality within his
work, it is haughtily scornful, at least in aspiration, and quite
unlike Amis's – which we might compare with Woody
Allen's. Jim's motives are embarrassment, revenge, humiliation, repression. As Maugham pointed out in his letter
about the book, Jim is 'woefully unable to deal with any
social predicament'; this is not true of Waugh's characters;
the latter are much more likely to drink champagne than 'six
beers at a public house'.

Waugh's comedy makes a cult of elegance, dexterity,
brilliance, command; that is why we can speak of mime as
well as farce in his work. In Amis elegance and dexterity
belong to the enemy, and the farce is much more physical,
clumsy, and undignified. And if Jim is a naif, like Paul
Pennyfeather, he is not a Pierrot figure; because he is too
aggressive – he has no grace as a victim. Moreover, none of
the women are Colombines. They are tougher than the
men, not more fragile, and – in various ways – embodiments of intelligence and moral force.

Thematically, Amis's satire picks targets which are the
social antithesis of Waugh's. For instance, the long set-piece
at the end of *Lucky Jim*, the drunken speech that sets out to
be in praise of Merrie England, and becomes an attack upon

it. Amis's set-piece is a satire on that disgust with the
modern world which Waugh proclaimed, and on his fondness for medieval chivalry and the Roman Catholic church.
And this is prepared for throughout the book by the
mockery of the Welches' love of genteel culture and the arts,
especially French literature and picturesque survivals from
pre-industrial England. All this had a clear anti-dandy
character in 1954. It is no accident that in their last encounter
at the end Welch and Bertrand, standing rigid and with
popping eyes, 'had a look of being Gide and Lytton Strachey,
represented in waxwork form by a prentice hand'. (p. 251)
Gide and Strachey were, like Maugham, liberating uncles to
the dandies and aesthetes of Waugh's generation, substitutes
for the oppressively orthodox fathers they rebelled against.
They were therefore enemies of Amis's generation.

Above all the two books differ because of the moral
realism of the Amis, and the importance of the moral problem it discusses. Jim has so strong a sense of pity and
responsibility, his mind and feelings are so dominated by
the image of those virtues, that he finds Margaret Peel more
attractive than Christine Callaghan.

> Dixon moved closer and saw that her hair had been
> recently washed; it lay in dry lustreless wisps on the
> back of her neck. In that condition it struck him as
> quintessentially feminine, much more feminine than the
> Callaghan girl's shining fair crop. Poor old Margaret, he
> thought, and rested his hand, in a gesture he hoped was
> solicitous, on her nearer shoulder. (p. 76)

It is, incidentally, no accident that pity and responsibility are
so much the characteristic virtues of the heroes of *The Heart
of the Matter* and Waugh's trilogy. Pity and responsibility are
for Amis whited sepulchres, seeming virtues which cover
masochism. When Jim thinks that he is doomed to lose
Christine and end up with Margaret, in some sense by his
own choice,

He remembered a character in a modern novel Beesley
had lent him who was always feeling pity moving in
him like a sickness, or some such jargon. The parallel was
apt; he felt very ill. (p. 185)

That novel was, or should be, by Greene. And if at the level
of the theme Amis is dissenting from Greene, at the level of
form he is different from Waugh, by setting a moral problem at the heart of his comedy.

It is also typical that the problem is treated pedagogically,
and that Jim's preceptor is a woman (and he in turn instructs
Christine). When he dismisses as adolescent the insistence
on sexual desire as a criterion in choosing a marriage partner,
Carol Goldsmith disagrees, and tells him,

after the maturity of my twenties was over I began
going back to that way of explaining things with a good
deal of relief. And justification, I'd like to think, too.
I'm rather keen on that formula these days, as a matter
of fact . . . You'll find that marriage is a good short cut
to the truth. No, not quite that. A way of doubling back
to the truth. (pp. 124–5)

Jim is much impressed.

These things helped to give her presence a solidity and
emphasis that impressed him; he felt not so much her
sexual attraction as the power of her femaleness. (p. 123)

This is, if not a Lawrentian, then an Orwellian note to strike,
a note evocative of the main tradition of the serious novel,
and quite out of Waugh's range. Amis is claiming some
alliance with that nineteenth-century liberal tradition in the
novel. And it is notable how often, even in Amis's latest
work, where everything else seems to have changed, his
heroes are instructed and put down at the hands of a
woman.

Having learned this lesson, Jim applies it to his own

attraction to failure. He must find within himself the courage of his own desires. On a taxi-ride which he persuades Christine to take with him, he resolutely stifles his self-punishing impulse to feel that she *ought* to disapprove the trick by which he procured the taxi for them.

> This ride, unlike most of the things that happened to him, was something he'd rather have than not have. . . . It was one more argument to support his theory that nice things are nicer than nasty ones.
> (p. 140)

This line of thought, deriving from the moral problem discussed, leads to the concept of luck announced in the title.

> It was all very bad luck on Margaret, and probably derived, as he'd thought before, from the anterior bad luck of being sexually unattractive. Christine's more normal, i.e. less unworkable, character no doubt resulted, in part at any rate, from having been lucky with her face and figure. But that was simply that. To write things down as luck wasn't the same as writing them off as non-existent or in some way beneath consideration. Christine was still nicer and prettier than Margaret, and all the deductions that could be drawn from that fact should be drawn; there was no end to the ways in which nice things are nicer than nasty ones. It had been luck, too, that had freed him from pity's adhesive plaster. . . . (pp. 242–3)

Incidentally the comic pedantries of Amis's prose, the obtrusive shifts of level in discourse – clumsy by comparison with Waugh – derive from or relate to his determination to combine realistic moral analysis with farcical comedy.

It is worth pointing also to the lovableness of Amis's hero – something for which there is no equivalent in Waugh's farces – and the simplicity, the sexual orthodoxy, of the central erotic action; boy meets girl, boy pursues girl, boy gets girl. (Again, there is no equivalent for this in Waugh – or for that matter in Kipling, Lawrence or Joyce.) Amis is clearly aiming at a general not a special audience, or at least offering a simple and not a sophisticated gratification, in terms of plot.

Among the specific comic tricks, to compare with Waugh's Commedia techniques, one can mention the faces Jim privately pulls to relieve his feelings; of course a classic expression of humiliation, repression, embarrassment; with the natural sequel of being found out, of having them seen. After pulling one elaborate and terrible grimace he sees that 'four witnesses of his actions were posted at the long window some yards away; they were (left to right) Christine, Bertrand, Mrs Welch, and Margaret.' (p. 179)

There are the fantasies of revenge, and the outbreaks of schoolboy rudeness, equally reflective of humiliation. There are the images, visual and aural. 'The other's clay-like features changed indefinably as his attention, like a squadron of slow old battleships, began wheeling to face this new phenomenon. . . .' (p. 9) Or the elaborate explanation of how Bertrand pronounces 'see' as 'sam'.

Most important, perhaps, are the practical jokes, because they persist all through Amis's career, and because they are morally ambiguous from the beginning. It is the Amis character who plays these tricks, and though they are excused on the grounds of all he has suffered from those he now attacks, they are also accused as cruel. Even in *Lucky Jim*, much the happiest and most innocent of Amis's comedies, Jim is gratuitously cruel to Evan Johns, and the reader is called upon to notice that and to condemn him. In later books this effect is much more developed, and the reader is made very uncomfortable by the intensity of dislike (of others, but also of himself) which the author reveals by the means of these tricks. It is also worth noting that

Waugh, though his sense of humour was certainly just as cruel, does not make so much use of the practical joke, and certainly does not attribute it to the one character that represents himself. Practical joking only appears in the war trilogy, and it is Ritchie-Hook who plays such tricks, not Guy. If we go back to Kipling, on the other hand, we *shall* find stories in which practical jokes are a prominent part of the writer's technique, and are performed by the writer's representative. In this way, as in others, Amis is closer to Kipling than Waugh was.

But in 1954 that would have seemed a very strange connection to make, because everything else in *Lucky Jim* attached the author to quite the opposite literary party to Kipling's. And the next two novels also expressed the moral-social viewpoint of *Lucky Jim*. The point of *That Uncertain Feeling* (1955) is that marriage is the supreme form of the erotic relationship, and that a nice simple girl like the hero's wife is more worth having than the rich and glamorous Elizabeth Gruffydd-Williams, who seduces him. Amis perhaps allows himself slightly more Waugh-like freedom of mockery here, as in this presentation of a quite sympathetic character.

> a man in his late 40s with a dark-red face and thick lips came by degrees into the room. Every straight grey hair in his abundant crop seemed the same length, making his head look as if it belonged to a little furry animal or shaving brush. Seeing a strange woman, he dropped his head and hunched his shoulders . . . 'How do you do' he said in a hoarse high-pitched voice with a strong North Walian accent; not an imitation, but the way he habitually talked. (p. 14)

This can remind one of Waugh's morally reckless mimicry of the Welsh in *Decline and Fall*. But Amis's major sympathies in *That Uncertain Feeling* are still made clear and firm, for Socialism and against the ruling-class – in literature, against the neo-romantic aestheticism of Dylan Thomas. This was a kind of Socialist realism, identified with all that was anti-imperialist in British life.

GEORGE ORWELL

The other author we can associate with the early Amis is George Orwell. I have pointed out that the latter was the object of great admiration by John Wain and the whole group of their friends. But what makes Orwell relevant here is rather his development of the technique of Socialist realism to a point where Amis could adapt it to his own purposes. What was humorously condescending in Wells, and in Joyce allied to bravura technical displays, in Orwell became the key in which a novelist could orchestrate a wide range of 'normality', while presenting and analysing moral-social problems.

We can take the 1939 novel, *Coming Up For Air*, as sufficiently representing this aspect of Orwell's work, although his other books, including the essays, contributed as much to this fictional idea of 'the normal man', which was so useful to Amis and his friends. *Coming Up For Air* begins, 'The idea really came to me the day I got my new false teeth.' And the unromantic indignity of false teeth is one of the most frequently sounded notes; another is the brisk movement and colloquiality of the prose.

I remember the morning well. At about a quarter to eight I'd nipped out of bed and got into the bathroom just in time to shut the kids out. It was a beastly January morning, with a dirty yellowish-grey sky. Down below, out of the little square of bathroom window, I could see the ten yards by five of grass, with a privet hedge around it and a bare patch in the middle, that we call the back garden. There's the same back garden, same privets and same grass, behind every house in

Ellesmere Road. Only difference – where there are no
kids there's no bare patch in the middle. (p. 3)

In *Lucky Jim* – and in most of his other novels – Amis
chooses a persona much closer to his own than this, one
which gives him more freedom to use his own experience,
but he puts the same stress on 'ordinariness' – experience
that is decidedly less exciting than expectation would have
wished, but is accepted or at least asserted, vigorously,
anti-romantically.

Orwell's narrator is called George Bowling, and describes himself as the athletic bouncing kind of fat man,
always the life of the party. This cuts off the writer's natural
association with the sensitive outsider, whether Paul Morel
or Stephen Dedalus, the quivering sensibility, the misfit or
victim of life; and allows the novel and the reader to discuss
general, in some sense public, experience. This was important to Amis in *Lucky Jim*. He was then fighting the same
battle against the 'gentlemen' left over from the empire as
Orwell had.

Bowling foresees the war and the bombs soon to come.

Seems a pity somehow, I thought. Miles and miles of
streets, fried-fish shops, tin chapels, picture houses,
little printing-shops up back alleys, factories, blocks of
flats, whelk stalls, dairies, power stations – on and on
and on. Enormous! And the peacefulness of it! Like a
great wilderness with no wild beasts. No guns firing,
nobody chucking pineapples, nobody beating anybody
else up with a rubber truncheon. (p. 24)

The exclamations and naïveté there are like Wells (and
Bloom) and unlike Amis. But the understatement (much
less literary than Hemingway's) was a valuable contribution
to Amis's Socialist realism. And another such contribution
is the complementary habit of grotesque exaggeration.

Their voices were quite different, too. Shooter had a
kind of desperate, agonized bellow, as though someone
had a knife at his throat and he was just letting out his
last yell for help. But Wetherall had a tremendous,
churning, rumbling noise that happened deep down
inside him, like enormous barrels being rolled to and fro
underground. However much noise he let out, you
always knew he'd got plenty more in reserve. The kids
nicknamed him Rumbletummy. (p. 33)

This is humour prepared for delivery in a pub, and credible
as the product of an ordinary man. Amis's is not that, but is
nearer to it than to Waugh's Latinate elegance.

This normality is in some ways coarse-grained and male-
chauvinist. Bowling says,

Thank God I'm a man, because no woman ever has that
feeling. [He explains] And it's a wonderful thing to be a
boy, to go roaming where grown-ups can't catch you,
and to chase rats and kill birds and cheek carters and
shout dirty words. It's a kind of strong, rank, feeling, a
feeling of knowing everything and fearing nothing, and
it's all bound up with breaking rules and killing things.
(p. 75)

On another occasion he says that killing things is about as
near to poetry as a boy gets. And when he describes a girl;

There was something about her black dress and the
curve of her breast against the counter – I can't describe
it, something curiously soft, curiously feminine. As
soon as you saw her you knew that you could take her
in your arms and do what you wanted with her. She
was really deeply feminine, very gentle, very
submissive, the kind that would always do what a man
told her, though she wasn't either small or weak.
(p. 121)

What Amis does with this sort of theme is more exploratory and dialectical, but it is like Orwell (and unlike Waugh) in its assertion of 'the normal' at the cost of the sensitive, the ordinary at the expense of the extraordinary. We are probably meant to imagine Lucky Jim in terms like those Bowling gives us about himself: 'An alert young chap with a round, pink, snubby kind of face and butter-coloured hair'. (p. 113)

In generational terms, Orwell was of course more like Waugh; they were in fact born in the same year and knew many of the same people – indeed, they knew each other and respected each other. And there are passages in *Coming Up For Air* which can remind one of Waugh; especially reminiscent nostalgic passages, for instance about boyhood reading, for both were expert cultural historians. But by and large Waugh and Orwell made opposite choices and stood for opposite values. That is why Amis was able to make so much use of Orwell in his dialectical repudiation of Waugh.

LATER AMIS

But the later Amis changed radically, and became almost the opposite of what he had been. The change began with *Take a Girl Like You* (1960) with its Restoration feeling for seduction as a masculine prerogative, and its godfather figure, who inducts the Amis-representative into masculine licence. Of course this prerogative is questioned, in some sense deplored, by the novel, but still it is asserted. The gentleman rogue, so sharply criticised in earlier Amis novels, here becomes a hero or model.

We see the favoured characters defiantly profess right-wing opinions, militarism, and luxury; while those who remain left-wing, pacifist, and puritan are mocked for doing so. And the Amis-representative attaches himself to a man, Julian Ormerod, who carries the former traits to an extreme. At one point we are told that, with his 'frowning but just-smiling expression, cold rather than crafty but crafty as well, he resembled the kind of British-film villain who ought by rights to be allowed to make a fool of the hero.' (p. 84) This occurs at a moment when the Amis-figure is transferring his allegiance to Ormerod from more innocent friends, and the suggestion of value-reversal – of *preferring* the villain – is clearly intended. Julian Ormerod is not a Kipling hero; but he is part way along the curve towards the Kipling heroes we are to meet in *The Anti-Death League*, from the starting point of *Lucky Jim*.

Then came *One Fat Englishman*, whose hero, Roger Micheldene, is categorically awful – a kind of opposite to Lucky Jim, but clearly just as much the author's representative. It was also significant that Micheldene was a Roman Catholic; the *Times Literary Supplement* said that Amis's God the Tormentor was as savage as Graham Greene's. Later it was said that *The Anti-Death League* was 'on the edge of Greeneland'. This was another affiliation it would have been paradoxical to predict in the days of *Lucky Jim*. Amis was now in alliance with those people who had been his enemies at first.

Moreover, from the days of *The Anti-Death League* on, he positively invited his readers to assimilate him to Evelyn Waugh – by his right-wing politics, his blatant polemics, his militarism, his publicity-seeking, his legal suits, his reaction against both left-wing liberalism and the cult of youth. He made himself known as a connoisseur of wine and food, clothes and snuff. He made himself into a dandy of the English kind – a dandy-gentleman. He made himself the ruling class's jester.

In 1967 he and his friend Robert Conquest publicly supported America's role in Vietnam. He said he had been disillusioned with Russia in 1956, and was dissatisfied with Harold Wilson's educational policies and the dominance of the state in England. He was also disenchanted with intellectuals who 'buy unexamined the abortion-divorce-homosexuality-censorship-racialism-marijuana package; in a word, the Lefty'. By this disenchantment, 'I am driven into grudging toleration of the Conservative party, because it is the party of nonpolitics, of resistance to politics.' Experience, he said, is a Tory.

Literarily, moreover, Amis invoked Waugh's name. In a short article on 'My Kind of Comedy' in *The Twentieth Century* for July, 1961, he said that the prime targets of his humour had been bores and right-wing things; and that his sense of what was funny had been limited by 'my tender political conscience'. But now, he said, he had begun to find Evelyn Waugh funny: 'Evelyn Waugh makes fun of things I feel strongly about, but then I made the discovery that we agree about certain basic things. He makes the sort of character I dislike behave in a way I like. . . .' And more and more after that, Amis dealt with 'the sort of character I dislike', Waugh characters. He also said he felt an affinity with Fielding, Anthony Powell, and Iris Murdoch; which adds up to a definite turn away from Socialist realism. His audience had been his generation of young men; but now his performance began to appeal to men of power and position, like Kipling's and Waugh's.

Looking back, of course one sees certain signs even in *Lucky Jim* of what was to come. Besides the things I have already mentioned, there is the feeling for Bill Atkinson and for Julius Gore-Urquhart. The former is a figure of 'archaic ferocity', whom Jim likes and reveres for 'his air of detesting everything that presented itself to his senses', and for his power to intimidate those who intimidate Jim himself. The latter is a millionaire who is able to change Jim's fate entirely with a wave of his wand, and whose favour Jim is lucky enough to win (he blushes to feel himself approved by this man, long before there is any practical advantage to be expected from it). Both these men stand for a forcefulness, and an indifference to ordinary criteria, including morality, which Jim eagerly admires and aspires to himself. They become his godfathers, promising him masculine privilege. This points in quite a different direction from his moral education of Christine. And this is the direction in which his career went – towards in-jokes for the master-class.

THE ANTI-DEATH LEAGUE

This is what we see again in the longest and most ambitious of his novels, *The Anti-Death League*, which also announces an allegiance to Waugh, and to figures and forces we can associate with Waugh. Indirectly, it affiliates Amis to Kipling.

This work is anyway important in Amis's career because in it he for once essays major themes and gives them a broad treatment. Those themes can be defined as anger at death and suffering; rebellion against God and against any scheme of ideas which offers to explain the universe and its moral economy; and feeling for the beauty and pathos of those structures in which men huddle together to create the order and kindness they fail to find outside – notably the army and the church. Each of these themes receives a multiple treatment, embodied in a number of characters and events, which naturally differ from each other, but can be added together. Both the dignity of the themes and the multiplicity of the treatments are unlike Amis's other novels, and could remind one – but for other differences – of the most ambitious novelists of the twentieth century.

The theme of death and its arbitrariness is announced at the very beginning, with a cat getting ready to pounce on a bird, and the shadow of a plane suddenly darkening the landscape ominously. (Such high-flown symbolism is very unlike *Lucky Jim*, obviously.) This theme is then related to the sufferings of the patients (including two of the major characters) at the mental asylum which is the setting for this first scene, and which is run by a man at first presented as stupid and dogmatic but later condemned as a sinister villain (a conception crude enough to suit a James Bond movie). Of these two patients, one is later deprived of his lover by the latter's accidental death; the other finds a lover, but in their first love-making a cancer is discovered in her breast. Meanwhile the group of officers who are the story's central characters are involved in an operation which involves their using nuclear weapons, and engaging in biological warfare.

The theme of protest against God, religion, theology, philosophy, or any explanation of life, is carried by James Churchill, a young officer, and by Willie Ayscue, the unit's chaplain: and by the unknown author of a deicide poem; and by the organizer of the Anti-Death League which is proposed in the camp. The poem and the proposal are anonymous, but are later revealed to be the work of Max Hunter, another officer.

The theme of the army (the civilizing mission of institutional life) is carried by the courtesy, mutual kindness, dignity, and cheerful rituals of these men, so often displayed in the officers' mess and at dinner together. Occasionally there are more romantic images of their moral elegance; Hunter and another officer, Ross-Donaldson, playing piquet and drinking iced champagne while the nuclear weapons are being tested; Captain Leonard abducting Catharine from hospital so that she can bring Churchill out of his condition of catatonic despair. The theme of the church is concentrated in Ayscue, who does not believe in God, has had no religious experience, and feels no power in the church, but still tries to bring spiritual consolation to those in his charge.

The character who most fully represents Amis in the story is Max Hunter, the subversive. It is he who talks most nearly the way the book talks. Visited in the asylum, he tells his friends:

> 'In a brief circuit of fifty yards or so I came across no fewer than three very amorous couples, and that was without trying to come across them. Quite the

contrary. I was virtually threading my way. I get the
impression everybody's at it all the time. It's no more
than you'd expect in an environment like this.' [And
when someone says 'Not everybody, surely?', he
replies] 'Not everybody, no. I question whether the
catatonics do much in that way, and no doubt the
senility wards have a stainless record,' (pp. 17–18)

Though this is the voice of the novel speaking, it is not the
voice of *Lucky Jim*. Amis's prose has changed; it is now
dandified, the epigrams and paradoxes, one might say, curl
up at the edges, keeping contact with ordinary experience to
a minimum.

That is not the only voice. The book begins with sen-
tences of a much more studied objectivity.

A girl and an older woman were walking along a
metalled pathway. To their left, beyond a strip of grass,
was the front of a large high building in grey stone.
Reaching its corner, at which there was a pointed turret,
brought them in view of a square of grass. . . . (p. 11)

This is a prose it seems fair to call Hemingwayesque,
because of its continuous suggestion that if the speaker
allowed himself any expressiveness his voice would rise to a
scream. And it seems right to invoke Hemingway's name
also because one whole sub-plot, and sequence of dialogues,
is clearly borrowed from *A Farewell to Arms*. This of course
confirms our sense of Amis's tendency, since Hemingway is
the most famous masculinist and militarist writer of
modern times.

There is then more than one voice in the novel, and one of
its most striking features – which it shares with other late
Amis novels – might be called polyphonality, in the sense in
which Bakhtin applies that term to Dostoevsky. Characters
in the book change their labels, their natures, as Amis
changes his thesis, and one is constantly reminded of the

fictionality of the fiction, and so of the dialectical relation of author to reader – of author to text. In this case, Dr Best *becomes* as the novel proceeds a cartoon of villainy; Leonard ceases to be a case of stupidity and tunnel vision, and becomes a naïve but decent human being; Ross-Donaldson is revealed at the end as a monster of impersonality under a suave surface.

For an analogy, surprising as it may seem, we might turn to Jean Genet. Sartre writes, in an essay on Genet's plays,

> With practise, Jean Genet has managed to transmit to his thought an increasingly rapid circular movement (7) . . . It is the element of fake, of sham, of artificiality, that attracts Genet . . . (8) . . . The spectator is warned that the actors are trying to deceive him as to their sex (9). . . . In his novels he betrayed his characters by warning the reader 'Watch out. These are the creatures of my imagination. They don't exist' (10). . .

We can think of L. S. Caton, revived from *Lucky Jim*, to be slaughtered in this later novel. And Amis does (as indeed Kipling does) challenge the reader dialectically. As much as Genet, he insists that there is no comfortable position for the reader to assume to his subject-matter – that being a reader is a false position – but that ceasing to read won't save you either.

Amis's trickiness seems to derive from something in his situation as an entertainer of the master-class, some moral-psychological unease that is more than his alone. That something characterized Kipling's and Waugh's situation also, and *their* work is tricky, but less modernist in style.

Modernism has never been fully welcomed or acclimatized in England, and its reflection in literature is partial and easily overlooked. But it is important to our argument because it is one of the major ways artists have disaffiliated themselves from the ruling class, and therefore from imperialism. (Because it also disaffiliated them from the working class, its political character is nevertheless ambiguous.) In France, at least according to French critics, the writers/readers renounced their social allegiances in the second half of the nineteenth century. But in England their loyalties merely divided, even after 1918. We find a pyrrhonism as total as Beckett's in Forster's account of the Marabar caves in *Passage to India*: but it is allied to social comedy, with all that genre's implicit loyalty to social norms. We find a Commedia art as brilliant as Brecht's in Waugh's entertainments, but it is allied to social conservatism. We find a use of vaudeville as bold as Brecht's or Genet's in Kipling, but it is allied to a master-class politics. And so we find the polyphonality of Dostoevsky or Genet in *The Anti-Death League*, but allied to a scrupulous modesty of intellectual ambition, a most British self-limitation. Amis can only be a partial modernist, because his relation to his rulers is (ambivalently) loyal.

For of course Amis's book is more like Waugh than like Genet or Sartre. The likeness can be seen in the concern both men share for the church and theology; in the love of the regiment, as the type of human society at its best; in the importance of adventure action, including killing, as a test for the main characters; and even in the importance of drinking – now no longer six beers at a public house, but pink gins and champagne, surrounded by rituals. Amis now identifies with, takes his characters from, the people in charge. In *Lucky Jim* they had been the villains or at least the counter-players; but in this novel there are no ordinary soldiers in the centre of the stage, only officers.

In an unpublished essay called 'Writers at War', Evelyn Waugh praised the military life; because the soldier is his rulers' natural enemy, and is immune to the emotions of the crowd. 'Army life with its humours, surprises, and loyalties, its ferocious internal dissensions and its lack of all hate for the ostensible enemy, comprises the very essence of human intercourse. . . .' This seems to be exactly Amis's idea in choosing and depicting his group of characters in *The Anti-Death League*. Soldiers are and are not ruling class; they embody the best of authority and responsibility, but stand outside the fake consolations of society.

The villains of the novel represent inhuman systematization, notably Best, and Leonard till Amis forgives him; his thematic place *should* be taken by Venables, the scientist who invented the plague which Operation Apollo is designed to spread, but so many explanations are crammed together at the end of the action that such issues never become real – the reader never connects the actions with their real perpetrators. What is said to happen loses touch with what Amis more deeply means. The theological theme also has many twists and turns in the last four pages of the book. There is thus much undeveloped thematic material in the book, and one suspects that the author had planned something much longer than he wrote. Like Waugh, Amis lay under the ban of artistic impotency, that incapacity for the large themes and forms which we saw first in Kipling.

AMIS AND KIPLING

After *The Anti-Death League*, Amis seems to have made up his mind that he could not write novels, and must devote himself to the minor forms of fiction. His publishing record seems to make that plain, for, even ignoring some peripheral works, we can point to a remarkable variety of minor genres he has attempted. There is for instance the ghost story, or story of the supernatural – *The Green Man* (1969); the detective story – *The Riverside Villas Murder* (1973); a James Bond thriller – *Colonel Sun* (1968); historical fantasy – *The Alteration* (1977); future fiction – *Russian Hide and Seek* (1980); science fiction – he for several years coedited an annual anthology; the geriatric-mortuary novel – *Ending Up* (1974); as well as what we can more loosely call light fiction – *I Want It Now* (1968), *Girl, 20* (1971) and so on.

This turn toward entertainments and away from novels will remind us of Waugh. More specifically, it will remind us of Kipling, who was remarkable for the variety of the sub-genres of fiction he practised. And indeed we find that Amis has written an appreciative book about Kipling.

In the introduction, dated January, 1975, he thanks the publishers for commissioning the book from him: 'If they had not done so, I might never have fully discovered the work of a great English writer.' Like Waugh in his corresponding phase, Amis here treats art as entertainment, and his stress in presenting Kipling falls on the latter's skills as a writer, but their political sympathy is also evident.

> A powerful underlying message of the Ballads
> [Kipling's 'Barrackroom Ballads'] is that freedom,
> order, art, learning and everything we call civilization
> depends in the last resort on the activities of a few score
> thousand commonplace, ignorant, vulgar, violent men
> whom it is all too easy to despise. Tommy Atkins'
> sardonic comment on the cheapness of 'making mock of
> uniforms that guard you while you sleep' has a
> formidable relevance today. It was good then too.
> (p. 64)

From the beginning, some of Amis's fictional preferences could have reminded us of Kipling. He always liked to play games with the reader, as for instance in the short story about a mock Parliamentary session in an army unit, which begins in such a way that the reader supposes it is a real Parliamentary scene; or the moment in *That Uncertain Feeling* in which a passage of poetic dialogue from a play is continued by a remark from one member of the audience to another, with no signal of interruption. He has always played jokes and surprises on the readers, and given them clues, though this has become much more striking a feature of his later work. This is characteristic of Kipling, and most uncharacteristic of Joyce and Lawrence and Doris Lessing.

Thematically too Amis followed Kipling in the cult of
laughter. This is more than achieving humorous effects, or
even designing whole stories to be humorous. Both these
writers, and Waugh, ascribe to laughter functions most
people reserve for serious thought. It is a matter of ascribing
importance to laughter, and developing a theory or a theology of humour. Kipling, for instance, has a rather remarkable poem, 'The Necessitarian', in which he says:

> I know not in whose hands are laid . . .
> The very Urns of Mirth
> Who bids the Heavenly Lark arise
> And cheer our solemn round –
> The Jest beheld with streaming eyes
> And grovellings on the ground;
> Who joins the flats of Time and Chance
> Behind the prey preferred,
> And thrones on Shrieking Circumstance
> The Sacredly Absurd.
>   . . .
> Yet it must be, on wayside jape,
> The selfsame Power bestows
> The selfsame power as went to shape
> His Planet or His Rose. (XXVII, p. 102)

It is obvious that there, however 'ironically', laughter is
being exalted to the level of the sacred. And the same is true
of the following passage from Waugh's *Officers and Gentlemen*, which describes Guy and a friend laughing over an
absurd dinner-party they have just attended – laughing so
hard their driver thinks them drunk.

> Tommy and Guy were indeed inebriated, not solely nor
> in the main by what they had drunk. They were caught
> up and bowled over together by that sacred wind which
> once blew freely over the young world. Cymbals and
> flutes rang in their ears. The grim isle of Mugg was full

of scented breezes, momentarily swept away and set
down under the stars of the Aegean.

Men who have endured danger and privation
together often separate and forget one another when
their ordeal is ended. Men who have loved the same
woman are blood brothers even in enmity; if they laugh
together, as Tommy and Guy laughed that night,
orgiastically, they seal their friendship on a plane rarer
and loftier than normal human intercourse.

There we see both love and war subordinated to laughter,
which is implicitly elevated to the rank of imagination or
poetry. I don't know of passages in Amis quite like that – he
might well consider that theme sufficiently treated by his
predecessors – but he clearly follows them in the importance
and function he ascribes to laughter.

At the end of *Lucky Jim*, for instance, Jim and Christine
meet the Welches on the street.

The incident was almost closed when he saw that not
only were Welch and Bertrand both present, but
Welch's fishing-hat and Bertrand's beret were there too.
The beret, however, was on Welch's head, the fishing-
hat on Bertrand's. In these guises, and standing rigid,
with popping eyes, as both were, they had a look of
being Gide and Lytton Strachey, represented in
waxwork form by a prentice hand. Dixon drew in
breath to denounce them both, then blew it all out again
in a howl of laughter. His steps faltered; his body sagged
as if he'd been knifed. With Christine tugging at his arm
he halted in the middle of the group like a man with the
stitch, his spectacles misting over with the exertion of it,
his mouth stuck ajar in a rictus of agony. 'You're . . .'
he said. 'He's . . .'. (p. 251)

Everything about the story promises us that this laughter
will seal the union between him and Christine, in the way

Waugh describes. In nearly all his novels Amis presents his representative sharing such moments – sharing the stories of his predicaments and his reprisals with the woman he loves; or failing to share them, as in *Jake's Thing*, and thereby breaking the bond between them. Laughter is erotic; laughter is marriage.

In the *Lucky Jim* passage, the joke upon Welch and Bertrand is played by Someone, as Kipling might say, 'Who joins the flats of Time and Chance/Behind the prey preferred.' More characteristically and more challengingly, in both Kipling and Amis, it is the author's representative who plays a trick upon a victim, and invites the audience to join in the laughter. This of course lays bare the element of cruelty in practical joking. But the two differ in the key role Amis assigns to women as appreciators of such jokes, in what I have called the erotic character of his laughter, but should perhaps be called the heterosexual character. In Kipling and Waugh the joke unites men, and constitutes a masculine world; and indeed in Amis the woman appreciates, not initiates. The difference between the authors is, however, significant, and relates to the way Amis and not Kipling punishes himself in public for his joking, the way he continues to put himself into his novels and to arraign and condemn himself.

In terms of serious opinion, Amis has moved towards Kipling (that is, to the right) in cultural politics as in regular politics. His critical essays had always, from 1957 on, expressed a very irritable consciousness of Leavis, Orwell, and Lawrence. Lawrence seems to have been always a bête noire for Amis, Orwell a former hero whose claque irritated, Leavis something in between. Amis was always keenly aware of their anti-dandy movement, and in some sense lived with his mind turned towards it, but his awareness led him as much to a sense that he was different as to any sense of comradeship. What happened in the 1960s is that he aligned himself with Waugh and the dandies positively, though still self-punishingly. In 1959 he had objected to *Lolita* on moral grounds as sadistic, allied to the charge that it was too 'aesthetic'. But in 1965 he wrote a James Bond adventure story, and said how much he had always admired Ian Fleming's work, morally and aesthetically.

In some sense, moreover, Amis continued to represent his generation even as he changed. The other brilliantly talented writer among the Angry Young Men, Philip Larkin, has gone through a similar evolution. In his poetry, in his two early novels, in his critical prose, in what he seems to have meant to Amis, Larkin was at first an anti-Waugh writer, a plain man as literary intellectual; an influence working in the same direction as Orwell, Leavis, and Lawrence. But in the 1960s he began implicitly to ally himself with Waugh's friend, John Betjeman, as a poet, just as Amis allied himself with Waugh. (And behind Betjeman we can see Kipling, the master of light verse.) In 1959, on *Listen*, Larkin described Betjeman as 'one of those rare figures on whom the aesthetic appetites of an age pivot and swing round to face an entirely new direction'. And in 1971, introducing Betjeman's *Collected Poems*, Larkin asks, can it be that Betjeman will dominate the second half of the twentieth century as T. S. Eliot did the first? He calls Betjeman's the most extraordinary poetic output of our time, praises his advocacy of 'the little, the obscure, the disregarded', and lauds his work as a preserver of the past. In these phrases we glimpse presumably the affinity Larkin feels between his own meanings and Betjeman's. He seems to feel a formal debt to the poet for whom, as he says, 'the modern poetic revolution has simply not taken place'. Of course such questions of form bear on the poetry's cultural meaning. Larkin says that in this century English poetry went off on a loop-line that took it away from the general reader; and presumably he feels that Betjeman, who stayed close to that reader (in our terms, to the book-buyers) will be a father figure to the English poets yet to come. All this is close to what Waugh says, in *The Ordeal of Gilbert Pinfold*, about the importance of the technical masters who have perfected the minor forms; Amis has said, similarly, that John D. MacDonald, of thriller fame, is by any standards a better writer than Saul Bellow; and the creative policy this judgment implicitly recommends is what Amis has prac- tised. It is a policy of deliberate provincialism, of imagina- tive defeatism.

Within these limits, Amis's work has continued to be interesting. *Girl, 20*, for instance, addresses 'issues of the day', notably the cult of youth, and declares the author's position boldly and honourably. Its first chapter is entitled 'Imperialist, Racist, Fascist', and in it the author's repre- sentative is accused of being all three, by a black man; when he fails to respond, the other man tells him that it is a bloody serious accusation, asking if he does not care about these accusations, these labels. He replies,

> 'No I don't. Nor a communist or a bourgeois or anything else. I just don't care about any of that, you see.'
>
> He looked at me in pure amazement. 'But these are some of the great issues of our time.'
>
> 'Of your time, you mean. The great issue of my time is me and my interests, chiefly musical. Can we go indoors now?' (p. 19)

Clearly this declaration is aimed at the reader as much as at the other character; and if it seems barrenly defiant, it is genuinely courageous.

Unfortunately the defiance has grown, as Amis has found himself more and more alienated from the liberal ortho- doxy of the reading public, without becoming any more fruitful of alternative self-definitions. Its only ally as a mode of self-expression has been self-laceration; Amis has defied the censure of others but inflicted his own more and more savagely. In *Jake's Thing* (1978) his representative comes to the conclusion that he is a male chauvinist pig. He does not merely apply that label to himself; he does not merely admit that from a feminist point of view it fits him; he adopts that label, he adopts that point of view and condemns himself from it. But the moral dignity Amis wins for himself here he loses in his treatment of the plot and subject matter of the novel; the self-condemnation is then felt largely as depression.

Probably his most successful piece of fiction is *The Green Man*, and it is appropriate that its final moment, its climax, is a moving expression by the central character of the wish to die.

> Death was my only means of getting away for good from this body and all of its pseudo-symptoms of disease and fear, from the constant awareness of this body, from this person, with his ruthlessness and sentimentality and ineffective, insincere, impracticable notions of behaving better, from attending to my own thoughts and from counting in thousands to smother them and from my own face in the glass . . . when I died I would be free from Maurice Allington for longer than that. (pp. 252–3)

AMIS AS WAUGH

But the expectation and the wish for death is only incidental to *The Green Man*, while it is central to *Ending Up*, which can therefore claim the dignity of representing Amis as he represents his generation and his country. (It is significant that there have been other such novels of death and dying in England recently, like Muriel Spark's *Memento Mori*.) In this novel, all the characters are old, and are living together, in circumstances which exacerbate their mutual irritabilities and richly develop their meannesses. And the character in whom the irritability and meanness is most striking,

Bernard Bastable, is the one who represents Amis.

This is made clear above all by the similarity between Bernard's dialogue and the narrator's prose. When his sister Adela calls him by name, he replies 'What?' and she repeats it, thinking he hasn't heard. 'I heard you say my name. I was asking in effect what you wanted, not for a repetition of what you have said. As my use of a falling rather than a rising inflection might have suggested.' (p. 10) Two pages later, the narrator remarks about Adela, '18th century timber-frame was what she called the style of the house when asked, and sometimes when not.' And on page 28 he mentions the radio. 'Bernard was listening to it now, or sat nearby while there issued from it, slightly off frequency, a short play about putatively comic clergymen.' None of the other characters talk in that tightly controlled diction which suggests a fury of irritation.

It is moreover clear that Bernard's cruel humour, his practical jokes, are the source of the book's action; and that they are recognizably akin to those of *Lucky Jim*, though now so far from charming. For instance, in order to set George at odds with Marigold, he induces the former's dog to tear up a letter directed to the latter; which is not unlike Jim's treatment of Evan Johns' magazine. Bernard is of course punished for this; it turns out that he had given the dog the wrong letter – one intended for himself – and moreover Marigold guesses what he was up to. Self-punishment can be expected from Amis, and is sometimes merely painful; but in this novel the punishment is worked out in the plot, in terms of farce, and is not so directly inflicted as elsewhere upon the reader's moral sensibility. And later Bernard succeeds in soaking Marigold's cat and blaming it on Shorty, whereupon Bernard goes to his bedroom 'where he laughed till he cried'.

The farce is genuinely black, genuinely distasteful, and genuinely grim. The old people (principally but not exclusively Bernard) so yield to the temptation to tease and

humiliate each other that they are finally responsible for
each other's deaths. This responsibility is largely accidental,
even in Bernard's case, but he is different because of the
activism of his malice; and he is punished for it.

> The daylight had just begun to fade. Bernard, wincing
> with pain and effort, propped the ladder against the far
> side of the house and laboriously mounted it. At the
> top, he reached up and cut the telephone wire with the
> pair of pliers he had found, laughed with great
> abandonment, lost his balance and fell.
>   He had broken something, something large. There
> was also a lot of what must be blood. Crying out with
> pain now, he crawled a little way, just far enough to be
> out of sight of anyone approaching the front door of the
> cottage, and found he could crawl no further.
> (pp. 173–4)

The story-telling is instinct with compassion. Of Adela
we are told, 'She had never been kissed with passion, and
not often with even mild and transient affection. This she
explained to herself as the result of her extreme ugliness.'
(p. 13) Marigold – though thoroughly selfish – is terrified by
the loss of her memory. 'Marigold had loved her husband
for 48 years; so, at any rate, she would have said, and would
have meant it. Now she could not remember their first meet-
ing, their engagement, their wedding. . . .' (p. 143) Even of
Bernard we are told that he had thought, when told he had
only three months to live, that he would now prize things
outside himself, knowing he would soon lose them. 'That
might have been some compensation for having had to be
Bernard Bastable, for having had to live.' Of course this
note is immediately counteracted by the opposite. 'There
was the sound of Adela's car returning. He limped quickly
off towards the kitchen in confident hope of an opportunity
to ridicule and distress her.' (p. 164)
Indeed, there is something more impressive than com-

passion in the novel; there is a steady recognition of the virtues of these humiliated and self-humiliating people. Adela had wished 'as she still occasionally found herself doing, that her brother would let her love him, but of course it was too late for that.' (p. 13) George is genuinely grateful to those who help him. Marigold can on occasion show some feeling for Adela, whom most of the time she mercilessly exploits. While Shorty, who had long before been Bernard's batman and lover, is little short of a saint. Though he much dislikes Marigold, when he finds her upset at the sight of a dead pheasant, he immediately withdraws the suggestion that they should cook it.

> He had instantly grasped that Marigold's action was the result of genuine feeling, not of any desire to make an impression, and in the second place that that feeling was not caused simply by confrontation with a dead pheasant. (p. 66)

As a work of art, therefore, *Ending Up* successfully controls and indeed turns to profit the sense of misery, both individual and general, out of which it arises. It is as successful on its own terms as *The Green Man*. But those terms are harrowing ones. As a document, both personal and cultural, it is very painful. (The cultural reference, out from these old people, living in Tuppeny Hapenny Cottage, to the English people, now living in their island, is entirely implicit – but that is the purity and the strength of the metaphor.)

The most striking and poignant aspect of the story is the cultural specification of Bernard, which must in some sense be the way Amis sees himself. He presents Bernard as a belated member of Kipling's master-class.

> In the past, he had been a man of many interests. The athletic ones – fives, racquets, cricket – had gone when they had had to go, and he did not want to read about them. Military tactics and strategy, the history of the

> Empire, anything connected with India (the land of his
> birth and early childhood and of eight years' service
> between the wars), pioneers in aviation, chess, the life of
> the Duke of Wellington, the works of George Meredith,
> all had gone too, thoroughly and for good, even though
> they had not had to, or not in any obvious sense. To try
> any of them these days, to look at *Kim* or *The Egoist*,
> was to come up against something with as little point as
> a railway platform conversation between a departing
> traveller and the man seeing him off. So all he did was
> pass the time. (p. 72)

The empire had gone, and with it all kinds of 'interests',
from Kipling and Meredith to chess and India. Bernard's
civilization – Amis's civilization – has gone, and with it the
rich culture which had beforehand seemed quite independent of any institutional support. If we turn from that
passage to Evelyn Waugh's self-portrait as Gilbert Pinfold,
we cannot but be struck by the likeness; a likeness first in
boredom, and then in furious irritability.

> His [Pinfold's]strongest tastes were negative. He
> abhorred plastics, Picasso, sunbathing, and jazz –
> everything in fact that had happened in his own lifetime
> . . . He looked at the world *sub specie aeternitatis* and he
> found it flat as a map; except when, rather often,
> personal annoyance intruded. Then he would come
> tumbling from his point of observation. Shocked by a
> bad bottle of wine, an impertinent stranger, or a fault in
> syntax, his mind like a cinema camera trucked furiously
> forward to confront the offending object close up with
> glaring lens, with the eyes of a drill sergeant inspecting
> an awkward squad, bulging with wrath that was half
> facetious, and with half simulated incredulity; like a drill
> sergeant he was absurd to many but to some rather
> formidable. (pp. 14–15)

The *Ordeal of Gilbert Pinfold* was published in 1962, just twelve years before Amis's book. The two personal predicaments are similar in their painfulness, but what concerns us here is the implicit public reference. The two predicaments owe some of their resonance to their reference to the two authors' achievements and public careers in the past; and to a reference through those to the public condition of literature and culture. And it is the final poignancy that Amis's career should have begun as a contradiction of and antithesis to Waugh's.

DORIS LESSING: THE RETURN FROM THE EMPIRE

WITH THE LAST OF my six writers, we come, if not full circle, then at least to the most clear-cut confrontation with the starting point, Kipling. Lessing, born in the empire, like Kipling, speaks for and to the empire as much as he did, but with an opposite orientation. Far from being an imperialist, she is not even anti-imperialist, as that term applies to, say, E. M. Forster. Lessing's subject is what comes *after* the judgment upon empire – the tragi-comedy of a life committed a priori and without hesitation to fighting her own country's imperialism. Her earliest books deal with that life as lived in an African colony, the later ones with ex-imperial London; and in the latter the theme of explicit anti-imperialism is often minor; but in fact her subject is always England's ruin – ruin in the wake of empire.

The most important characteristic of English history after 1945 – one which I have sufficiently asserted already – was the decline of every sort of English power. But almost equally important, and intricately interwoven with this, was the arrival in England of immigrants from all over the ex-empire. This was an ironic and judgmental event; just when the imperial country began to shrink and wither, to feel poor and cramped, to lose its margins of freedom, both overseas and at home, just then her former subjects, her clients and serfs, arrived in great numbers to claim their share of her diminishing privilege.

There were two groups of them, different in numbers and

in influence. There were a few white colonists and administrators, who could disappear into the national scenery,
and who had official and semi-official allies to help them
adjust to the new poverty. And there were many non-white
colonized, who stood out against the national scenery, as
dramatically different, and were allowed to drift into
ghettoes and into serf labour. Doris Lessing's fiction drew
authority over the general reader from 'representing' both
groups.

Immigrants from the West Indies, and soon after from
India and Pakistan, and then from the ex-colonies of Africa,
began arriving in England very soon after the war ended.
They took over various highly visible occupations, like
driving the city buses and clerking the post offices, and lived
in various areas of London, like Southall and Notting Hill.
In the North of England, in some industrial towns, they
became the industrial proletariat, or its larger half, threaten-
ing the native born workers' security. They filled many
whole classrooms and indeed many whole schools; necessarily bringing with them a new range of cultural problems.

They therefore became the symbol in the popular eye of
the manifold modern troubles with the British economic
and social system. A number of proto-Fascist movements
arose, offering to defend English values against being
swamped. (In such movements there were several representatives of the ex-colonial ruling class.) Riots became a
feature of English city life in certain places and times, after
some decades when they had been almost unknown, and the
cultural character of the police (and other forces of law and
order) became much more grim and aggressive.

And as far as readers and writers are concerned, the
immigrants replaced the native working class as an
embodied reproach to the privileged. The system of literature which gradually developed in the eighteenth and nineteenth centuries, with the domestic novel as its supreme
form, attracted to it (indeed derived from, to a significant

degree) a critical and intellectual interpretive tradition which we can label 'cultural'. (Raymond Williams has made a study of this tradition in his book *Culture and Society*.) For these thinkers, the working-class reader (even more the *potential* reader) became a figure of great imaginative force. He/she was the living criterion for judging the novelists' and the critics' work. Their work was good if it did justice, or brought advantage, to him, and vice versa. Their calling was to restore to him the treasure of English literature, pre-empted by the ruling class; and to test that literary gold against his experience – did Jane Austen take the life of the poor seriously enough to justify our responding to her wit? That work-grimed hand on a 'classic' volume, that cloth-capped face bent over it, became the icon of a great critical movement that climaxed in mid-century in the work of F. R. Leavis, Raymond Williams, and Richard Hoggart. But at just the moment of climax, that icon was challenged by another, that of the recent immigrant. It was his hand, reaching up to the shelf in the public library, which now represented conscience to readers and writers. And Doris Lessing spoke to that conscience, as no native-born writer could.

Doris Lessing belongs by birth to the white settlers, and her arrival in London in 1949 fits into a pattern of the way the white women writers of several generations born in the empire made their way to that city (seen as the centre of the English literary system) as soon as they could break free. But by political conviction and commitment she belonged to the oppressed, the colonized, and the revolutionaries. Indeed, the London she lived in was not so much literary as radical; she lived among political exiles – from East Europe, from McCarthy's America, from colonial and ex-colonial states.

But what her writing represented was not either group so much as the experience of colonial life seen from the inside, illuminated with the moral realism long directed at English life as a fictional subject, and not with Kipling's frontier humour. And this was the body of experience which the daily news charged with special significance for the English reader – news of the Third World but also news of troubles at home. Without writing explicitly on such topics, Doris Lessing spoke for and to them. By the same token, she spoke for and to the women's movement. She spoke to all the students of Lawrence's exploration and celebration of eroticism. Her audience we may call, like Lawrence's, the party of culture, hostile to the powers in control of civilization; but with a more political slant in her case than in his. Her fiction stood in the 'right' relation to all these issues; while for instance Kingsley Amis's stood in the 'wrong' relation. This rightness or wrongness is not a matter of, simply, the two writers' opinions on particular issues; it is rather the angle of incidence of the two sensibilities, the way they choose to take hold of a topic, and what that implies about their relation to themselves and to their readers. Amis's fiction does not offer to bear upon black- or brown-skinned readers' experience; implicitly it excludes them. Doris Lessing's fiction does not exclude those others; implicitly it invites them in.

Doris Lessing was born Doris Tayler in Kermanshah, Persia, in 1919. The date and place refer us directly to history – the history of the British empire. Her father had served in the Great War, which had been a horrifying experience (he lost a leg in battle) but which had 'rescued' him in his own mind from a stifling life as a bank clerk. He married his nurse (the standard wartime romance) and as soon as the War was over, they went out to Persia to work in a bank there; Persia was in effect a British protectorate then; and there his first child was born.

Doris Lessing has often portrayed her parents in her fiction, and these portraits have a character of being historical clichés, both psychologically and sociologically. Both the father and the mother are thoroughly English and thoroughly of their period. He is a combination of Wells's dreamily humorous and inarticulate husbands with Kipling's shy military charmers; she is the jolly but anxious school-girlish matron, not so kindly treated in literature – Forster's British matrons of *Passage to India* come closest to serious treatments of the type.

Such human clichés do of course occur, and colonial conditions seem to fix or even exaggerate them. The impor-tant thing is that Lessing felt them to be clichés even as she lived with them; which means that they fit into her – and indeed our – categories of thought with a neatness that paralyses her imagination. And her categories of explana-tion refer to the history of the empire. In thinking of Martha Quest's father, for instance, one cannot but remember the famous war propaganda poem of 1915, 'The Volunteer', by Herbert Asquith, the Prime Minister's son.

> Here lies a clerk who half his life had spent
> Toiling at ledger in a city grey,
> Thinking that so his days would drift away
> With no lance broken in life's tournament.

This is a Kipling conception, in some sense a Kipling poem; the clerk will now, when killed as a soldier, 'join the men of Agincourt': become a military caste hero. Mr Tayler survived; but he carried a loyalty to war inside him, and infected his daughter with it.

In 1925 the Taylers were home in England on leave, and were so attracted by the image of Rhodesia given by the Imperial Exhibition in London that they bought a farm there, to grow tobacco and maize, and to seek adventure while also making money, according to the myth of empire. Lessing has described their waggons going to the farm, piled high with English furniture, Persian rugs, a piano – Mrs Tayler played Grieg and Chopin – again according to the myths of colonial adventure. But their experience did not correspond to those myths. The farm did not pay, the life was lonely, Mr Tayler felt defeated and became hypo-chondriacal, Mrs Tayler suffered a neurotic illness and then pulled herself together and took command of the family. The daughter grew up in sympathy with the father, but finding him fail her; in irritation with the mother, but admiring her strength and feeling her pathos. What she resented most was the resignation they both equally expressed, and her determination was not to accept an inadequate fate herself.

This family pattern seems to repeat one we can make out in the biographical background of several women writers of the empire. It repeats, for instance, that of Elspeth Huxley, who lived in and wrote about Kenya; that of Olive Schreiner (her father was a missionary) of South Africa; that of Jean Rhys of Dominica and Katherine Mansfield of New Zealand. There were of course variations in the individual cases; in Mansfield's case the quite large variation that the father was successful. But when you add to these specifications the image of the girls educating themselves through books – books about England – and setting off for England as soon as they could, you have a striking similarity. In all these cases the girl's talents are early recognized and fostered to redeem or raise the family's social fortunes; and in some she recognizes the source of the strain between her parents as the challenge of the frontier (the myth of the empire) which her father has failed to meet.

Lessing grew up, then, on a farm; but as she says in *Martha Quest* (her first autobiographical novel) the word farm meant, even to her, something quite different from what she saw about her; 'farm' meant small green fields in England, not the veldt. The English words never fitted the experience of the colonists, and this discrepancy has been a motif of English writing since 1945. This is often humorous, though not without an underlying guilt about the cultural pluto-cracy implied; we are told how odd it is to teach Words-worth's 'Daffodils' to Egyptian students who have the most

inappropriate notion of that flower; but Lessing – typically –
takes seriously both this motif and all the other incon-
gruities of frontier experience. 'The myths of this society are
not European. They are of the frontiersman and lone wolf
. . . the simple and brave savage defeated after gallant fighting on both sides; the childlike and lovable servant.' Such
myths *are* of course European, despite what Lessing says;
they only seem not to be because the European empires kept
their frontiers at a distance; white America, for instance, had
such myths.

Lessing attended a convent school in Salisbury and then
spent some painful years with her parents. She was a difficult child, with a more easily loved younger brother. Nearly
all her subsequent writing bears the scars of that experience
of herself as difficult, and some of her most characteristic
locutions express both settled exasperation, and guilt about
that exasperation. 'Not even *he* could believe *that* . . . She
could not believe that he was *really* going to . . .' Other
people's behaviour is always exceeding her heroine's worst
expectation, dashing her minimal hopes.

Soon she left home to earn her living in Salisbury. The
historical associations of the city and the colony both were
classically imperialist. Salisbury was a British statesman at
the time when Cecil Rhodes was acquiring the land of the
Matabele and the Mashona which was given his name. In
Martha Quest, Lessing describes Salisbury's Founders Street,
named 'to commemorate those adventurers who had come
riding over the veld to plant the Union Jack, regardless of
the consequences to themselves or to anybody else . . .'
(p. 81)

During the war years she married twice; when she left her
first husband she had also to give up her two children by
him; when she left the second she kept the child by that
marriage and brought him to England with her. This
second husband was a German called Lessing, a leading
figure in the circle of Communists to which she belonged,

who were openly active in the colony during the years of England's wartime alliance with Russia. After the war this man went to East Germany, and later returned to Africa as the country's ambassador to Uganda, in which capacity he was killed by Idi Amin. This is a biographical equivalent for that immersion in the crucial history of her time which we feel in Doris Lessing's fiction.

She arrived in London in 1949 with the manuscript of a novel about race relations in Africa and their interaction with sexual fears and obsessions, which was published in 1950 under the title *The Grass is Singing*. This book had a considerable popular success (it was reprinted seven times in five months) and also established her reputation among left-wing intellectuals in London. It was the empire 'seen from the inside' and 'seen realistically', in the simplest sense. Lessing, however, soon became dissatisfied with it, for moral/political as well as aesthetic reasons; as she explains in some of the most impressive passages of *The Golden Note-book*. But unlike her protagonist in that novel, Anna Wulf, Doris Lessing did not suffer from a writer's block in consequence. In 1951 she published a collection of short stories about Africa, and in 1952 *Martha Quest*, the first volume of five with the collective title *Children of Violence*.

At this stage of her career we can compare her with two other important writers of the post-war period, V. S. Naipaul and Paul Scott. Naipaul, though ten years younger, arrived in London at about the same time as she – her passage having been delayed by the war. He is a Trinidad Hindu, who was as eager as she had been to exchange his birthplace for London, the capital of literature. 'I knew Trinidad to be unimportant, uncreative, cynical . . . the threat of failure, the need to escape; this was the prompting of the society I knew.' He, like Lessing, read prodigiously as a child, and in his imagination relocated in Trinidad settings the stories he got from Jane Austen, Dickens, Wells; but never tried the reverse – never tried to translate a Trinidad story into fictional terms; because he saw fiction as something exclusively English. In later years – living in London – he like she found a way to write about that early experience. He has a fine autobiographical novel, *A House For Mr Biswas*, and several other books about Caribbeans at home and abroad. He has been as alert to world events as she, and as profoundly depressed by recent history.

Paul Scott was born in England two years before Lessing, and educated at an English prep school. He is thus much closer to Waugh and Amis in heritage. But he served as a soldier in India during the war, and has written about the imperial or ex-imperial subject since. 'My interest in the closing years of the British power in India is probably due to my feelings that, in India, the British nation came to the end of themselves as they were and have not yet emerged from the shock of their own liberation.' His *Birds of Paradise* is about William Conway, who never again recaptures the freedom and beauty he knew during his childhood in the India dominated by England. Then in 1966 began his four-part *Raj Quartet*, about the last months of British rule there – a sequence which can be compared in several ways with Lessing's *Children of Violence*.

These were the narratives that carried authority, this was the subject matter which conferred authority on its narrator, in England in the post-war years. In *Golden Notebook* Anna Wulf remarks that what she and her friends want from novels is reportage; and the examples she gives make it clear that what they want information about is communities of the underprivileged or of revolutionaries. She opposes such fiction to the 'philosophical' novel which she associates with Thomas Mann, and which she herself would like to write. But in fact she was able to combine the two by writing about colonial life.

THE NOVELS

In *Martha Quest* (1952) and the novels that followed, Doris Lessing tackled Kipling more directly than any of his other successors had done. Or rather, Martha Quest did so, not Doris Lessing; and it was Kiplingism she attacked, not Kipling. She does not mention his name, and unlike Amis and Waugh she has never come to exploit his literary heritage; but the socio-political complex of ideas he stood for is omni-present in her fiction, as what her heroines rebel against. They are born into a society and world view dominated by Kiplingism, and hate it.

The figures in the novels we associate most directly with Kipling are perhaps Mr and Mrs Maynard. They are introduced in *Martha Quest* in connection with the Salisbury Sports Club, a Kiplingesque Colonial institution which Lessing subjects to brilliant erotic analysis and mockery. It was Mrs Maynard who first thought of founding a Sports Club in Salisbury, and this is typical of the way the Maynards direct and control the life of the city. She is described as 'large, strong-minded, black-browed and energetic, the wife of a magistrate; and she was a lady.' (p. 131)

Mr Maynard, who remains one of Martha's counter-players throughout the series, is equally large, strong-minded, black-browed and energetic; and a gentleman. He watches over Martha's activity as a Communist with benevolent irony, but when he expresses his own political philosophy, it is that of Kipling's administrators. In *A Ripple From The Storm* (1958):

'Good God', he exclaimed, really angrily, speaking
from his depths. 'What do you suppose you are going to
change? We happen to be in power, so we use power.
What is history? A record of misery, brutality, and
stupidity. That's all. That's all it ever will be. What does

it matter who runs a country? It's always a bunch of knaves administering a pack of fools.' (p. 46)

In Chapter I of *Martha Quest*, Lessing presents her heroine (herself) as an adolescent challenging her mother silently by reading first Havelock Ellis in her presence, and later a book called *The Decay of the British Empire*. Her mother rightly recognizes the challenge and angrily complains about Ellis, and Epstein, the sculptor – whom together we can take to represent anti-Kiplingism – that highbrow art and liberated thought which displaced Kipling's kind of culture. This was art and thought in attack upon the ruling class. Martha's 'devotional' reading is Thoreau and Whitman, which she reads 'like the Bible'. These may seem classic and harmless enough, but she sees them as 'the poets of sleep and death and the heart', which suggests the private function they have for her, of rebellion and retreat. Her father is presented as being obsessed with the memory of the Great War, especially the battle of Passchendaele. Through him Martha often found that she unwillingly '. . . was seeing, too, the landscape of devastation, shattered trees, churned and muddy earth, a tangle of barbed wire, with a piece of cloth fluttering from it . . . and feeling . . . a frightening excitement.' (p. 90) Through him, she too is a Child of Violence, though all her conscious and voluntary attitudes are directed against it. It is the violence of the old empire, of Kipling's England.

Martha has an episode of religious mysticism early in this volume which remains undeveloped, for her youth and young adulthood are dominated by two conflicting ideologies, both anti-religious or anti-transcendental – one is eroticism and the other revolution. Her father does not recognize these and treats her as just a pacifist of the 1920s; he threatens her with a new war which he says is coming, and which will show her how wrong, how self-deceiving and irresponsible, she is.

Of these two ideologies (both anti-imperialist, anti-Kipling) we may associate that of revolution with the influence of the Jewish brothers who lend Martha books, Joss and Solly Cohen. It is thanks to them and their books that when, much later, she is shown a copy of the *New Statesman*, she has a strong feeling of 'warmth and security'; she has found the brotherhood of which she has long been an unconscious member. When a young man of the Sports Club tells her that he too reads that magazine, she takes his hand in unselfconscious delight; and insists he come home with her to look at her books. In fact, the reasons she marries him – disastrously – have much to do with his reading the *New Statesman*; and that disaster is a judgment upon the political ideology by the erotic mind.

The other ideology, eroticism, is allied to the literary influence of D. H. Lawrence. Indeed, it is sometimes hard to know if one should say to oneself, about a feature of her fiction, 'This is Lawrence', or whether she is inspired by some other author from the erotic movement; in any case, the erotic idea is something Lessing has thoroughly absorbed and made her own. But there can be no doubt that in general Lawrence is a major, indeed the major, influence. In *The Grass is Singing*, an important stage in developing the white woman's sexual obsession with the black man occurs when she comes upon him washing himself – as in the scene in *Lady Chatterley's Lover* where Lady Chatterley surprises Mellors. In *Martha Quest* the central passage for fixing the relationship between the two authors is this, about Martha's expectations of sex.

> Martha, final heir to the long, romantic tradition of love, demanded nothing less than the quintessence of all experience, all love, all beauty, should explode suddenly in a drenching, saturating moment of illumination. And since this was what she demanded, the man himself seemed positively irrelevant . . . (p. 184)

Clearly, this is the long tradition of the *novel* of love, but in the sexualized and feminized form which Lawrence gave it – the novel of desire; a form which Lessing was to carry one stage further than Lawrence had. Thus Martha is disgusted – 'shocked and furious' – to find that Douglas, the *New Statesman* reader, is still a virgin at the age of thirty. For Martha and Lessing sexual activity has become a moral duty. This is perhaps implicit in Lawrence, but never explicit.

Lessing also draws on Lawrence in her depiction of the colonial personality. Lawrence wrote brilliantly in this vein in *Kangaroo*, 'Saint Mawr', and elsewhere. What he and Lessing insist on is the deliberate immaturity of the colonial man, his cultivation of youth. At this point again we can evoke Kipling, the great myth-maker of the colonies, who shaped their young-man image. And we can say that Lessing evokes Lawrence to help her refute Kipling – help her establish a tone of voice and point of view which will reveal the sleaziness of that image.

Her diagnosis is more acutely erotic than Lawrence's, and stresses the convention which made colonial men claim irresponsibility – claim to be creatures of appetite, impulse, whimsy, wild young colts who knew they needed to be bridled – while the girls were assigned responsibility – they were to be figures of maturity, authority, wisdom, compassion. Lessing brilliantly depicts the crudeness and artificiality of this division of roles, while Lawrence is more concerned with colonial-style politics. But both writers equally emphasize the gap between colonial behaviour and the standards of 'culture' as they understand it. (This admission of a concern about culture is reluctant in both writers.) Lessing says that at the Sports Club all the romances, flirtations and quarrels were public.

These terms, however, were never used, for words are
dangerous, and there was a kind of instinctive
shrinking, or embarrassment, against words of emotion,

or rather, words belonging to that older culture, to
which this was an attempt at providing a successor.
(p. 137)

In *A Proper Marriage*, Lessing tells of Martha's first
marriage, which immediately made itself felt as an error,
and her growing involvement with the Communist group
in Salisbury. In *A Ripple From the Storm* she describes their
work, putting her stress on the moral enthusiasm they
generated among themselves.

These days she always woke early, and with delight, no
matter how late she had been in getting to bed. For the
first time in her life waking was not a painful process of
adjustment . . . before she had opened her eyes she was
already poised forward in spirit, thinking of the
moment when she would rejoin the group and her
friends (p. 25).

In *The Golden Notebook*, writing about the same experience, she makes the same point.

I don't think people who have never been part of a left
movement understand how hard the dedicated socialists
do work, day in and day out; year in, year out. . . . And
part of our duty was to explain to anyone with any kind
of spark that life was a glorious adventure. . . . I doubt
whether any of the people we took on will forget the
sheer exuberance of our conviction in the gloriousness
of life, for if we didn't have it by conviction we had it on
principle. (p. 91)

But she also stresses the split in their experience, the moral
paradox which corrupts their enthusiasm. 'At the back of
my mind when I joined the Party was a need for wholeness,
for an end to the split, divided, unsatisfactory way we all

live. Yet joining the Party intensified the split.' (*Golden Notebook*, p. 161) And the scene of the pigeon-shooting in that novel is a powerful dramatization of that paradox and corruption.

Even in *A Ripple From the Storm* the writing about the Communist group, if generous in places, is essentially diagnostic and written from outside and from out-of-sympathy. At the end of the book, Martha marries Anton, who is the leader of the group, but a man of no erotic dignity. She feels nothing for him erotically, and blames her disastrous mistake in part upon the ideological atmosphere and personal confusion of the group. The position from which Lessing writes is erotic. She will say about Martha, 'There is a type of woman who can never be, as they are likely to put it, "themselves", with anyone but the man to whom they have permanently or not given their hearts.' (p. 33)

The next novel, *Landlocked* (1958), is the story of Martha's first passionate love affair, which is described much less critically and is described from the erotic point of view. Lessing's description of sexual and carnal behaviour and consciousness is more naturalistic than Lawrence's; and in harmony with this, Martha's lover, Thomas, is not only erotically attractive to her, but is a Dionysian ecstatic of sex; but both changes are a natural development further on in the erotic movement.

Martha now sees her marriages as 'terrible crimes', and eroticism as a matter of moral law, though a law most people break.

> How strange it was – marriage and love; one would think, the way newspapers, films, literature, the people who are supposed to express us talk, that we believe marriage, love, to be the desperate important deep experiences they say they are. But of course they don't believe any such thing. Hardly anyone believes it. We

want them to believe it. We want to believe it. Perhaps people will believe it again. (pp. 154–5)

This is something we can imagine Ursula Brangwen or Connie Chatterley saying. The difference is, of course, that Martha Quest is writing this novel – that the woman in Lessing's case is also the intellectual and the artist – that Martha is Birkin as well as Ursula. But this difference too is very obviously the next step on in the direction Lawrence opened up. What has every woman said, in the last twenty years, reading Lawrence, but, 'Why shouldn't Ursula be a writer? Why should the human qualities be distributed this way, with the intellectual and artistic powers going to the man?' Doris Lessing took that step on behalf of all her woman readers.

Thomas is a gardener, as Mellors was a gamekeeper, and the atmosphere of the garden and the greenhouse is associated with their love-making. But he is also a Zionist, a political man, involved in a system of political hatreds; and in the issue these hatreds prove themselves more powerful than his love for Martha. When he sees his political enemy, his face becomes 'black, clenched, hurtful. . . . She felt as if she had never really known Thomas and as if loving him were a mistake if not worse.' (pp. 139–40) Martha looks at this other man and knows that 'he is an enemy too strong for her.' (p. 146)

At the end of this novel, therefore, Martha is defeated again, as she was at the end of the preceding one. These defeats are the links between the different novels in the sequence. This time, of course, her faith has not been proven wrong, only not strong enough to overcome this resistance. But still she has been defeated, and disillusioned about the power of the erotic values she still believes in. After this defeat she goes to England. But the story of what happened to her there, *The Four Gated City*, was not published until 1969, and in between came *The Golden Notebook*, which treated all this autobiographical material in a different way.

The Golden Notebook is probably the most important single fiction published in England since the War, and all the six constituent parts of the book essentially succeed, or, one may rather say (since four of them are too diffuse to have an essence), have their successes. The book's first lines in the first 'Free Women' section announce the theme. The two women, we are told (Anna and Molly) are alone together. 'The point is' said Anna, as her friend came back from the telephone on the landing, 'the point is, that as far as I can see, everything's cracking up.' (p. 3) This theme is developed in a number of materials, a number of contexts. Within the 'Free Women' sections it is dramatized above all in the behaviour of Tommy, Molly's son, who deliberately becomes psychotic, in revenge upon his mother.

At the same time as we follow this sequence of events, we read, in the sections from the Black Notebook, about the tension of mutual malice and self-contempt which held together a group of young Communists in Africa – their ironic relish of their forced hypocrisy, the ruling class luxuries they combine with their revolutionary activities. Anna also enters in this notebook items about her novel based on that experience, *Frontiers of War* – items about proposals to adapt it for film or television which would (voluntarily and maliciously) betray the story they profess to admire; but she also analyses her own inspiration in writing it – her secret nostalgia for the violence she was overtly condemning.

> The novel is 'about' a colour problem. I said nothing in it that wasn't true. But the emotion it came out of was something frightening, the unhealthy, feverish illicit excitement of wartime, a lying nostalgia, a longing for license, for freedom, for the jungle, for formlessness. . . . When I think back to that time . . . I have to first switch something off in me; now, writing

about it, I have to switch it off, or 'a story' would begin
to emerge, a novel, and not the truth. (pp. 63–4)

The poignancy of this, for Anna Wulf as novelist, for Doris
Lessing, is of course the resistance it signals to writing again.
But it is important to her as political and moral being too.
She continues:

> Nothing is more powerful than this nihilism, an angry
> readiness to throw everything overboard, a willing-
> ness, a longing to become part of dissolution. This
> emotion is one of the strongest reasons why wars con-
> tinue. And the people who read *Frontiers of War* will have
> had fed in them this emotion, even though they were
> not conscious of it. That is why I am ashamed, and why
> I feel continually as if I had committed a crime. (p. 64)

In the Red Notebook we read about the splitting and
splintering of political groups, and the counterplay of truth
and lie, moral enthusiasm and cynicism, each corrupting the
other, among Communists. When she rejoins the party, her
first interview

> both pleased me – being back in the fold, so to speak,
> already entitled to the elaborate ironies and complicities
> of the initiated; and made me suddenly exhausted. I'd
> forgotten, of course, having been out of the atmosphere
> so long, the tight, defensive, sarcastic atmosphere of the
> inner circles. (p. 155)

In the Yellow Notebook we see, reflected in fictional
form, Anna's love affair with a man who is determined from
the start not to commit himself to her, and the strain this
creates, out of which she splits herself into psychic parts.
And in the Blue Notebook we see Anna's sessions with a
Mrs Marks, Jungian psychoanalyst, who sees her cure
exclusively in terms of her starting to write again – to
resume her sacred vocation as artist – while Anna is deeply

ambivalent, deeply split, about the value of art. She describes Mrs Marks's room:

> The walls are covered with reproductions of
> masterpieces and there are statues. It is almost like an art
> gallery. It is a dedicated room. It gives me pleasure, like
> an art gallery. The point is, that nothing in my life
> corresponds with anything in this room – my life has
> always been crude, unfinished, raw, tentative; and so
> have the lives of the people I have known well. It
> occurred to me, looking at this room, that the raw
> unfinished quality in my life was precisely what was
> valuable in it and I should hold fast to it. (pp. 236–7)

And we may see *The Golden Notebook* as an attempt to
combine the form of art and meaning with the 'raw, un-
finished, tentative' quality she values. But from the point of
view of the book's theme, the point of the blue notebook
sessions is that psychoanalysis fails as much as politics and
eroticism to heal the split and to prevent the crack-up.

This summary of the first part of the book is enough to
indicate the way the four main notebooks function to
develop the theme. The other two sections have a different
relation to the whole and a different consistency; they are
more concentrated ('Free Women' an aesthetic whole, the
Golden Notebook restricted to a few days' events and a
single relationship) and they sum up, impose order on,
develop to a climax, what is diffuse or inert elsewhere.

The presence of Lawrence is as much to be felt here, as it is
in *Children of Violence*. The form of 'Free Women' is very
Lawrentian; it is impossible to imagine that it could have
begun the way it did if *Women in Love* had not begun the
way it did. The doctrine of sexuality also is Lawrentian,
despite the connotations of Free Women. In the Yellow
Notebook, we are told that Ella 'floated darkly on her love
for him, on her naivety, which is another word for a spontaneous creative faith (p. 211) . . . *What Ella lost during those*

five years [of her unhappy dependence] *was the power to create through naivety.'* (p. 212) Indeed, the Yellow Notebook even decides that all her unhappiness derives from her trying to abandon 'conventional' behaviour – trying to be 'free'. Anna and Molly talk of 'real women' and even 'real men', in a way that would shock a sexual liberationist. And the treatment of homosexuality is very hostile/old-fashioned. Indeed, the relationship depicted in the Golden Notebook between Anna and Saul may be seen as a conflict and coming together of the Lawrentian mode of eroticism, embodied in Anna, with that Promethean mode which has been better expressed in American literature – in, for instance, Hemingway's and Faulkner's fiction.

The book's ultimate message is in these words, spoken by Paul, one of the young men in the African group:

'Comrade Willi, would you not say that there is some principle at work not yet admitted to your philosophy? Some principle of destruction?' Willi said, in exactly the tone we had all expected: 'There is no need to look any further than the philosophy of the class struggle,' and as if he'd pressed a button, Jimmy, Paul and I burst out into one of the fits of irrepressible laughter that Willi never joined. (pp. 427–8)

This laughter is of course as alien to Lawrence as to Marx.

The virtues of the novel are Lessing's virtues: it presents a body of experience acquired at the crucial frontiers of modern life – the political, the psychotic, the erotic, and so on – and that experience has been passionately criticised; the themes and motifs which recur in these different areas have been identified; and then a structure has been invented, to make the meaning of the experience cumulative.

The weaknesses are superficial, though blatant. The dialogue is often implausible, and rarely positively right. The men characters are unreal exemplifications of ideas, and much less substantial (in their artistic realization as well as in their moral qualities) than the women. The wording, in narrative and dramatic passages, is often muddy and graceless (not in analytic and expository passages). And of course it is all overwhelmingly long, and sometimes repetitive.

None of this prevents it from being a great novel, and Lessing from being Lawrence's heir. The differences in quality between the two – the greater charm and distinction, variety and vitality of Lawrence's art and intelligence – may derive from Lessing's doubts about art. She did not suffer Anna Wulf's writer's block; but her faults as a writer may be other symptoms of an inner conflict about the act of writing. The roughness of her writing's texture sometimes suggests that a will to write is over-riding a resistance. Her early guilt and misery, tied as it was to her will to write, may have always haunted her pen. Clearly she could not hear the call to write as clearly or innocently as Lawrence could.

After *The Golden Notebook* and *The Four Gated City*, Doris Lessing wrote *Briefings for a Descent Into Hell*, which is about a man who loses touch with reality but finds a world of illusion which is preferable, and *The Summer Before the Dark*, which is about a hitherto responsible wife and mother who explores areas of freedom and adventure in the London of the 1960s. Then, after *Memoirs of a Survivor*, which I shall discuss in more detail, she wrote the four-volume science fiction or future fiction, *Canopus in Argos*. Of this body of work only *The Summer Before the Dark* could be called a novel, and even that strains towards other forms of fiction at times. Lessing was clearly moving out and away from the novel form, in this period.

But if we say that, we must add that she was from the beginning a writer on her way out – always leaving behind some subject or some faith – always preparing to leave even as she began, like Martha in her marriages. She wrote about the end of colonialism and the Africa she would soon leave; she wrote about political commitment from an erotic standpoint, and then about eroticism from the point of view of defeat in that faith. She wrote about the value of health and wholeness after the experience of crack-up and sickness, and about London from a point in a future when London had broken down. It was a natural climax that she should write a novel about the boredom of personal relations and politics, of the traditional subject matter of novels.

And Lessing's emotionally quiet and politically quietist withdrawal from the revolutionary theme of her times, from the post-imperial subject, seems to characterize the English experience, for it can be seen in Scott and Naipaul also. One way to understand the English experience is to contrast it with the French. England extricated herself from her empire, after 1945, with comparative dignity; comparatively speaking, it was another Glorious Bloodless Revolution, a Glorious Bloodless Renunciation; she did not suffer any equivalent for France's bitter Algerian war, and then Vietnam war. (The partial equivalent for England, in Northern Ireland, could not seem post-imperial, for various reasons.) English political feeling in general, and that relating to post-imperialism in particular, was much less extreme. This was reflected in, or represented by, the intellectuals' treatment of such feeling. England had no equivalent for Jean-Paul Sartre and his existential Marxism, for Jean Genet and his 'The Blacks', or for Franz Fanon and his *The Wretched of the Earth*. In fact, the English equivalents were Lessing, Naipaul, Scott (none of whom were politically activist, even in their writings) and figures like Raymond Williams and Edward Thompson, who were much more at peace with certain elements in their native culture.

Thus if we look at Scott's *Division of the Spoils* (the last volume of his *Raj Quartet*) we shall find a strong contrast drawn between the actual peaceful withdrawal of the English from India and what might have happened. The retaliatory violence that imperialism should have provoked was miraculously averted, the guilty past exorcised. Dmitri

Bronowsky, one of the novel's *raisonneurs*, describes Ronald Merrick (its villain) by saying that perhaps he hoped 'that his murder would be avenged in some splendidly spectacular way, in a kind of Wagnerian climax, the raj emerging from the twilight and sweeping down from the hills with flaming swords . . .' (p. 571)

Some such thing might easily have happened, we realise, and Scott stresses the horrifying violence which did break out between Muslims and Hindus, and the miraculous and undeserved exemption of the English from this.

The British withdrawal was a lucky escape; it is not presented as morally triumphant. The author's representative, Guy Perron, looks down on India from the plane in the last paragraph, 'the India his countrymen were leaving, the India that was being given up. Along with what else?' And the answer suggested is responsibility and the extra dimension of dignity that goes with that.

No longer the rulers of India, the English there have already begun to squabble among themselves, we are told. 'Universally popular as the English are in India now, among themselves there emerges this dissension. The old solidarity has gone because the need for it has gone.' (p. 554) Perron reports one of them as saying, 'now we've all got to get used to living like carpet-sellers in Cairo' (p. 557), and when he tells Bronowsky this the latter agrees, saying, 'We're all émigrés now.' This man, himself a White Russian émigré, who has been adviser to an Indian prince, represents an extreme of detachment, dandified intelligence, self-knowledge, self-limitation, consciously shrunken feelings; and this is the model towards which the British themselves will now tend. The ex-rulers of the British empire will become as lightweight, historically and morally speaking, as those of the Russian empire.

The last action of the book is a massacre of Muslims by Hindus, on a train which also carries Perron and Sarah Layton, the chief woman character. One of the men killed is

Ahmed Kassim, their friend and travelling in their compart-ment. They let him go to his death, and their passivity is clearly attributed to their loss of responsibility as English, their liberation from the heroic duty of imperialists.

The sympathies of the reader are controlled above all by this question of responsibility. There is for instance an important contrast drawn between Sarah and her sister Susan, who is irresponsible. They are Sense and Sensibility; the contrast between them is as crucial as that between Elinor and Marianne Dashwood, and Scott is as decided as Austen in preferring Sarah and Sense. And this is the choice Kipling would have made; Sarah is a figure like his 'William the Conqueror', in the story of that title. Lessing, moreover, in *Memoirs of a Survivor*, also presents a heroine who is equally characterized by responsibility.

Naipaul is also close to Lessing, but on the other side of her talent. He is concerned with the corruption of the *non*-WASP members of the ex-empire, the victims of the empire. He writes the reportage Lessing says her friends want to read as fiction. Not that he is politically radical – quite the reverse, by most standards – but his subject-matter is the activity of the new nations' intellectuals, and movements like Black Power. He stands in the right relation to the new subjects, the relation of concern. In his long essay, 'Michael X and the Black Power Killings in Trinidad', he investigates a subject which he later used for his novel, *Guerillas, Guerillas*.

This is the story of Michael X (born Michael de Freitas) who came to London in 1957 as a Trinidad seaman, aged 24. He discovered the Black Power movement, and became one of its leaders and poets, and was popularized by the liberal press. In 1971 he returned to Trinidad famous – for being famous in England – set up a commune there, and then committed a series of murders. This essay (with its obviously reactionary moral) appeared in a volume which included similar investigations of affairs in Argentina, and in Zaire.

Naipaul is as reactionary as Amis, in what he has to say about Michael X, but he seems radical because he does write about him.

Naipaul's fiction as well as his journalism has focused on such Third World subjects, always stressing the fragility of the civilized order now so freely attacked by radicals of all sorts. Conrad is the only earlier writer who meditated on Naipaul's world, he says; all the other great novelists wrote about highly organized societies, with a high level of law and order. Naipaul feels himself doomed to be different, and therefore to be ineffectual as a novelist. He complains that 'The novel as a form no longer carries conviction. . . . The great societies that produced the great novels of the past have cracked.' (p. 227) He says he has felt the ground of society move under his feet, in warning of earthquake. He has seen the old politics replaced by 'The new politics, the curious reliance of men on institutions they were working to undermine –'. (p. 226) This makes him claim Conrad as his predecessor; but he could as well claim Kipling.

In *The Mimic Men* (1967) he describes a Caribbean politician's career in London first as a student and later as an exile – someone who might well have been a character in *The Golden Notebook* or *The Four Gated City*. This character says, 'My career is by no means unusual. It falls into the pattern. The career of the colonial politician is short and ends brutally.' (p. 10) The book's title refers to an inauthenticity in him and men like him, beginning in their school days, in a British-style school.

> Everything that touched on our everyday life excited laughter when it was mentioned in a classroom: the name of a shop, the name of a street, the name of street corner foods. The laughter denied our knowledge of these things to which after the hours of school we were to return. (p. 114)

(Such laughter and its destructiveness is one of Lessing's

preoccupations, as we have seen.) When this man returns to
his island, he finds it to be as fraudulent as he himself is:

> on the morning of arrival I saw through each porthole
> the blue, green and gold of the tropical island. So pure
> and fresh! And I knew it to be, horribly, man-made; to
> be exhausted, fraudulent, cruel, and above all, not mine.
> (p. 60)

This man, and Naipaul himself, is a reactionary. He is
anti-anti-imperialist. In fact he is an imperialist. At the end
he thinks he may spend the next ten years writing the
history of the British empire; and he says, 'The empires of
our time were short-lived, but they have altered the world
for ever; their passing away is their least significant feature.' He scorns the orthodox liberal scholarship about
imperialism: 'on the subject of empire there is only the
pamphleteering of churls.' (p. 38) He makes a secret identification with the Aryan conquerors of Central Asia, and sees
himself as of warrior caste.

In his book about the history of Trinidad, *The Loss of El
Dorado* (1969) Naipaul in his own person is sympathetic
above all to Raleigh, the English imperialist adventurer,
whose writing about Guinea 'suggests mines, and gold,
spaciousness, enamelled forests, a world in which the
senses, needs, life itself, can be extended. The book is part of
the world's romance.' (p. 86) In this, of course, Naipaul goes
much further than Lessing and Scott, who associate themselves only with the ruling class's fate of responsibility;
Naipaul endorses also that class's romance of conquest and
expansion, and repudiates the imputation of imperialist
guilt. But the three of them belong together by contrast
with the French intellectuals mentioned before. The English
reaction to the loss of empire, for all its intensity and bitterness, was politically quietist.

MEMOIRS OF A SURVIVOR (1975)

This is in many ways a different sort of fiction from Lessing's early work. It is non-political and non-erotic. It is assertively non-autobiographical, non-personal, and describes the future and not the past. It employs the techniques of fantasy and rejects those of realism (nothing is named, not even London or the narrator). And its values are in some sense symbolic and mystical. Thus it is not a novel at all. Is Lessing's development, then, following Waugh's and Amis's, towards Kipling? Not entirely; because though she discards the role of revolutionary, she does not assume reactionary views; and though she turns away from the novelist's responsibilities, she does not accept the role of entertainer of the ruling class. Her tendency is in some sense mystical.

Thus even this book's most novelistic moments – when the writer persuades us to grieve over other people's grief – are very different from parallel moments in the early work. The moment which impresses me most is when the narrator hears crying from the room beyond the wall of her apartment.

> I heard the sobbing of a child, a child alone, disliked, repudiated; and at the same time, beside it, I could hear the complain of the mother, the woman's plaint, and the two sounds went on side by side, theme and descant.
>   I sat listening. I sat by myself and listened. It was warm, over-warm; it was that final hot summer.
>   (p. 148)

The crying is that of the child whom Emily had been. Emily, a girl who has come to live with the narrator, is now nearly fifteen. The narrator has deduced, from her personality, that as a child she had been denied love, by her mother, and has been forced into prematurely 'ironic' attitudes and feelings of responsibility.

One morning, soon after the sobbing begins to be heard, she joins the narrator at work, 'brisk and lively', but also looking 'tired, as well as full of energy';

> she had not yet bathed, and a smell of sex came from her. She was fulfilled and easy, a bit sad, but humorously so. She was, in short, a woman, and she sat wiping plums with slow easy movements, all the hungers, drives, and the needs pounded and hunted out of her, exorcised in the recent love-making. And all the time that child was crying . . . 'Can't you hear someone crying?' I asked, as casual as could be, while I was twisting and turning inwardly not to hear that miserable sound. (pp. 148–9)

But she can't. It is only the narrator who is accessible to two and more schemes of time, levels of reality. Such writing is on the far side of the novel, verging on the mythic and the legendary, turning away from psychological and sociological realism, and psycho-social explanations of the characters.

> I let my palms move over to the wall, slowly, inch by inch, but I did not find a way in that day, nor the next; I never did find that weeping child, who remained there, sobbing hopelessly alone and disowned, and with long years in front of her to live through before time could put strength into her and set her free. (p. 151)

What the narrator did find, she says, was something inevitable, even banal. That crying child:

> Who else could it possibly be but Emily's mother, the large cart-horse woman, her tormentor, the world's image? . . . Up went the little arms, desperate for comfort, but they would be one day those great arms that had never been taught tenderness. . . . (p. 151)

And one of the elements in this narrator's (this novel's)

structure of sensibility is a positive disinclination for personal relations and their analysis and everything else that
characterizes novelistic experience. When she begins to tell
us it was the mother who was crying, she breaks off in a
boredom that has some element of revulsion.

> I never found Emily. But I did find . . . the thing is,
> what I did find was inevitable. I could have foreseen it.
> The finding had about it, had in it as its quintessence,
> the banality, the tedium, the smallness, the restriction,
> of that 'personal' dimension. (p. 151)

She has talked before of the personal dimension and how
she dislikes it. She finds behind the wall both the personal
history that explains Emily, and an impersonal space, or
series of empty spaces; and she hates the first and loves the
second.

> One, the 'personal', was instantly to be recognized by
> the air that was its prison, by the emotions that were its
> creatures. The impersonal scenes might bring
> discouragement of problems that had to be solved – like
> the rehabilitation of walls or furniture, cleaning, putting
> order into chaos – but in that realm there was a
> lightness, a freedom, a feeling of possibility. Yes, that
> was it, the space and the knowledge of alternative
> action. One could refuse to clean that room, clear that
> patch of earth; one could walk into another room
> altogether, choose another scene. But to enter the
> 'personal' was to enter a prison, where nothing could
> happen but what one saw happening, where the air was
> tight and limited, and above all where time was a strict
> unalterable law and long. . . . (p. 42)

That note of weariness is sustained, though blended with
other notes, of responsibility, of engagement, and together
they make a new voice for fiction – the voice of the old
woman.

What this book has to tell the student of Doris Lessing is perhaps primarily that she had revised her image of herself. Of course she does not appear in the novel – that freedom from the personal is largely a matter of the absence of Martha Quest, Anna Wulf, et al. But still the childhood and family situation which the narrator fantasizes about Emily, to explain her, is strikingly like the family and childhood of Martha Quest and Doris Lessing. The jolly but anxious mother, the silent resigned father, the girl who feels guilty and rejected, the younger brother who seems to be preferred; all these are familiar. But the character, the typology, assigned to the girl who is the product of this upbringing is now English middle class, even upper middle class. Emily is not, as Martha was, primarily a rebel, a victim, a passionate truth-seeker or 'final heir to the long tradition of love'; she is primarily an anxious controller of others, a servant of the community, the person who takes responsibility and authority. At four she had 'intensely serious, already defensive eyes' (p. 43). And we see her thus.

Moreover, the narrator's sympathies are with those in charge, those cut off by responsibility from full membership in the group.

It is striking that she portrays Emily's lover Gerald, the leader of a street gang, in the same terms.

> From near by, this young chieftain was not so
> formidable; he seemed harassed, he was even forlorn
> . . . one saw a very young man, overburdened and
> over-responsible and unsure, asking for support, even
> tenderness. (p. 108)

And one can of course remember that Martha Quest married Anton, Anna Wulf married Willi.

There is moreover a great gulf set, in the book, between Emily-and-Gerald and the Ryans, a slum family whose life-pattern is discussed at length, as totally feckless. This is the categorization the novel observes, opposing the

responsible to the irresponsible – the administrator's categories. Something like the opposite was true of Lessing's
earlier books. Of course I remember that Lessing's early
heroines are often said to do welfare work; that is what
Anna turns to at the end of *The Golden Notebook*. But in
those cases such work was subsumed in the larger category
of radical politics; social distress was presented as somebody's fault, as the fault of 'them'. In this book, as the
narrator says, 'they' have been replaced by 'it', the enemy by
the catastrophe, anger by patience. Here that suggestion of
original sin, made as a horizon to the analysis in *The Golden
Notebook*, is the centre or starting point of the myth.

If one accepts this suggestion, that Lessing is here
identifying herself as someone implicated in the privileged
and ruling class, then one finds a further poignancy in the
Edwardian (or Imperial period) furniture and clothes fantasized for Emily; and in the Edwardian style of the fantasy
itself – the style of Edwardian books about and for children
– there is an echo of Barrie or the Kipling of 'They' about the
transparent wall and the world beyond it and the children
there. Changing the African farm for the Edwardian nursery,
she changes innocence for guilt.

Moreover, the natural symbolism of painting walls,
cleaning house, gardening and cooking, so widespread in
Lessing's earlier books, is here replayed in a more powerful
and concentrated but self-diagnostic form. The book makes
a symbolic antithesis between white paint (and white cur-
tains, white baby-clothes, white bedspreads) and the
brown, the dirt, of the faeces with which the baby smears
herself. House-painting in the role of Martha Quest and
Anna Wulf, it is hinted, Doris Lessing was acting out the
anxiety of cleanliness, driven by the fear of dirt, a fear
derived, via her family, from her class, with its duty to
maintain standards and represent the social ideal.

What the book shows us if we take the view of the history
of the novel is Lessing saying goodbye to the novel form. At

the end, she, Emily, Gerald, their attendant animal, and the
Presence behind the wall, move away from us into a legendary and emblematic land, away from people and cities and
actuality. Her imagery here seems to owe something to
T. S. Eliot in 'Ash-Wednesday', and it would be appropriate
that this late Lessing should make some alliance with that
poet in her withdrawal. The earlier Lessing, the Martha
Quest and Anna Wulf (who lived in the same London of the
1950s as Eliot) cannot be conjoined with him in the imagination. What could Anna have said of *The Cocktail Party* or
The Confidential Clerk? It was Lawrence, not Eliot, who
then commanded her imagination. But since *Memoirs of a
Survivor*, Lessing has not turned back to Lawrence or the
novel form; or to realism or to life-values as she would have
defined them. She has stayed in the world of fantasy, in its
characteristic modern form, future fiction. She too, like
Kipling's heirs, had to turn away from the novel to fiction.

And what the book shows us, if we take the view of the
history of England and the empire, is Lessing saying goodbye to the WASP enterprise, the spread of the modern
system. This may sound like less of a change from the early
Lessing than the other things we have described, but this is a
goodbye, not a denunciation or a repudiation. There is no
anger expressed, and no self-dissociation from those responsible – if anything, as we have seen, there is a self-
association. Above all, there is a lingering, in a sense a
loving, last recapitulation of the themes of the WASP myth,
of that adventure story which was the energizing myth of
the British empire.

We can see this in terms of *Robinson Crusoe*, the archetype
of the modern adventure, which is evoked in many passages
of *Memoirs of a Survivor*. Gerald and Emily are both presented to us wearing skins, like illustrations to Defoe's
story, for instance, and Gerald is presented to us thus:

[Gerald] swaggered there with the knives in his belt, his

whiskers, his strong brown arms. Good Lord, how
many centuries had we overturned, how many long
slow steps of man's upclimbing did Emily undo when
she crossed from my flat to the life on the pavement!
And what promise, what possibilities, what
experiments, what variations on the human theme had
been cancelled out! (p. 150)

Then the do-it-yourself enthusiasm so strong in *Robinson
Crusoe* is replayed in *Memoirs of a Survivor*. The narrator
describes houses in London which were as if the technological revolution had never occurred at all; where shrubs
and flowerbeds had been cleared away and where only
vegetables were now grown.

There was even a little shed in which a few fowls were
kept. . . . But they were about to get a hive of bees. . . .
The place was a conglomeration of little workshops:
they made soap and candles and wove materials and
dyed them; they cured leather; they dried and preserved
food; they reconstructed and made furniture. (pp. 104–5)

Here Lessing shares in Defoe's enthusiasm for making
things, in her own, more melancholic way. In other places
she more simply expresses the melancholy of seeing so
much civilization destroyed.

I cannot begin to give an idea of the mess in those rooms
. . . heaped with cracking and splintering furniture. . . .
Once I saw in the centre of a formal and rich room –
French, Second Empire, as lifeless as if it had been
arranged for a museum – the remains of a fire built on a
piece of old iron, some sleeping bags left anyhow, a big
pot of cold boiled potatoes near the wall in line with a
dozen pairs of boots. I knew the soldiers would come
back suddenly, and if I wanted to keep my life I should
leave. Already there was a corpse, with dried blood
staining the carpet around it. (p. 159)

Thus *Memoirs of a Survivor* can be seen as an inverted and reverted form of *Robinson Crusoe* and of Defoe's fiction in general. Instead of a man alone on an island, we have a woman not alone in a city; instead of an entrepreneur, a survivor; instead of a sense of a beginning, a sense of an ending; instead of a young narrator an old one; instead of a technology and economy being built up before our eyes, we have them being broken down; instead of the London of *Moll Flanders*, the new Rome, a great growing labyrinth of excitements and extremes, we have a broken social machinery, half-empty, about to become a ruin; instead of the beginnings of the British empire, and the modern world system, and the new technology, we have their endings.

That is why it is an appropriate book to form the last in the series I consider here. And that is also why the old woman's voice is so appropriate to it. When the question of feminism is raised, it is put by, wearily.

And now I suppose it must be asked and answered why Emily did not choose to be a chieftainess, a leader on her own account? Well, why not? Yes, I did ask myself this, of course. The attitudes of women towards themselves and to men, the standards women had set up for themselves, the gallantry of their fight for equality, the decades-long and very painful questioning of their roles, their functions – all this makes it very difficult to say, simply, that Emily was in love. . . . There was nothing to stop her. No law, written or unwritten, said she should not, and her capacities and talents were every bit as varied as Gerald's or anybody else's. But she did not. I don't think it occurred to her. (p. 109)

There is even an explicit, though unstressed, wish for death. When Emily for the first time takes a shirt of the narrator's without permission, the latter is delighted and feels it as a liberation.

This is more mine than yours, says the act of the theft; *more mine because I need it more; it fits my stage of life better than it does yours; you have outgrown it.* . . . And perhaps the exhilaration it releases is even a hint of an event still in the future, that moment when the person sees in the eyes of people the statement – still unconscious, perhaps: *You can hand over your life now; you don't need it any longer; we will live it for you; please go.* (p. 59)

We can hear there again the echo of Eliot; we can hear the weariness of the responsible class; above all we can hear the end of empire.

[8]

THE FALL OF
KIPLING'S SHADOW

AFTER THE GREAT WAR, the empire understood as a spread of
possessions was clearly about to break up, to decay, or – to
take the most hopeful view – to transcend, to become a
Commonwealth. And understood as England, the imperial
country, it was clearly shrunken – Englishmen felt
shrunken, their houses and rooms felt too big for their
inhabitants. In *The Heart of the Matter* Graham Greene describes the law courts as 'a great stone building like the
grandiloquent boast of weak men. Inside that massive frame
the human being rattled in the corridors like a dry kernel.'
(p. 7) And Orwell asks somewhere what has happened to
the breed of guardsmen he remembers as a child, their chests
like barrels and their moustaches like the wings of eagles.

Literature in this period was dominated by the reaction
against Kipling and adventure. This to some degree
separated literature off from the rest of life, for non-literary
readers largely continued to like what they had liked before.
There was one law in the academy and the critics' circles,
but another in the libraries and the publishing houses. One
example is H. M. Tomlinson's 1912 autobiographical
account of a journey across the Atlantic and up the Amazon,
called *The Sea and the Jungle*. This had eight new editions or
reprints in the USA alone in the 1920s, including one in the
Modern Library. There were more in the 1930s and an
Armed Services Edition during the war. In 1964 the *Time*
Reading Program, a subscription publishing venture,

brought it out in an edition of a hundred thousand, with a
new preface by V. S. Pritchett. This was re-published in
1982.

   This is a publishing history which at least rivals that of
Sons and Lovers, published a year later; but whereas Lawrence's novel plainly owed its continued popularity to
critical acclaim and to assignment in innumerable college
courses, Tomlinson's book has probably never been
assigned or critically discussed. (Incidentally, since
Tomlinson was a follower of Kipling, his book is consider-
ably more elaborate stylistically than Lawrence, and a
slower read.) We see here an appetite for books – and
specifically Kiplingesque books – which was independent of
critical opinion.

   But a change had taken place, which was bound to be
important to all writers of talent and ambition. One way
this change made itself felt was in attitudes to London, the
imperial city, which had felt very oppressive to our first
three writers. We may take Rupert Birkin's feeling about
London, as expressed in *Women in Love*, to be Lawrence's.
As his train pulled into the station, Birkin

> was filled with a sort of hopelessness. He always felt
> this, on approaching London. . . . 'I always feel
> doomed when the train is running into London. I feel
> such a despair, so hopeless, as if it were the end of the
> world' . . . At length they were under the huge arch of
> the station, in the tremendous shadow of the town.
> Birkin shut himself together – he was in now. (pp. 53–4)

What he felt is presumably what Joyce put more explicitly,
about his one visit to London in 1902. He told a friend, 'I
remember how I disliked it all and I decided that I never
could have become part of English life, or even have
worked there, for somehow I felt that in that atmosphere of
power, politics, and money, writing was not sufficiently
important.' (Arthur Power, *Conversations with James Joyce*,

p. 64) Their calling, as writers, was to resist the pressure of empire, to assert the counter-value of literature.

Kipling of course did not take that tone, since he had allied himself to empire, had taken the vow of service to its master-class. But that vow did not resolve all his feelings, some of which were certainly akin to Lawrence's and Joyce's. He probably felt what Dick Heldar puts into words in *The Light that Failed*: 'What a city to loot!' It was a tremendous challenge to him, and filled at least Dick with resentment and aggression, as well as pride and awe.

The second three writers took a very different attitude to London, and the contrast they form with the first three makes the latter three seem a unit too. Waugh, we are told by his biographers, was so filled with excitement at the prospect of a trip to London, even in his last years, that he was beside himself; and in all his novels it is a place of magic – a harder, brittler, more meretricious magic than Oxford or the great country houses embody, but then all magic is brittle in Waugh. Amis's hero in *Lucky Jim* finds happiness at the end of the novel by going to London; and there are many scenes in his other early novels of the central character exulting as he arrives there from the provinces. Later in both men's work – during the war or after – there comes the sense of London as impaired, impoverished, impeded, an ailing organism needing to be cherished and protected. And this last feeling is of course an important theme in Doris Lessing's *Four Gated City* and *Memoirs of a Survivor*. For all these three, London was first a welcoming centre where congenial friends were likely to be gathered – a place of escape; and later a sad old remnant of the past – the ex-imperial city.

If we now look back over these six authors, and the others we have linked with them; and if we study the dialectic of their relations with each other and with the pressures of empire; then we see a striking pattern emerge. Of the three novelists of imperial England, the one who had most influence upon those coming after was not Lawrence or Joyce but Kipling. And this is remarkable not only because of the preference most readers would give to Lawrence or Joyce, but because Waugh, Amis, Lessing (indeed all the other five) were in their early work sharply hostile to Kipling. Moreover, their hostility was not of that ambivalent kind which often conceals love or admiration, and signals intense engagement with the precursor. Waugh, Amis, and Lessing show comparatively few signs of having really read Kipling (obviously the later Amis is an exception to this). Their hostility, which was profound, was directed at 'all he stands for'.

One might also be struck by how little Lawrence and Joyce have counted for, at least with these major successors, considering their character early on as brilliant rebels, and later as canonized saints and heroes of literature. On both counts they were the obvious models for young writers who wanted to rebel against empire, and empire-in-literature – against Kipling – but they were not followed. (Lessing of course is an exception here, with her primary debt to Lawrence.) Waugh and Greene might as well never have read Lawrence and Joyce; and whatever Amis may have learned from Joyce's socialist realism, via Orwell, or from Lawrence's presentation of women, is hypothetical and anyway secondary in importance.

But influence and tradition move in mysterious ways; probably one should not make too much of this apparent lapse. The influence of Lawrence and Joyce, amplified by critics and teachers, was perhaps too formidable to be directly avowed or even directly encountered, by attempting anything comparable. Probably the pattern of disconnection between them and their successors should be stressed only as a part of the larger pattern of Kipling's positive connection with them.

But preliminary to the argument for his paradoxical presence to later writers must come the reminder of his obvious, his platitudinous, absence. Kipling was banished from the courts of literature in the first decade of this century. As Eliot said, in 1919, his name was no longer mentioned, except as a term of abuse – 'Kiplingism', like 'Fascism' some years later. None of our five major novelists talk about him, with the partial exception of the late Amis. (Among the other writers discussed here, Orwell – always different – has an interesting essay on Kipling.) Here the fact of the absence, its cause, and its significance are all obvious. Kipling rebelled against the law of literature which forbade any overt alliance with the ruling class, which insisted that writers fly the flag of resistance or else no flag at all, and so he was exiled. What we need to insist on about that law is only its sudden emergence from the shadows of discretion, and the severity of the punishment which sanctioned it.

And perhaps there should be a word too about the theory of influence I am implicitly employing. The younger writers' reaction against Kipling was against what he stood for, against his political and social opinions, or those attributed to him; and not against his personality, his artistic achievement, his deeply and in-detail-felt presence. Thus the resistance to him of Waugh and Amis (though they clearly 'understood' Kipling sympathetically) is not of that existential or psychoanalytic kind described by Harold Bloom in *The Anxiety of Influence*. Their resistance and their yielding both were unfraught with feelings of anxiety.

Their relation to him is more like the interaction described by Jacques Lacan in his essay on 'The Purloined Letter'. There a configuration of roles proves so strong that when one actor, by taking some decisive action, moves out of his place, he slips into one of the other notches or sockets, and begins to act from new motives – to have that other nature. In our (more historical) case, Waugh wins the place of public entertainer by his memory of Kipling – he displaces the latter; but as a result of his success in that action, he finds himself taking up those attitudes and attributes he mocked before. And Amis displaces Waugh, wins the place from him, and finds himself taking up Waugh's attitudes, turning into Waugh. In Lacan's analysis, the issue is always 'who has the phallus?'; in our case, what is at stake is Harlequin's phallic sceptre.

This then is the final doom of empire, understood in literary terms, the shadow of Kipling falling over subsequent men of talent, the curse of a disbelief in the saving powers of the imagination, a resignation to the function of entertainer. Unless a writer can commit himself to an attack on empire, he will be compelled by any public success he achieves to adapt himself to that identity of entertainer, to minor genres and minor truths. After Kipling, only a representative of a disinherited class like Lawrence (who had also his ideology of Woman) or of a disinherited race like Joyce (who had also his ideology of Art) or of a disinherited sex like Lessing (who had also the experience of colonialism) could write novels. The others had to content themselves with fiction, and within fiction with slight themes and small forms. (For the example of *Ulysses* reminds us that there are possibilities of massiveness in fiction too, though they proved to be beyond the reach of these English writers.)

By a curious coincidence, which cannot be quite accidental, a strong feeling emanates from the late work of these writers that they feel themselves rejected, and rightly so; they feel – they seem to say – that they have made monsters of themselves. The striking cases of this are Waugh's self-portrait as Gilbert Pinfold, and Amis's as Bernard Bastable. And there is plenty of other evidence of the same sort; Guy Crouchback knows that he alone of the English in his town in Italy is not *simpatico*; Jake in *Jake's Thing* knows that no one can stand him. We do not feel this about Lessing and Lawrence and Joyce, difficult as their last years were. The portrait of Mellors in *Lady Chatterley's Lover* does not strike that note; nor does the portrait of the narrator in *Memoirs of a*

Survivor. On the other hand, Kipling does. He was too discreet, too guarded about himself, to make any such *statement*; but the photographs of him after 1918 persuade us to align him with Waugh and Amis.

To some degree, this is a personal grief we see in each case, and separable from the literary pattern I am tracing; as such, it is irrelevant – or we would feel impudent in discussing it. But to some degree theirs is a literary grief, the grief of being rejected by their confraternity of readers and writers; something which must be felt emotionally by men like these, in so far as they are writers.

In reading each of them, one fancies one can feel the audience narrowing further with each successive book, the function of the author narrowing, the scope of the themes, the reach of the intentions, diminishing. After all, one source of the greatness of the literary calling is the writer's sense that he is speaking to many people and telling them something important. Losing that sense, he loses his vocation. It is true that the coming of film and television has narrowed down the audience for all writers, of every persuasion. And it is true that nowadays we associate the isolation of an Amis with the fact of the new foreign-born population of England, for whom he defiantly does not write. But Waugh's jokes had a minority orientation back in 1928, and kept it even when in bookselling terms he had a large audience. Indeed, Kipling's work had and has often a minority feeling to it, though he had a world audience of 'a hundred million Anglo-Saxons'. Such feelings derive from the writer's consciousness of the dissent and disapproval of his colleagues – of other writers, of the liberal world of reading, and the vocation of writing. That larger audience was the gallery – its applause was irrelevant, or worse. All three writers were very successful in selling books. But the world of letters is different from the book-buying public. And though talented writers probably always *quarrel* with the former, they rely on its soon coming round to appreciate

them; or at least the scorn of the world of letters soon
withers them.

Lawrence and Joyce and Lessing in their different ways all
believed that individual experience can be so transfigured
by being transcribed that it becomes a source of radiant
power – that it alters other people's lives. Kipling, Waugh,
and Amis did not believe that. Paradoxically – and in paradoxical ways – they *achieved* something of that sort –
Waugh's laughter, Kipling's myths, did alter lives – but
fundamentally they did not believe. For them, truth/beauty/
goodness were always partial and illusory, were always
deferred presences. They believed instead in structures; in
the army/the church/the empire. (There is much in their
work to remind us of the French structuralist and post-
structuralist critics, but they lack the intellectual zest and the
intellectual radicalism which gives the latter their vitality.)
Such a belief is of course atheism from the viewpoint of
art-as-resistance, art as Art. It leaves the 'believer' face to
face with power, with *Realpolitik*.

Kipling, Waugh, and Amis all came too close to power, to
empire, for their health as novelists. This was not a case of
the artist gazing upon the sun and searing his sight with it.
Lawrence and Lessing both have their insights into power,
as piercing as anything in Waugh and Amis. The relevant
myth here is Icarus or Hippolytus, and the sun's attribute is
heat, not light. These writers flew too high in the social sky,
associating themselves with the political sun and its
triumphal progress across the heavens; their wax melted,
their wings dropped off, and they fell. Art, it seems, is not
for writers or readers who acknowledge themselves loyal
members of a ruling class; if you serve that class, you can
only entertain. The artists of the novel must either proclaim
resistance, or implicitly enact it, even if only by staying in
the shade of private domestic concerns, turning their backs
on power, seeing only its image reflected in the pools of
personal relations.

In 'A Propos of *Lady Chatterley's Lover*' Lawrence says,

> Christianity brought marriage into the world: marriage
> as we know it. Christianity established the little
> autonomy of the family within the greater rule of the
> state. Christianity made marriage in some respects
> inviolate, not to be violated by the state.

Lawrence is of course concerned with marriage as the theme
of his *novel*; he presents his kind of fiction as the force which
sustains these values in the modern world.

> It is marriage, perhaps, which has given man the best of
> his freedom, given him the little kingdom of his own
> . . . the foothold of independence on which to stand and
> resist an unjust state. . . . Make marriage in any serious
> degree unstable, dissoluble, destroy the permanence of
> marriage, and the Church falls. (*Phoenix II*, pp. 502,
> 501)

It is surely clear enough that the 'Great Tradition' in the
novel did in fact take up the task of celebrating marriage and
giving it enormous meaning. This was the great work of
Tolstoy and Lawrence, and early Lessing and even Joyce,
and all those who in lesser ways followed or accompanied
them; and in Lawrence's essay one sees the usually implicit
intention of resisting the state, the empire, power, for once
made explicit.

But for the other three we are concerned with, empire and
power were irresistible. What fiction could be made of that
realization? Kipling is the most important practitioner as
well as the initiator of the new fictional strategies, and it is of
interest to try to specify *how* his influence has been exerted –
how later writers were induced to follow the same paths.
Such influence is as much impersonal as personal. The
entertainer of the master-class must do certain things, and
cannot do certain others, whoever he may be. (Though
what Kipling did was also stamped with his personal

signature, whether or not Waugh and Amis recognized it.) The two forms of Kiplingism I want to draw attention to are to be found, one in the area of laughter, and the other in that of cliché. The novelist who cannot believe in life-values is likely to broaden the function of laughter, and to dramatize the clichés of experience.

The theme of laughter has already been discussed, in the chapter on Amis, but it is worth reconsidering it in relation to the themes of power and cliché. Laughter is the classic way to resolve irresolvable tensions, to deal with the morally impossible, to make sense out of that which does not make sense. Or perhaps it is more exact to say that it is the obvious alternative to the other classic way, which is tears. Laughter and tears are equally partial life-responses, though we lack a word for laughter equivalent to sentimentality; and as far as British literature goes, laughter has characterized the twentieth-century novel as much as tears characterized that of the nineteenth. Recognizing the irresistibility of power, yielding to the repetition and cliché in all our experience, these three writers could not get beyond laughter, and tried to make it substitute for other values.

Kipling has many joke and practical joke stories, from the *Soldiers Three* series, and the Pyecroft sequence, to late work like 'Dayspring Mishandled' (1928) and 'Aunt Ellen' (1929). He has many poems about laughter, like 'The Legend of Mirth', and 'The Playmate'. From the last I take these lines:

> . . . The secret mirthful fellowship,
> She, heralding new-framed delights,
> Breathes, 'This shall be a Night of Nights'.
> Then, out of Time and out of Space,
> Is built an Hour and a Place,
> Where all our earnest, baffled Earth
> Blunders and trips to make us mirth;
> Where, from the trivial flux of Things,

Rise unconceived miscarryings,
Outrageous but immortal, shown,
Of her great love, to me alone.   (*Limits and Renewals*)

In Waugh's case, we might take a fine passage describing
Virginia Troy's laughter in *Unconditional Surrender*.

Virginia's spontaneous laughter had seldom been heard
in recent years; it had once been one of her chief charms.
She sat back in her chair and gave full, free tongue:
clear, unrestrained, entirely joyous, with a shadow of
ridicule, her mirth rang through the quiet little
restaurant. Sympathetic and envious faces were turned
towards her. She stretched across the table cloth and
caught his hand, held it convulsively, unable to speak,
laughed until she was breathless and mute, still gripping
his bony fingers. . . . 'Oh Peregrine,' said Virginia at
last with radiant sincerity, 'I love you.' (p. 136)

One sees there how laughter turns into or transcends love.
Of course Virginia does not love Peregrine; but she does
love laughter, and the implication is that she loves it enough
to love a man for it. Something similar is true of Amis's
love-relationships, as I have said; they are based on the
shared anecdotes and exploits of laughter.

And of course at a lower level of emotional intensity,
laughter has always been recognized as the bond that holds
together the compatible and separates off the incompatible.
There is a striking case of this in *Officers and Gentlemen*,
where a piece of drunken foolery by Job, the porter at
Bellamy's, brings even his stupid brother-in-law in
laughing harmony with Guy, and marks off the absolute
unacceptability of Air Marshal Beech, who doesn't see the
humour of it.

Of course these writers know the inadequacy of this
laughter. Virginia Troy is the emblem of treachery in
Waugh's trilogy; she has ruined Guy's life, and her laughter

is the way she had done it; Waugh's celebration of that laughter is generous and rueful. And in Amis's novels there usually comes a time when the woman he cares about refuses to join in the hero's laughter; when the reader refuses to laugh; because the writer has given him the cue that this has gone too far. Amis knows, as Waugh knew, that he is chained to the stake of comedy, unable to move beyond that limit. And it is the pathos of all twentieth-century England that that laughter was not enough.

But there is a significant difference in Doris Lessing's treatment of the same theme. There is plenty of laughter in *The Golden Notebook*, for instance. In the Free Women sections laughter was a main mode of action, uniting Anna and Molly against Richard. Their laughter too, like that of Tommy and Guy on the isle of Mugg, was 'orgiastic', all-absorbing, marital. But against the other major actor in that story, Tommy, their laughter was no use and dried up. In fact he could use *his* evil laughter, the giggle of spite, against them. The self-destructive laughter of the group in Africa is similarly stressed. And in nearly all Lessing's novels there is a similar point made. Her work begins in the effort to escape from such laughter, to escape Kipling's or Waugh's or Amis's company. She insists on a fuller response.

The other theme, of cliché, is more general and cultural in scope. It seems that, after 1918, English culture gradually became riddled with cliché. The sense of *déjà vu* in matters of history and literature, of contemporary society and human types, of rhetoric and even of everyday vocabulary, became so oppressive that people could hardly speak or write at all. On the topics their fathers had considered important or intimate, they had recourse to quotation marks and allusions and ellipses, to ironies and eccentricities of tone, to lispings and gigglings and affectations, because so many big words felt too philistine to use, and yet there was no way to renew them – no reason to believe one ever could replace or

renew the large meanings. This conviction spread sufficiently to amount to a profound imaginative and intellectual
defeatism, and can be located at widely spaced and uncon-
nected points of English culture. One can see a likeness
between the habits of a certain kind of quoting, in matters of
literature, a certain sense of period, in matters of history, a
certain preoccupation with class and manners; but other
new habits seem too disparate to connect by any 'explanation' less vague than that there was 'a turn to cliché'.

By a cliché I mean primarily a standardized opinion, a
judgment expressed in a phrase or sentence so standardized
as to deprive it of all intellectual sincerity. But I also mean
the taste or enthusiasm behind that judgment and also the
object of that taste whether aesthetic or not. A poem or a
building or an emotion or an institution like marriage can all
become clichés, by becoming the object of a standard enthusiasm. When this happens a sensitive person must keep
silent about them, or make them the butt of hostile irony, or
– and this is what English culture after 1918 mostly did –
play with them: ring the changes on them, invert them,
exaggerate them, interweave and embroider them, stand
them on their heads. And by extension cliché means the
quotation, allusion, example, by means of which – like so
many handles – these ideas are grasped in order to be played
with.

Understood that way, cliché points immediately to
Kipling. Orwell pointed out in the 1940s that

> Kipling is the only English poet of our time who has
> added phrases to the language . . . [He cites] half a
> dozen phrases coined by Kipling which one sees quoted
> in the gutter press or overhears in saloon bars from
> people who have barely heard his name. . . . (George
> Orwell, *A Collection of Essays*, p. 133)

Orwell points out that these phrases are consciously clichés,
for their users.

what the phrases I have listed above have in common is that they are all of them phrases which one utters semi-derisively . . . but which one is bound to make use of sooner or later. Nothing could exceed the contempt of the *New Statesman*, for example, for Kipling, but how many times during the Munich period did the *New Statesman* find itself quoting that phrase about paying the Dane-geld? The fact is that Kipling, apart from his snack-bar wisdom and his gift for packing much cheap picturesqueness into a few words ('Palm and Pine' – 'East of Suez' – 'The Road to Mandalay') is generally talking about things that are of urgent interest.' (ibid., p. 134)

And one thing which Orwell almost says is that these phrases are *designed* to be used semi-derisively, that they are consciously clichés for Kipling too. They have always a sardonic or parodic edge, complementing their romanticism. The way that Brecht was able to take over Kipling's technique so completely shows that the 'snack-bar wisdom' and the 'cheap picturesqueness' come labelled as such.

And Kipling's command of cliché extended beyond language to cover human types, landscapes, and situations. One can point to examples in his fiction, like *Soldiers Three*, but the more striking evidence comes from other people's testimony, and from life. For instance, Rupert Brooke wrote to Eddy Marsh just before the war, from Tahiti,

It is all incredibly like a Kipling story, and all these people are very self-consciously Kiplingesque. Yesterday, for example, I sat in the Chief Engineer's cabin with the First Officer and a successful beach-comber lawyer from the white man's town in Samoa, drinking Australian champagne from breakfast to lunch. (A. Curtis, *Somerset Maugham*, p. 98)

And in *The Moon and Sixpence* (1919) Maugham wrote,

'There were men scattered about the outlying parts of the Empire who would never have been just what they are except for him' (Kipling).

Finally, let us look at Leonard Woolf, who at twenty-eight had 1000 square miles to rule in Ceylon and 100,000 subjects. Woolf was not a soldier, and indeed belonged to the political and cultural party opposite to Kipling's, but he saw himself in the same caste-terms as Kipling saw his heroes. He presents himself in *Growing* (published 1961) as melancholy, fond of solitude, fond of animals, strongly sexed, hot-tempered, a strong administrator who was complained of but respected by the natives.

What makes this doubly interesting is that Woolf shows us something of conscious choice and effort in this military caste personality. He felt himself to be essentially very unlike the Anglo-Indians he worked with. On the ship going out he had learned to improve the social façade behind which he hid his intelligence, and to deal with Ceylon civil servants, and planters. 'The process is what is popularly known as "making a man of him." It made, let us say, finally a man of me, though the man was, and has remained, three-quarters sham.' (p. 37)

But in a story he tells, and the way he tells it, about a police magistrate he lived with called Dutton, one meets the manly Woolf, the Kipling Woolf. He says Dutton reminded him of Leonard Bast, in *Howard's End*: and with good reason, for Forster drew exactly the same figure. Dutton read cheap editions of great books, wrote dreadful poetry – about 'fays' – and played the piano badly. His talk of women and love made Woolf 'feel slightly sick'.

Given a job in England with the post office or the inland revenue, Dutton would have been happy, Woolf says, because there his colleagues would have been small timid men like himself. 'In Ceylon he lived the life of a minnow in a shoal of pike. The basis of his character was timidity, which, as so often, was compensated underneath by boundless self-conceit.' (p. 65) He had been a scholarship boy, and had risen above his parents' station in life.

Unfortunately this meant that he was given the kind of education which completely addled his fairly good brain and destroyed every chance of his becoming a rational person. . . . Literature, art, music, poetry, history, mathematics, science, were pitchforked into his mind in chaotic incomprehensibility. . . . (p. 66)

He was denatured by 'the undigested, sticky mess of "culture" which they provided for him. His roots began and ended in Peckham, while his mind was full of Keats.' (p. 66) He married a missionary, Miss Beeching, who later complained to Woolf of her husband's impotence.

This is a very Kiplingesque story: this man and Leonard Bast, and Septimus Smith in *Mrs Dalloway*, are all descended from Kipling's Cockney clerks, like the man in 'The Greatest Story'. They are drawn the way Kipling drew and saw that figure. The anecdote is full of caste feeling; what little men like this lack is the caste element of temperamental fire and form; they are, to use Hindu terms, Banias trying to be Kshattriyas. Lacking that element of style, that feeling for form, they should never have been given access to the world of the imagination.

Woolf pays tribute to Kipling as the poet of Anglo-Indian society, but grudgingly, and in a way that denies him any insight into men like himself. He says he could never decide whether Kipling had copied colonial society exactly or whether his social world in Ceylon was copying Kipling. 'In Kipling's stories and our conversations there was the same incongruous mixture of public-school toughness, sentimentality, and melancholy.' (p. 46) But the real Woolf, he implies, did not take part in those conversations. All seven years in Ceylon, Woolf felt he was acting a part; he couldn't really have become an imperialist, he felt, – not 'a white ruler of our Asiatic empire'.

Woolf could only use Kipling's categories ironically, and yet he could not escape from them. He belonged to Kipling's world, the world of cliché, psychologically as well as by situation, and to deny that was in effect to lie. And that seems to be typical of the failure of the English intellectual response to Kipling: because he dealt in cliché, they thought they could escape him by irony, though they had no alternative to offer.

Perhaps most strikingly, Kipling's expertise with cliché gives him a close relationship with a group who felt themselves to be his bitterest enemies – the dandy enemies of empire of the 1920s and 1930s. Because one of the supreme laws of their sensibility was to sharpen one's sense of cliché, of the obvious, of the platitudinous, Kipling was (covertly) one of their great teachers, as well as overtly their butt.

Let me offer two quotations, from Waugh and from Orwell. First of all, Waugh in *Labels*, 1930, discussing a 'sense of period' and thus putting his finger on the meaning of 'culture', as the English use the term.

I do not really know how genuine or valuable this sense of period is. It is a product of the English public school and University education; it is, in fact, almost its only product which cannot be acquired far better and far more cheaply elsewhere. Cultured foreigners are lacking in it, and so are those admirably informed Englishmen whose education has been at secondary schools, technical colleges, and the modern Universities, or at the Royal Naval Colleges of Dartmouth and Greenwich. I am inclined to think that it is practically useless. It consists of a vague knowledge of History, Literature, and Art, an amateurish interest in architecture and costume, of social, religious, and political institutions, of drama, of the biographies of the chief characters of each century, of a few memorable anecdotes and jokes, scraps of diaries and correspondence and family history. All these snacks and tidbits of scholarship become fused together into a more or less homogeneous and consistent whole, so that the cultured Englishman has a sense of the past, in a continuous series of clear and pretty *tableaux vivants*. This Sense of the Past lies at the back of most intelligent conversation and of the more respectable and worse-paid *genre* of weekly journalism.

Those *tableaux vivants* and that sense of the past are to be found in Kipling's *Puck of Pook's Hill* and other stories and poems. And note how general is the function – 'lies at the back of most intelligent conversation' – which Waugh ascribes to this Sense of the Past. It is the material core of all English culture.

While Orwell, in 'Such, Such, Were the Joys', showed us how that Sense of the Past was taught, and so how it could be counted on to be there at the back of every upper-class Englishman's mind, uniting them and distinguishing them from the men of 'the secondary schools and the technical colleges'. He described how boys at his preparatory school were prepared to take the examination for the Harrow History Prize.

They were the kind of stupid question that is answered by rapping out a name or a quotation. Who plundered the Begams? Who was beheaded in an open boat? Who caught the Whigs bathing and ran away with their clothes? . . . Disraeli brought peace with honour. Clive was astonished at his moderation. Pitt called in the New World to redress the balance of the Old. . . . I recall positive orgies of dates, with the keener boys leaping up and down in their places in their eagerness to shout out the right answers, and at the same time not feeling the faintest interest in the meaning of the mysterious events they were naming. . . .
'1587?' 'Massacre of St. Bartholomew!' etc.

Orwell's commentary stresses the 'factuality' of this history, but we must be just as struck by its picturesque legendariness.

With Orwell at St Cyprian's was Cyril Connolly. Orwell won the Harrow History Prize for St Cyprian's one year, Connolly the next. And Connolly went on at Eton to win the Rosebery History Scholarship to Balliol. In 'A Georgian Boyhood' (1938) he says,

> I had an excellent memory, I could learn by heart easily, gut a book in an hour and a half of arguments, allusions, and quotations . . . and remember them for just long enough to get them down in an examination paper. I was the perfect examinee.

As a literary critic, Connolly may be said to have made his life-work out of elaborating this sensibility into a quasi-ideology. He combined a strong sense of period of the kind Waugh describes with the sensibility of a dandy, to use his own phrase. 'The London I like best is the one I can find in books where it lies embalmed between 1760 and 1840, the dandies still outnumbering the slums and the fog as yet barely invented.' But in an essay of 1963 Connolly expressed also the rebelliousness of the dandy, saying that England in the 1960s was no longer recognisable as the country he had rebelled against as a young man. 'Can this be the ferocious figure who tried to bend us to his will – the England of the 1930s, the Establishment a group of poker-faced prefects who know there is going to be a beating?' (*Suicide of a Nation*, ed. A. Koestler, London, 1963)

Thus this anti-imperialist dandyism did not die in the 1920s, nor was its cultural material confined to history of the past. It was a sense of the present and future too. It was the English imagination. And in the fiction of the period, it is notable how many novels describe literal *tableaux vivants* or historical pageants to largely but not entirely comic effect. The most famous is no doubt Virginia Woolf's *Between the*

Acts, which is all built round such an event; but there were also Nancy Mitford's *Wigs on the Green,* Anthony Powell's *From a View to a Death,* and others.

At this point again one can put one's finger on the Kipling source, for behind all these pageants and masquerades is surely his historical fantasy; and behind all these country houses stand those he depicts in 'They' and 'An Habitation Enforced' and 'My Son's Wife'. This is not to say Kipling as distinct from other celebrants of English history was the inspirer of this later work, but Kipling as representing the others. And he represents them by the right of his success in the genre; surely no one has done better with history as tapestry, as mural, as stained glass, with the short story as ceremony, as tournament, as Court of Beauty? Kipling's signature is on the form, recognized or not. Just so his signature is on the habit of quotation and allusion.

Such allusion is not only a matter of vocabulary, it is also a matter of concept and factual detail, description and characterization, all of which are likely to be extremely compressed, complex, and suggestive. In *Puck* the allusion is predominantly historical and literary in direction, and the book is a triumph of vivid and richly intricate evocation of the English past. In this aspect of his work Kipling is quite worthy to be put beside Scott and Shakespeare. These stories are in fact Kipling's Foundation Epic; except of course that these are short stories and at an opposite extreme from the epic poem in most formal terms. (That paradox – the fragmentariness of Kipling's form, combined with the monumentality of his themes, is the shape of his achievement.)

Once Kipling had written – and been so widely read – it followed naturally that the habit of quotation and allusion should become a particularly prominent one, and a particularly revealing index of intellectual distinction in England. Virginia Woolf's novels and her Common Reader essays are a high-level example of this, applied to literature. She makes constant allusion to and quotation from a narrow range of books, mostly English and French, and mostly eighteenth- and nineteenth-century 'classics' – a word which in itself sums up the taste we are talking about. Rosamond Lehmann's *Dusty Answer* has a whole section of quotations from English poets to evoke her heroine's experience of Cambridge. And Dorothy Sayers's characters engage in the most extraordinary contests and co-operations of allusion, again to a similar range of books. In intention, these authors offer us the opposite of clichés – they are always wincing away from the standardized – but in effect it is a banquet of *different* clichés, saved from commonplaceness by being played with. The effect of all three authors is to make the reader feel that a certain range of literature (one notably lacking in challenge, adventure, or contemporaneity) is the whole universe of intellectual achievement, the whole humanist tradition, and that all that spontaneity can mean is playing within it. The imagination is humbled, defeated, reduced to entertainment.

Thus one thing that has distinguished the English from the American sense of humour, sense of tact, sense of manners, has been the greater sensitivity of the former to clichés of behaviour. One example, which neatly ties the habit of quotation together with the confrontation with America, is the humour of Evelyn Waugh's *The Loved One* of 1946. The English poet, Denis Barlow, woos the American girl, Aimée Thanatogenos, by sending her poems. But she is so naïve, and he is so sophisticated, so intellectually dandified, that he copies out anthology war-horses, and changes the girls' names to Aimée, and claims them as spontaneous effusions of his own feelings for her. We are told that Aimée majored in Beauticraft, and took Art as a minor one year, though Psychology and Chinese were her real minors. Her mind is a mass of clichés, but naïve ones. She does not play with her clichés, and she knows nothing of the standardized culture he knows *so* well – so much *too* well. When Aimée discovers Denis's deception and reproaches him, he retorts:

> I should be disillusioned that I have been squandering my affections on a girl ignorant of the commonest treasures of literature. But I realize that you have different educational standards from those I am used to. No doubt you know more than I about science and citizenship. But in the dying world I come from quotation is a national vice. No-one would think of making an after-dinner speech without the help of poetry. It used to be the classics, now it's lyric verse. Liberal M.P.s constantly quote Shelley; Tories and Socialists don't get up and complain of being disillusioned when they learn that their ornaments are not original. They keep quiet and pretend they knew all the time.

This joke focuses shrewdly a general difference both nations have felt separating them – a very important feeling for England because it expressed the awareness that America had usurped the functions of health and vigour and responsibility for Anglo-Saxon manhood, and that Englishmen must be dandies. So it is interesting that the joke and the difference could be expressed so naturally in terms of literary clichés.

And in all this the hand of Kipling can be felt – though it was not named – the shadow of Kipling paralysing young English imaginations. Literary culture, manifested above all in the sense of humour of the educated, was hostile to enthusiasm and affirmation, was hostile to life-values. The sense of cliché turned in upon itself, and the only tactic available to the writer was to play upon the obvious, sardonically or romantically, in the ways Kipling had pioneered. Of course, great writers like Lawrence, Joyce, and Lessing did not fall into this pattern, but lesser writers did, and even some who were potentially major, like

Waugh and Amis. English culture after 1918 gradually lost imaginative life, and one is bound to see the shadow of Kipling falling dark across the landscape. But I use his name as we may name a disease after its first great victim. What Kipling confronted was something real. He faced up to the writer's complicity with power and privilege – the dependence of the public artist on the book-buying section of the master-class. His way of facing it (not of course the only way possible) was to accept the role of mythmaker and entertainer of that class, and the imaginative diminishment that went with that role. In England in the twentieth century it has been difficult to find any other way out of the artistic dilemma. Of those who disdained Kipling and his diminishment, most ended with less to be proud of than he; and the few who found a better way succeeded only for themselves, for the tragic dilemma still confronts each public artist.

BIBLIOGRAPHY

PREFACE

Woolf, Virginia, *Between the Acts*, New York, 1941.
Woolf, Virginia, *Mrs Dalloway*, New York, 1925.

[1] THE EMPIRE AND THE ADVENTURE STORY

Borrow, George, *Lavengro*, London, 1906.
Bowle, John, *The Imperial Achievement*, Boston, 1975.
Dinesen, Isak, *Letters from Africa*, Chicago, 1981.
Green, Roger Lancelyn, *Kipling: The Critical Heritage*, London, 1971.
Kipling, Rudyard, *The Light that Failed*, New York, 1969.
Morris, James, *Pax Britannica*, New York, 1978.

[2] RUDYARD KIPLING: THE EMPIRE STRIKES BACK

Brecht, Berthold, *Ges-annette Werke*, Frankfurt, 1967.
Carrington, C. E., *The Life of Rudyard Kipling*, New York, 1956.
Conrad, Joseph, *Last Essays,* London, 1926.
Conrad, Joseph, *The Rescue*, New York, 1925.
Conrad, Joseph, *Three Short Novels*, New York, 1960.
Esslin, Martin, *Brecht: The Man and His Work*, New York, 1961.

Hopkins, R. Thurston, *Rudyard Kipling: A Literary Appreciation*, New York, c. 1915.

Kipling, Rudyard, *Collected Works*, New York, 1941.

Kipling, Rudyard, *A Kipling Pageant*, New York, 1935.

Kipling, Rudyard, *Land and Sea Tales*, London, 1923.

Kipling, Rudyard, *The Naulahka*, New York, 1891.

Kipling, Rudyard, *Something of Myself*, Garden City, New York, 1936.

Kipling, Rudyard, *Stalky and Co.*, London, 1967.

Kipling, Rudyard, *The War and the Fleet in Being*, Garden City, New York, 1941.

Mason, Philip, *Kipling: The Glass, the Shadow, and the Fire*, New York, 1975.

[3] D. H. LAWRENCE: THE TRIUMPH OF THE SISTERS

Forster, E. M., *Howards End*, New York, 1921.

Forster, E. M., *Passage to India*, New York, 1924.

Lawrence, D. H., *Aaron's Rod*, London, 1922.

Lawrence, D. H., *Lady Chatterley's Lover*, New York, 1959.

Lawrence, D. H., *The Rainbow*, New York, 1960.

Lawrence, D. H., *Women in Love*, New York, n.d.

[4] JAMES JOYCE: THE EMPIRE OF ART

Brown, Malcolm, *The Politics of Irish Literature*, University of Washington Press, 1972.

Ellmann, Richard, *The Consciousness of Joyce*, New York, 1977.

Joyce, James, *The Letters of James Joyce*, 3 vols, New York, 1957–66.

Joyce, James, *The Portable James Joyce,* Introduction and Notes by Harry Levin, New York, 1966.

Joyce, James, *Ulysses*, New York, 1961.

Margariello, Dominick, *Joyce's Politics*, London, 1980.

Parrinder, Patrick, *H. G. Wells: The Critical Heritage*, London, 1972.

[5] EVELYN WAUGH: THE TRIUMPH OF LAUGHTER

Green, Martin, *Children of the Sun*, New York, 1976.
Greene, Graham, *The Heart of the Matter*, New York, 1974.
Waugh, Evelyn, *Black Mischief*, London, 1938.
Waugh, Evelyn, *Decline and Fall*, London, 1937.
Waugh, Evelyn, *A Handful of Dust*, London, 1948.
Waugh, Evelyn, *The Holy Places*, London, 1952.
Waugh, Evelyn, *A Little Learning*, Boston, 1964.
Waugh, Evelyn, *Men at Arms* and *Officers and Gentlemen*, New York, 1961.
Waugh, Evelyn, *Scoop*, New York, 1961.
Waugh, Evelyn, *Vile Bodies*, London, 1938.

[6] KINGSLEY AMIS: THE PROTEST AGAINST PROTEST

Amis, Kingsley, *The Anti-Death League*, London, 1968.
Amis, Kingsley, *Ending Up*, New York, 1976.
Amis, Kingsley, *Girl, 20,* London, 1971.
Amis, Kingsley, *The Green Man,* London, 1969
Amis, Kingsley, *Lucky Jim,* Penguin, London, 1961.
Amis, Kingsley, *Take A Girl Like You*, New York, 1960.
Genet, Jean, *The Maids. The Deathwatch*, tr. B. Frechtman, introd. J. P. Sartre, New York, 1954.
Orwell, George, *Coming Up For Air*, New York, n.d.
Waugh, Evelyn, *The Ordeal of Gilbert Pinfold*, London, 1962.

[7] DORIS LESSING: THE RETURN FROM THE EMPIRE

Lessing, Doris, *The Golden Notebook*, New York, 1968.

Lessing, Doris, *Landlocked*, New York, 1970.

Lessing, Doris, *Martha Quest,* New York, 1970.

Lessing, Doris, *Memoirs of a Survivor*, New York, 1975.

Lessing, Doris, *A Ripple from the Storm,* New York, 1970.

Naipaul, V. S., *The Loss of El Dorado*, London, 1969.

Naipaul, V. S., *The Mimic Men*, London, 1967.

Naipaul, V. S., *The Return to Eva Peron*, New York, 1968.

Scott, Paul, *Division of the Spoils*, London, 1975.

[8]   THE FALL OF KIPLING'S SHADOW

Connolly, Cyril, *Previous Convictions*, London, 1963.

Curtis, Anthony, *Somerset Maugham*, New York, 1977.

Koestler, Arthur, ed., *Suicide of a Nation*, London, 1968.

Orwell, George, *A Collection of Essays*, New York, 1954.

Power, Arthur, *Conversations with James Joyce*, London, 1974.

Waugh, Evelyn, *Labels*, London, 1930.

Waugh, Evelyn, *Unconditional Surrender*, London, 1964.

Woolf, Leonard, *Growing*, London, 1961.

INDEX